AUTOCAD® 2012
AND AUTOCAD LT® 2012

ESSENTIALS

AUTODESK® OFFICIAL TRAINING GUIDE

AUTOCAD® 2012
AND AUTOCAD LT® 2012
ESSENTIALS
AUTODESK® OFFICIAL TRAINING GUIDE

Scott Onstott

WILEY

Wiley Publishing, Inc.

Senior Acquisitions Editor: Willem Knibbe
Development Editor: Denise Lincoln
Technical Editor: Ian le Cheminant
Production Editors: Christine O'Connor and Nick Moran
Copy Editor: Elizabeth Welch
Editorial Manager: Pete Gaughan
Production Manager: Tim Tate
Vice President and Executive Group Publisher: Richard Swadley
Vice President and Publisher: Neil Edde
Book Designer: Happenstance Type-O-Rama
Compositor: Craig Woods, Happenstance Type-O-Rama
Proofreader: Publication Services, Inc.
Indexer: Jack Lewis
Project Coordinator, Cover: Katherine Crocker
Cover Designer: Ryan Sneed
Cover Image: © Manuel Gutjahr / iStockPhoto

Dear Reader,

Thank you for choosing *AutoCAD 2012 and AutoCAD LT 2012 Essentials*. This book is part of a family of premium-quality Sybex books, all of which are written by outstanding authors who combine practical experience with a gift for teaching.

Sybex was founded in 1976. More than 30 years later, we're still committed to producing consistently exceptional books. With each of our titles, we're working hard to set a new standard for the industry. From the paper we print on, to the authors we work with, our goal is to bring you the best books available.

I hope you see all that reflected in these pages. I'd be very interested to hear your comments and get your feedback on how we're doing. Feel free to let me know what you think about this or any other Sybex book by sending me an email at nedde@wiley.com. If you think you've found a technical error in this book, please visit **http://sybex.custhelp.com**. Customer feedback is critical to our efforts at Sybex.

Best regards,

NEIL EDDE
Vice President and Publisher
Sybex, an Imprint of Wiley

Dedicated to Jenn and Merlin

ACKNOWLEDGMENTS

A team of people has been instrumental in making this book the reality you are holding in your hands or reading on screen. I would like to express my sincere gratitude to the professional team at Sybex (an imprint of Wiley) for all their hard work.

It has been a pleasure working with Senior Acquisitions Editor Willem Knibbe and Pete Gaughan, Connor O'Brien, and Jenni Housh in the editorial department. I couldn't be more pleased to have this book published through Wiley and their top-notch group, which includes Developmental Editor Denise Santoro Lincoln, who thoroughly corrected my blunders; Technical Editor Ian Le Cheminant, who verified that all the exercises work as planned; Copy Editor Liz Welch, who ensured I used language properly; and Production Editor Christine O'Connor and Production Assistant Nick Moran, who transformed my Word docs and screen captures into the finished product.

About the Author

Scott Onstott has published five books with Sybex prior to the present title, including *Enhancing Architectural Drawings and Models with Photoshop, AutoCAD: Professional Tips and Techniques* (with Lynn Allen), *Enhancing CAD Drawings with Photoshop, Mastering Autodesk Architectural Desktop 2006,* and *Autodesk VIZ 2005* (with George Omura). Scott has worked on some 20 other technical books as contributing author, reviser, compilation editor, and/or technical editor.

Scott has a bachelor's degree in architecture from University of California, Berkeley, and is a former university instructor who now acts as a consultant, independent video producer, and contributor to popular industry websites. You can contact the author through his website: **www.scottonstott.com**.

Contents at a Glance

CONTENTS

CHAPTER 7   Organizing Objects   117

CHAPTER 8   Hatching and Gradients   139

CHAPTER 9   Working with Blocks and Xrefs   157

INTRODUCTION

The year 2012 marks the 30th anniversary of the first version of AutoCAD. AutoCAD's staying power is legendary in the ever-changing software industry. You can rest assured that spending the time learning AutoCAD is a wise investment and the skills you obtain here will be useful for years to come.

I wish to personally welcome you in beginning the process of learning AutoCAD. It will give you great satisfaction to learn such a complex program and use it to design and document whatever you dream up. You'll find step-by-step tutorials that reveal a wide variety of techniques built on many years of real-world experience.

The first 14 chapters apply to both AutoCAD 2012 and AutoCAD LT 2012. LT is Autodesk's lower-cost version of AutoCAD and has reduced capabilities. Chapters 15 through 18 are for AutoCAD only as they cover advanced tools not available in LT, including attributes, 3D navigation, 3D modeling, and rendering.

Who Should Read This Book

This book is for students, hobbyists, and professional architects, industrial designers, engineers, builders, landscape architects, or anyone who communicates with technical drawings in their work.

If you're interested in certification for AutoCAD 2012, this book can be a great resource to help you prepare. See **www.autodesk.com/certification** for more certification information and resources.

What You Will Learn

You'll gain a solid understanding of AutoCAD's features in this book. Each chapter features multiple exercises that take you step by step through many complex procedures. The goal of performing these steps on your own is to aim for an understanding that you can abstract into skills you can apply to many different real-world situations.

While each project presents different obstacles and opportunities, I urge you to focus on the concepts and techniques presented, rather than memorizing the specific steps used to achieve the desired result. The actual steps performed may vary in each geometric situation.

The best way to build skills is to perform the steps on your computer exactly as they are presented in the book during your first reading. After you achieve the desired result, start over and experiment using the same techniques on your own project (whether invented or real). After you have practiced, think for a moment about how you have achieved the desired result, and try to abstract the steps performed into concepts that you'll remember. Only then will you begin to own the knowledge and get the most out of this book.

Reader Requirements

You don't need any previous experience with AutoCAD to use this book. However, you'll need familiarity with either Windows or the Mac operating system and have the basic skills necessary to successfully use a graphical user interface and confidently operate a computer.

AutoCAD 2012 or AutoCAD LT 2012 System Requirements

The book is written for both AutoCAD 2012 and AutoCAD LT 2012. The following are system requirements for running either version on the different operating systems in which they are offered. See **www.autodesk.com** for the most up-to-date requirements.

General Windows System Requirements

- ▶ Microsoft Windows 7 Enterprise, Ultimate, Professional, or Home Premium
- ▶ Microsoft Windows Vista Enterprise, Business, or Ultimate (SP1 or later)
- ▶ Microsoft Windows XP Professional (SP2 or later)
- ▶ 2 GB of RAM
- ▶ 2 GB of free space for installation
- ▶ 1,280 × 1,024 true color video display adapter 128 MB or greater, Microsoft® Direct3D®-capable workstation-class graphics card; Pixel Shader 3.0 or greater required for 3D modeling
- ▶ Internet Explorer 7.0 or later

32-Bit AutoCAD 2012 for Windows

▶ For Windows Vista or Windows 7: Intel® Pentium® 4 or AMD Athlon® dual-core processor, 3.0 GHz or higher with SSE2 technology

▶ For Windows XP: Intel Pentium 4 or AMD Athlon dual-core processor, 2.0 GHz or higher with SSE2 technology

64-Bit AutoCAD 2012 for Windows

▶ AMD Athlon 64 with SSE2 technology, AMD Opteron® processor with SSE2 technology

▶ Intel® Xeon® processor with Intel EM64T support and SSE2 technology

▶ Intel Pentium 4 with Intel EM64T support and SSE2 technology

64-Bit AutoCAD 2012 for Mac

▶ Apple® Mac® Pro 4,1 or later; MacBook® Pro 5,1 or later (MacBook Pro 6,1 or later recommended); iMac® 8,1 or later (iMac 11,1 or later recommended); Mac® mini 3,1 or later (Mac mini 4,1 or later recommended); MacBook Air® 2,1 or later; MacBook® 5,1 or later (MacBook 7,1 or later recommended)

▶ Mac OS® X v10.6.4 or later; Mac OS X v10.5.8 or later

▶ 64-bit Intel® processor

▶ 3 GB of RAM (4 GB recommended)

▶ 2.5 GB of free disk space for download and installation (3 GB recommended)

▶ All graphics cards on supported hardware

▶ 1,280 × 800 display with true color (1,600 × 1,200 with true color recommended)

▶ U.S., U.K., or France keyboard layout

▶ Apple® Mouse, Apple Magic Mouse, Magic Trackpad, MacBook® Pro trackpad, or Microsoft®-compliant mouse

▶ Mac OS X–compliant printer

What Is Covered in This Book

AutoCAD 2012 and AutoCAD LT 2012 Essentials is organized to provide you with the knowledge needed to master the basics of computer-aided design. The book's web page is located at www.sybex.com/go/autocad2012essentials, where you can download the sample files used in each chapter.

Chapter 1: Getting Started   You'll take a tour of AutoCAD's user interface and learn to identify each of its parts by name. Chapter 1 is essential reading as you'll need to know the difference between workspaces, ribbon tabs, toolbars, panels, palettes, status toggles, and so on to understand the terminology used by your colleagues and in the rest of this book. In addition, you'll learn about how to match your industry's standard units to the drawings you'll be creating.

Chapter 2: Basic Drawing Skills   Learn how to navigate a 2D drawing with Zoom and Pan so you can zero in on areas of interest. You'll learn how to draw lines, rectangles, circles, arcs, and polygons; how to cancel, erase, and undo; and how to fillet and chamfer lines. In addition, you'll use two coordinate systems to specify the exact sizes of objects you are drawing.

Chapter 3: Using Drawing Aids   Drawing aids are something you'll want to learn how to do to create measured drawings with ease. The drawing aids covered with step-by-step exercises in this chapter include grid and snap, ortho and polar tracking, PolarSnap, running object snaps, the From snap, and object snap tracking.

Chapter 4: Editing Entities   This chapter teaches what you'll probably be doing most of the time in AutoCAD: editing the basic entities that you've drawn to make them conform with your design intent. Editing commands covered include Move, Copy, Rotate, Scale, Array, Trim, Extend, Lengthen, Stretch, Offset, and Mirror. In addition to these commands, you'll learn an alternative method for editing entities called grip editing.

Chapter 5: Shaping Curves   The landscape exercise in this chapter teaches you how to create complex curves with NURBS-based splines, curved polylines, and ellipses. By the end, you'll be able to shape curves to create almost any curvilinear form imaginable.

Chapter 6: Controlling Object Visibility and Appearance   You'll learn how to hide and reveal objects with properties and layers. Layers are essential to managing the complexity of design, and you'll use many different layer tools in this chapter's step-by-step exercises.

Chapter 7: Organizing Objects   By combining entities such as lines, polylines, circles, arcs, and text into blocks and/or groups, you can more efficiently manipulate more complex objects such as chairs, mechanical assemblies, trees, or any other organizational designation appropriate to your industry. You'll learn how to create and work with blocks and groups in this chapter.

Chapter 8: Hatching and Gradients   In this chapter you'll flood bounded areas with solid fill, hatch patterns, and/or gradients to indicate transitions between materials and to improve the readability of drawings in general.

Chapter 9: Working with Blocks and Xrefs   You'll learn how to access content from other files in the current drawing in this chapter. You'll also understand the important distinction between inserting and externally referencing content. In addition, you'll store saved content on tool palettes for simplified reuse.

Chapter 10: Creating and Editing Text   The written word is undeniably a part of every drawing. This chapter teaches you how to create both single- and multiline text, how to edit any text, and how to control its appearance through text styles and object properties.

Chapter 11: Dimensioning   You'll learn how to annotate drawings with specific measurements known as dimensions in this chapter. In addition to learning how to control measurements' appearance with dimension styles, you'll create linear, aligned, angular, and radius dimension objects.

Chapter 12: Keeping In Control with Constraints   This chapter teaches you how to add geometric and dimensional constraints to objects so that their ultimate form is controlled by mathematical formulas. The formulas in the example are as simple as adding two dimensions or calculating the diameter of a circle from its radius.

Chapter 13: Working with Layouts and Annotative Objects   AutoCAD has two environments you'll learn about in this chapter on layouts: modelspace and paperspace. You'll create floating viewports to display the contents of model-space in the paperspace of a layout. In addition, you'll create annotative styles and objects that always display the proper height no matter which viewport or annotation scale is selected.

Chapter 14: Printing and Plotting   From plotter drivers to plot style tables and page setups, you'll learn the intricacies of creating printed output to scale in AutoCAD. You'll plot in both modelspace and paperspace and even create electronic output that can be shared on the Internet.

Chapter 15: Storing, Presenting, and Extracting Data   Attributes, fields, and tables are the subjects of this chapter on managing data. You'll learn how to embed nongraphical data in blocks, how to dynamically link to that data in text fields, and finally how to display and format this same data in an organized fashion in spreadsheet-like tables.

Chapter 16: Navigating 3D Models   In this chapter you'll learn how to change your point of view while working on 3D models using the ViewCube, the Orbit tool, and SteeringWheel technology. In addition, you'll compose and save perspective views with cameras to help you visualize 3D models with added realism.

Chapter 17: Modeling in 3D   You'll learn the basics of surface, solid, and mesh modeling in this chapter by building the 3D geometry you navigated in the previous chapter. Each 3D toolset has its strengths and limitations, and you'll learn to use tools in each category to get the job done.

Chapter 18: Presenting Your Design   By assigning realistic materials, inserting artificial and natural light sources, and rendering the scene, you'll create realistic computer-generated imagery in this chapter. By approaching the final render in a series of ever more realistic test renders, you'll hone in on photorealistic output in stages.

Appendix: AutoCAD Certification   The appendix contains information about how to prepare for Autodesk certification exams using this book. The tables point you to the chapters where you'll find specific examples giving you practical experience with the topics covered in the exams.

The *Essentials* Series

The *Essentials* series from Sybex provides outstanding instruction for readers who are just beginning to develop their professional skills. Every *Essentials* book includes these features:

▶ Skill-based instruction with chapters organized around projects rather than abstract concepts or subjects.

▶ Suggestions for additional exercises at the end of each chapter, where you can practice and extend your skills.

▶ Digital files (via download) so you can work through the project tutorials yourself. Please check the book's web page at **www.sybex.com/go/autocad2012essentials** for these companion downloads.

Certification Objective
  The certification margin icon will alert you to passages that are especially relevant to AutoCAD 2012 certification. See the certification appendix and **www.autodesk.com/certification** for more information and resources.

CHAPTER 1

Getting Started

As we begin this chapter on getting started with AutoCAD, I'm reminded of a quote by Lao-Tzu: "A journey of a thousand miles begins with a single step." In much the same way, learning AutoCAD is something anyone can do by taking it one step at a time. And I promise AutoCAD is much easier than walking a thousand miles! Congratulations if you are reading this: You are now on your way. By the end of this book, you will have a solid understanding of AutoCAD.

▶ **Exploring the AutoCAD 2012 for Windows User interface**

▶ **Setting drawing units**

Exploring the AutoCAD 2012 for Windows User Interface

▶

AutoCAD for Mac has a user interface that is customized to the Mac experience. Although the Mac user interface is not covered in this book, its commands and capabilities are similar to those in AutoCAD for Windows.

Autodesk has released several versions of AutoCAD, including AutoCAD 2012, AutoCAD LT 2012, and AutoCAD 2012 for the Mac. The two Windows versions look nearly identical and function in almost the same way. The main difference is that LT doesn't support automation and some of the advanced 3D functions. The Mac version looks a bit different than its cousins but functions nearly identically to AutoCAD for Windows. Although this book was written using AutoCAD 2012 running on Windows XP Professional, you can use it to learn any of the current versions of AutoCAD.

Exploring AutoCAD's Graphical User Interface

Before you can use AutoCAD, you'll need to thoroughly familiarize yourself with its graphical user interface (GUI). The AutoCAD 2012 (for Windows) user interface is shown in Figure 1.1.

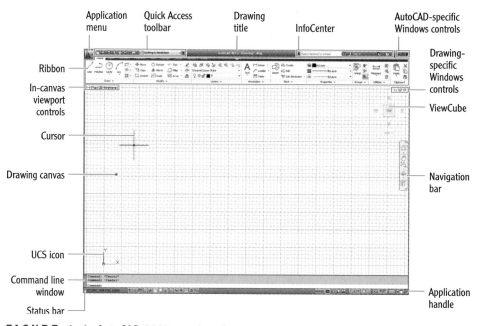

Application menu

Quick Access toolbar

Drawing title

InfoCenter

AutoCAD-specific Windows controls

Ribbon

In-canvas viewport controls

Cursor

Drawing canvas

UCS icon

Command line window

Status bar

Drawing-specific Windows controls

ViewCube

Navigation bar

Application handle

FIGURE 1.1 AutoCAD 2012 user interface

Let's now step through the basic user interface for AutoCAD:

Certification Objective

1. Click the Application menu. Type **polygon** and observe that the text appears in the search box at the top of the Application menu. The search results (see Figure 1.2) list many related commands. Search is useful when you're not sure how to access a command in the interface or what its exact name is.

FIGURE 1.2 Searching for commands in the Application menu

2. Click the red X at the extreme right edge of the search box to make the initial Application menu interface reappear; here you can create new or open existing drawings, export or print drawings, and more. Hover the cursor over Open and then click Drawing (Figure 1.3).

Certification
Objective

FIGURE 1.3 Opening a drawing
from the Application menu

3. Select the following sample file and click Open in the Select File dialog box:

```
C:\Program Files\Autodesk\AutoCAD 2012\Sample\
Sheet Sets\Manufacturing\VW252-02-0142.dwg
```

If you are using AutoCAD LT open any of the sample files located under: C:\Program Files\Autodesk\AutoCAD LT 2012\Sample. The Sheet Set Manager palette appears when the sample file is opened (see Figure 1.4). This palette automatically appears when you open any drawing that's a part of a sheet set. AutoCAD has many palettes to organize tools and reusable drawing content.

4. Click the Sheet Views tab along the right edge of the Sheet Set Manager and observe that tabs provide a means of accessing additional interface content. In its present state, the Sheet Set Manager is a floating palette. Drag its palette bar and relocate it on screen.

5. Click the Auto-hide toggle and watch the palette collapse to its vertical palette bar; this saves space on screen. Hover the cursor over the palette bar and watch the whole palette reappear so you can access its content. Now toggle Auto-hide off.

Sheet sets are not available in AutoCAD LT and are an optional feature in AutoCAD.

◄

◄

Drag floating palettes to a secondary monitor to maximize the drawing area on your primary monitor.

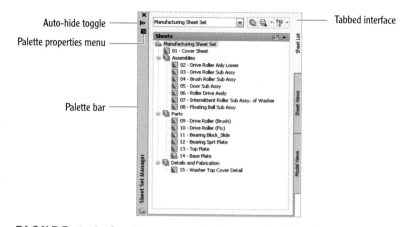

Auto-hide toggle

Palette properties menu

Palette bar

Tabbed interface

FIGURE 1.4 Opening a sample drawing reveals this palette.

6. Click the palette properties menu and select Anchor Left. The Sheet Set Manager palette is docked along the left edge of the user interface (see Figure 1.5). There are many options you can use to organize the user interface to match the way you work.

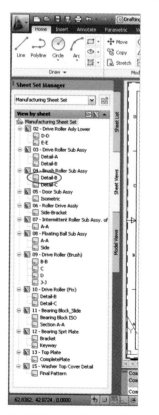

FIGURE 1.5 Docking a palette

7. Double click Detail-B under 04 – Brush Roller Sub Assy in the Manufacturing sheet set. A new drawing appears in the drawing window.

8. Click the Open button in the Quick Access toolbar. Select any drawing in the Manufacturing folder and click Open. If you are using LT, open any other sample file.

9. Click the Quick View Drawings button in the application status bar (see Figure 1.6). Move the cursor over the first drawing and observe that two smaller views appear above it; these are the highlighted drawing's spaces. Move the cursor over Model and its view enlarges. Click the model view icon to go there immediately. Use Quick View to navigate through open drawings and their spaces.

Certification Objective

◄

The Quick Access toolbar is a convenient way to open drawings, especially when you're not using the Sheet Set Manager.

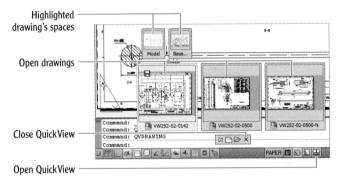

Highlighted drawing's spaces

Open drawings

Close QuickView

Open QuickView

FIGURE 1.6 Accessing open drawings and their spaces with Quick View

AUTOCAD DRAWING SPACES

AutoCAD has two types of drawing spaces: paper and model. Paperspace is a two-dimensional area analogous to and having the dimensions of a sheet of paper. Various sizes of "paper" can be created in individual layouts (see Chapter 13, "Working with Layouts and Annotative Objects"). Modelspace, on the other hand, is a single three-dimensional volume where everything is drawn actual size. Modelspace is typically scaled down in viewports and displayed in paperspace. Most of the drawing you will do in AutoCAD will be in modelspace. Both paper- and modelspaces are saved in the same drawing file.

Exploring AutoCAD's Workspaces

AutoCAD workspaces (not to be confused with drawing spaces) are stored sets of user interface controls, which include menus, toolbars, palettes, and the ribbon.

People use workspaces to quickly configure the interface for the task at hand. Let's take a brief look at AutoCAD's workspaces:

Although longtime users might feel more comfortable with the AutoCAD Classic interface, there are many advantages to using all the workspaces.

1. Select the AutoCAD Classic workspace from the drop-down menu on the Quick Access toolbar. The user interface changes dramatically (see Figure 1.7). The AutoCAD Classic workspace makes AutoCAD look similar to how it did in 2008 and before.

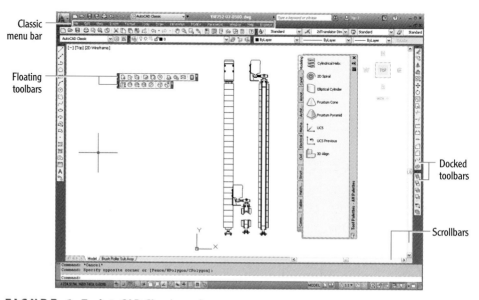

Classic menu bar

Floating toolbars

Docked toolbars

Scrollbars

FIGURE 1.7 AutoCAD Classic workspace

Certification
Objective

2. Drag a docked toolbar out from the edge of the screen and convert it into a floating toolbar. Select Tools ➤ Toolbars ➤ AutoCAD ➤ Dimension from the classic menu bar. Drag the Dimension floating toolbar to any edge of the screen and dock it.

Certification
Objective

3. Position the cursor over a docked toolbar button and right-click; a toolbar context menu appears. Select Object Snap from this menu (Figure 1.8).

4. Right-click in the drawing window and you'll see a different context menu. Right-clicking over most items, from the tool palettes to the status bar buttons, brings up other unique context menus. In the Classic workspace, right-clicking is the means of accessing numerous context-sensitive menus throughout the user interface.

3D Navigation
Array_Toolbar
CAD Standards
Camera Adjustment
Dimension
Dimensional Constraints
✔ Draw
✔ Draw Order
Draw Order, Annotation to Front
Find Text
Geometric Constraint
Group
Inquiry
Insert
✔ Layers
Layers II
Layouts
Lights
Mapping
Measurement Tools
Modeling
✔ Modify
Modify II
Multileader
Object Snap
Orbit
Parametric

FIGURE 1.8 Using the context menu to open toolbars

The AutoCAD Ribbon

AutoCAD has so many toolbars, palettes, and menus that finding the right tool for the job can seem like a job in itself. The ribbon was therefore an important feature that was introduced to AutoCAD. Autodesk adopted Microsoft's ribbon standard to organize the ever-increasing number of toolbars in a single special palette, making tools much easier to find. Let's now explore various ribbon modes and identify the user interface elements of each.

The ribbon isn't shown in the AutoCAD Classic workspace.

Certification Objective

1. Choose the 3D Basics workspace from the drop-down menu in the Quick Access toolbar. The ribbon replaces all the classic menus and toolbars (see Figure 1.9). Close the tool palettes and the Online floating toolbar.

Tabbed interface   Minimize ribbon

Typical panel

FIGURE 1.9 The full ribbon interface

2. Click the Minimize Ribbon button and observe the full ribbon change to display tabs and panel buttons (see Figure 1.10). Hover the cursor

over the panel buttons. The buttons expand to reveal all the tools shown on the full ribbon.

Panel buttons

Panel titles

Tabs

FIGURE 1.10 Ribbon modes

3. Click the Minimize Ribbon button again. The panel buttons change into titles. Again hover the cursor over the titles to reveal each panel's tools.

4. Click the Minimize Ribbon button once again. Hovering the cursor over the tabs doesn't have any effect. Click the Home tab to reveal the full panel temporarily. It disappears after you move the cursor away.

5. Click the Minimize Ribbon button one last time. The full ribbon interface is restored.

6. Click the Create button at the bottom of the Create panel to reveal additional tools. Hover the mouse over one of the tools to display a tooltip that identifies the tool and describes its function. Holding the cursor still a while longer reveals either a drawing or a video (without audio) that visually demonstrates what the tool does (see Figure 1.11).

7. Observe that the bottom of the tooltip shown in Figure 1.11 reveals the command name (SURFSCULPT in this case). The ribbon, menus, toolbars, and palettes are all graphical alternatives to typing commands.

8. Press and release the Alt key. Keytips appear on the ribbon (see Figure 1.12). Pressing any of the letter combinations activates that part of the GUI. Type **IN** and observe that the Insert tab is selected without moving the cursor.

9. Press the F2 key to open the AutoCAD Text window. The bottom line, Command:, is called the *command line*. It is the active line where commands appear regardless of whether they are typed or triggered from

Certification
Objective

▶

I recommend using the full ribbon interface until you learn where all the tools are. Using one of the minimized modes saves space on screen.

▶

AutoCAD is based on commands. If you know the name of a command, you can type it instead of finding it in the GUI.

the GUI. The complete history of commands scrolls upward as new commands are entered. Close the AutoCAD Text window. Three lines of this command history appear at the bottom of the user interface, just above the application status bar.

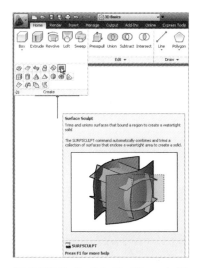

FIGURE 1.11 Tooltip and video

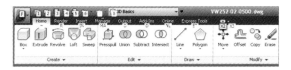

FIGURE 1.12 Keytips allow you to press keys to manipulate the ribbon with the keyboard.

10. The application status bar contains a coordinate readout on the left, a number of status toggle buttons, and various items, as shown in Figure 1.13. Click the application status bar menu and deselect Clean Screen; its button disappears. You can control which buttons appear using this menu.

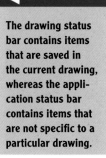

The drawing status bar contains items that are saved in the current drawing, whereas the application status bar contains items that are not specific to a particular drawing.

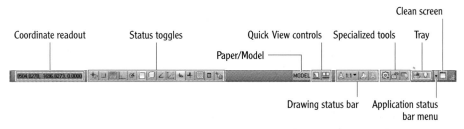

FIGURE 1.13 Application, drawing status bars, and the tray

11. Take a look at the InfoCenter at the top right of the screen (see Figure 1.14); this is where you connect to Autodesk and the larger community. Click in the search field and type **solid**.

Search box   Search button   Exchange

Autodesk online   Help
services

FIGURE 1.14 InfoCenter

12. Click the binoculars icon on the right of the search field and the AutoCAD Exchange dialog box appears. Multiple online books are searched and relevant results appear in the left panel. The description of the SOLID command appears in the right panel (Figure 1.15).

FIGURE 1.15 AutoCAD Exchange

13. Click the Help button on the right edge of the InfoCenter. The Help Table of Contents page opens in your browser. All AutoCAD documentation is accessible through this interface.

Setting Drawing Units

Before you start drawing, it's important to decide what one drawing unit represents in the real world. Architects in the United States typically equate one drawing unit with one inch in AutoCAD. You need to choose a unit type that matches your country's industry standard.

Architectural   As the name suggests, most architects will choose this type, which displays units in feet and inches. For example, 12 feet, 6½ inches is typed as **12´6-1/2˝**. The hyphen is used to separate inches from fractions of an inch rather than feet from inches.

Decimal   Metric users should select this type. One decimal unit can be equal to one millimeter, one centimeter, or any metric unit.

Engineering   Like the architectural type, engineering units feature feet and inches, but the inches are represented in decimal form—for example, 12´6.500˝.

Fractional   Woodworkers often prefer to set AutoCAD drawings in fractional units of inches because that is how their work is normally reckoned. For example, 12 feet, 6½ inches reads 150-½˝ in fractional units.

Scientific   For example, 12 million parsecs reads 12.000E+06 in scientific units, where 12.000 indicates 12 accurate to a precision of three decimal places and E+06 indicates the exponential function to the sixth power, or one million.

Let's set AutoCAD's drawing units:

1. Click the New button on the Quick Access toolbar. Click the arrow button next to the Open button in the Select Template dialog box and choose Open With No Template – Imperial (see Figure 1.16).

Certification Objective

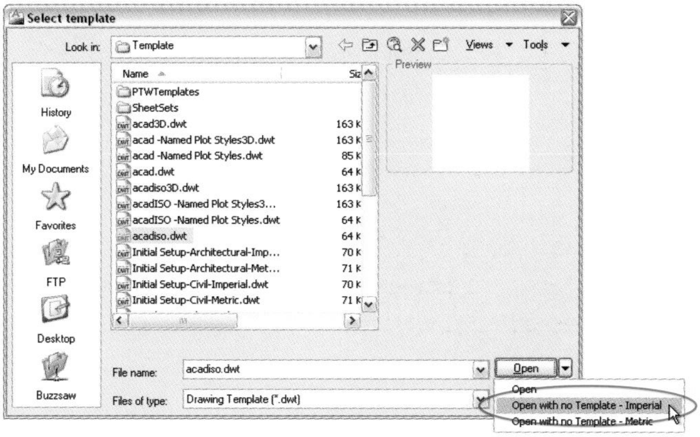

FIGURE 1.16 Opening a drawing with no template

You can press Enter or the spacebar to enter commands (command names never have spaces). Commands and their options can be typed in upper or lowercase.

2. Type **UN** and press Enter to bring up the Drawing Units dialog box (see Figure 1.17). UN is the command alias (abbreviation) of the UNITS command. Most commands have aliases that save on typing.

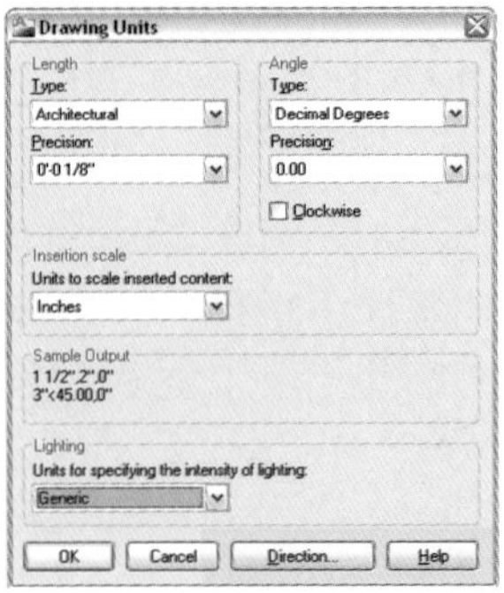

FIGURE 1.17 Setting drawing units

3. Select Architectural from the Type drop-down menu. I'm using Architectural in this book, but you should select the unit type that fits your industry when working professionally. Metric users should select Decimal length units.

4. Click the Length Precision drop-down menu and select 1/8″ (or 0 for metric). Set Insertion Scale to Inches and Angle Type to Decimal Degrees. Set Angular Precision to 0.00 (two decimal places).

5. Click the Insertion Scale drop-down menu and select Inches (or Centimeters for metric). Click OK to close the Drawing Units dialog box.

THE ESSENTIALS AND BEYOND

You have thoroughly explored the user interface and learned how to control the look and feel of AutoCAD to suit task-based workflows. In addition, you've learned how to create a new drawing and set the drawing units, and you're ready to get to the business of drawing.

ADDITIONAL EXERCISES

▶ Drawing templates are drawing files that store styles, layers, and settings that you want to keep consistent in every drawing you create. Set up the drawing units according to the way you work and save a new template file (.dwt). Then create a new drawing file (.dwg) based on your template and verify that the units are as expected. As you learn more about styles, layers, and settings later in this book, you can add your preferences to this template file. Be aware that templates do not affect preexisting drawings.

CHAPTER 2

Basic Drawing Skills

This chapter teaches you how to draw basic shapes such as lines, rectangles, circles, arcs, and polygons. You will learn how to correct mistakes, navigate two-dimensional space, and use coordinate systems to draw accurately. In addition, you'll perform your first editing by joining existing lines in straight, rounded, or angled intersections.

▶ **Navigating 2D drawings**

▶ **Drawing lines and rectangles**

▶ **Canceling, erasing, and undoing**

▶ **Using coordinate systems**

▶ **Drawing circles, arcs, and polygons**

▶ **Filleting and chamfering lines**

Navigating 2D Drawings

Unlike image editing programs where zooming in results in blurry pixilated images, you can zoom in forever in AutoCAD without suffering any loss in quality. However, to avoid getting lost in space you'll need to learn how to navigate with a variety of pan and zoom tools, which we'll explore here.

1. Go to the book's Downloads page at **www.sybex.com/go/ autocad2012essentials** and browse to Chapter 2; get the file Ch2-A.dwg or Ch2-A-metric.dwg, and open it in AutoCAD (see Figure 2.1). The Navigation bar is on the right edge of the user interface.

Certification Objective

2. Click the Zoom flyout menu on the Navigation bar and select Zoom In. The Zoom In button replaces the original button on the Navigation bar (which was Zoom Extents, incidentally); the last used tool appears on top. Click the Zoom In icon again and the view is magnified by another factor of 2.

> **Instead of changing the size of objects, Zoom merely increases the magnification on the canvas.**

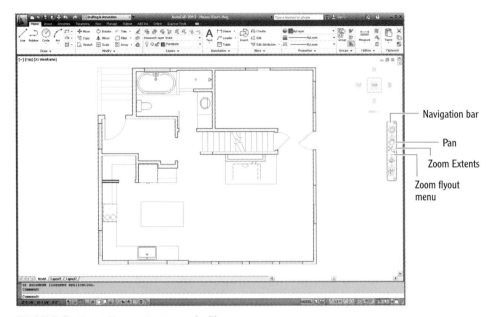

Navigation bar

Pan

Zoom Extents

Zoom flyout menu

F I G U R E 2 . 1 House-start sample file

3. Click Pan in the Navigation bar, drag the mouse from left to right, and then press Enter to end the command.

4. For an alternative method, press and hold the mouse wheel and pan the drawing to center the refrigerator on the canvas (as shown in Figure 2.2).

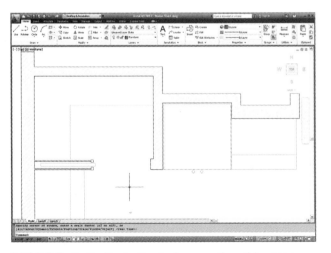

F I G U R E 2 . 2 Navigating to focus on the refrigerator

5. Select the Drafting & Annotation workspace if it is not already selected and then select the View tab in the ribbon. Click the bottom menu arrow in the Navigate 2D panel and select Zoom Realtime (Figure 2.3). Drag up in the document window to zoom in until the refrigerator fills the screen, and then press Esc.

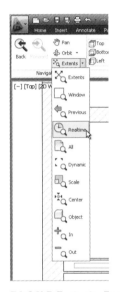

FIGURE 2.3 Zoom tools on the Navigate 2D panel of the View tab of the ribbon

> There are many ways to execute commands in AutoCAD so that you can find your favorite ways of working and become more efficient.
>
> ◄

6. Pan to the lower-left corner of the refrigerator using the scroll bars at the edges of the document window.

7. Select Zoom Window from the Navigate panel on the View tab. Click points A and B, as shown in Figure 2.4. The area of the rectangle you draw is magnified to fill the canvas.

8. Roll the mouse wheel forward to zoom in further and drag the mouse wheel if necessary to reveal the object in the lower-left corner of the refrigerator (see Figure 2.5).

> It's not good practice to create infinitesimal text objects; this was done only to demonstrate AutoCAD's infinite zoom capability.
>
> ◄

9. Type **z** and press the spacebar (Z is the command alias for the Zoom command). Read the prompt in the Command window:

```
ZOOM
Specify corner of window, enter a scale
factor (nX or nXP), or [All/Center/Dynamic/
Extents/Previous/Scale/Window/Object] <real time>:
```

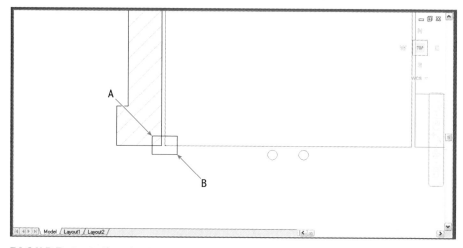

FIGURE 2.4 Zooming into a window

FIGURE 2.5 Secret text in lower-left corner of the refrigerator

You are looking at AutoCAD's roots in the form of command-line options. This interface was invented before the rest of the GUI and remarkably not only still functions, but is a very efficient means of working. Execute any of the options shown in square brackets by typing the capitalized letter. The option in angled brackets (real time in this case) executes by default if you press Enter without typing anything.

10. Type **P** and press Enter to execute Zoom Previous. Press Enter again to repeat the previous command (Zoom), type **P**, and press Enter again. Repeat this process until you can see the entire refrigerator again.

11. To see everything that has been drawn, you use Zoom Extents. Double-click the mouse wheel to Zoom Extents.

12. Position the cursor over the bathroom sink and roll the mouse wheel forward to zoom in. Notice that the view stays centered on the sink without having to pan (Figure 2.6). Drag the mouse wheel to make slight panning adjustments if necessary to center the target object on the screen.

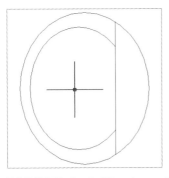

FIGURE 2.6 Directing navigation by positioning the cursor over the bathroom sink while zooming

13. Practice zooming into the kitchen sink, the stove, and the bathtub using various methods shown in this section. Leave the drawing file open for work in the next section.

> Navigation should become second nature to you so you don't have to think much about it and can focus on drawing.

Drawing Lines and Rectangles

The drawing commands you'll probably use the most in AutoCAD are LINE and RECTANGLE. You will begin by drawing some lines and rectangles without worrying yet about entering measurements.

Drawing Lines

Lines are the backbone of AutoCAD. Let's begin drawing lines.

1. In Ch2-A.dwg or Ch2-A-metric.dwg, zoom into the living room in the lower right of the floor plan so that empty space fills the canvas.

2. Turn off all status toggles in the application status bar. Status toggles are highlighted in blue when they are on and appear in gray when they are off (see Figure 2.7).

> You will use some of the status toggles in Chapter 3, "Using Drawing Aids."

FIGURE 2.7 All status toggles shown are off.

3. Type **L** and press Enter. Click two arbitrary points to define a line object. Observe the flexible segment (called a *rubberband*) connecting the cursor with the second point you clicked (Figure 2.8).

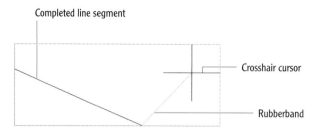

Completed line segment

Crosshair cursor

Rubberband

F I G U R E 2 . 8 Drawing a line

4. Click another point to draw your second segment. The prompt in the Command window reads

   `Specify next point or [Close/Undo]:`

   Type **U** and press Enter. The last point you clicked is undone but the rubberband continues to be connected to the cursor, indicating that you can keep drawing lines.

5. Click two more points and then type **C** and press Enter to create a closing segment between the first and last points. The close option automatically terminates the Line command so Enter is not required here, as it was in step 3.

6. Press the spacebar (or Enter) to repeat the last command. Click two arbitrary points to create a single line segment. Right-click to open the context menu and then select Enter with a left-click.

7. Open the Application menu and click the Options button at the bottom. Click the User Preferences tab in the Options dialog box that appears. Under the Windows Standard Behavior section, select Right-Click Customization and then in the new dialog box select Turn On Time-Sensitive Right-Click (see Figure 2.9). Click Apply & Close and then OK in the Options dialog box.

8. Select the Home tab in the ribbon and click the Line tool in the Draw panel. Click two points and draw another line. This time right-click quickly to terminate the Line command.

9. Right-click again to repeat the last command and then click two points on the canvas. Next, slowly right-click (holding down the right mouse button for longer than 250 milliseconds, to be precise) and you'll see the context menu shown in Figure 2.10. Left-click and press Enter from this menu to complete the Line command.

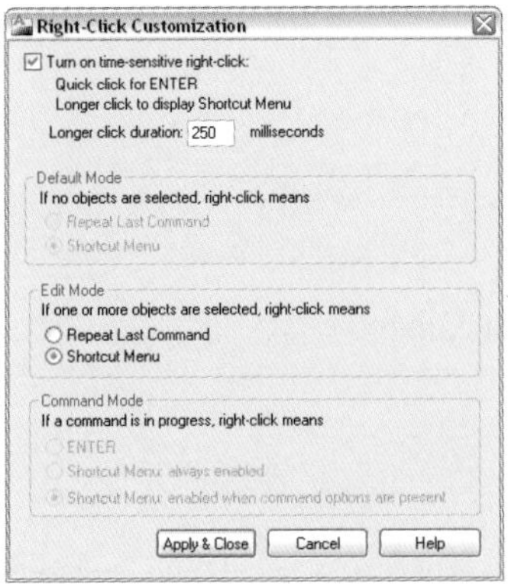

FIGURE 2.9 Turning on Time-Sensitive Right-Click for more efficient drawing

FIGURE 2.10 This context menu appears when you hold the right mouse button longer than 250 milliseconds.

Drawing Rectangles

Line segments are treated as individual objects, whereas the four line segments comprising a rectangle are treated as a single entity. Although rectangles can obviously be drawn with the Line command, specialized commands such as RECTANGLE are more efficient for constructing specific shapes and offer more options. Let's experiment now with this feature.

1. Click the Rectangle tool in the Draw panel and then click two opposite corner points on the canvas. The command automatically terminates when the rectangle is drawn.

   Certification Objective

2. Press Enter to repeat the last command. This time pay attention to the prompts in the Command window:

   ```
   Specify first corner point or
   [Chamfer/Elevation/Fillet/Thickness/Width]:
   ```

▷

Pay close attention to the prompts in the Command window to see what options are available and/or what specific input is requested at each step. After some practice you will anticipate command sequences and know what to do next without looking at the Command window.

▷

Do not type cm when using metric units; input numbers only.

3. Click the first corner point in the document window. A new prompt appears:

   ```
   Specify other corner point or
   [Area/Dimensions/Rotation]:
   ```

4. Click the other corner point and the command is finished. You had the opportunity to execute a number of options before you clicked the first point, and again more options appeared after you clicked the first point but before the second point terminated the command.

5. Type **rectang** (the command alias for the RECTANGLE command) and press the spacebar. Type **F** and press Enter to execute the Fillet option. The command prompt reads as follows:

   ```
   Specify fillet radius for rectangles <0.0000>:
   ```

6. Type **2″** (or **5** cm) and press Enter.

7. Click two points to draw the rectangle. The result has filleted corners (see Figure 2.11).

First click ⟶　　　　⟵ Second click

FIGURE 2.11 Rectangle drawn using its Fillet option

8. Draw another rectangle and observe that it also has rounded corners. Some options such as the fillet radius are sticky; they stay the same until you change them. Zero out the Fillet option by pressing the spacebar, typing **F**, pressing Enter, typing **0**, and pressing Enter again. Click two points to draw a sharp-edged rectangle.

9. Save Ch2-A.dwg or Ch2-A-metric.dwg by clicking the Save button in the Quick Access toolbar.

DRAWING RECOVERY MANAGER

Occasionally something goes wrong with AutoCAD and it crashes. The next time you launch AutoCAD, the Drawing Recovery Manager will automatically appear, allowing you to recover damaged drawings that were open (and possibly corrupted) when the program unexpectedly came to a halt.

Canceling, Erasing, and Undoing

Making mistakes in AutoCAD is entirely acceptable if you know how to cancel, erase, and/or undo what you've done wrong. The following exercise will show you how to do all three:

1. Type **L** and press Enter. Click two points on the canvas and then press the Esc key; the LINE command is terminated but the single segment you just created remains. The Esc key will get you out of any running command or dialog box.

2. Type **E** and press the spacebar. Click the line created in step 1 and then right-click; the segment is erased.

   Certification Objective

3. Click the Line tool in the Draw panel, click four points on the canvas (making three segments), and then right-click to finish the LINE command.

4. Click each of the segments, one at a time. Blue grips appear on the lines' endpoints and midpoints (see Figure 2.12). Grips are used for editing, and you'll learn more about them in Chapter 4, "Editing Entities." In the meantime, it's helpful to know that if you press the Delete key, the lines are gone.

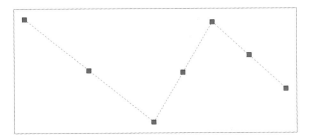

FIGURE 2.12 Selecting lines before deleting them

5. Click the Undo arrow on the Quick Access toolbar (see Figure 2.13). The lines you deleted in step 4 reappear.

Undo ⌐   ⌐ Redo

FIGURE 2.13 Undo and Redo

6. Click the Redo button and the lines disappear again.

7. Click the Undo button's menu arrow. A list of all the commands you've issued in this session appears. Select the bottom item in the list to undo all the way back to the moment when you opened Ch2-A.dwg or Ch2-A-metric.dwg.

Using Coordinate Systems

AutoCAD's virtually unlimited number of undo and redo actions means that it is a very forgiving program. However, you can't undo past the point when you opened an existing file; in other words, undo and redo actions are not stored in the file but in volatile RAM.

Certification
Objective

AutoCAD uses the same Euclidean space you learned about in the Geometry class of your youth—but don't panic, I don't expect you to remember any theorems! You can draw objects in Euclidean space using the following coordinate systems: Cartesian, polar, cylindrical, and spherical (the last two are rarely used so they won't be covered in this book).

Cartesian coordinates are useful for drawing rectangles with specific length and width measurements. Polar coordinates are used most often for drawing lines with specific lengths and angles with respect to horizontal. Once you learn coordinate system syntax, you can use the systems interchangeably to draw accurately in any context.

In the Cartesian system, every point is defined by three values, expressed in terms of distances along the x-, y-, and z-axes. In two-dimensional drawings, the z-coordinate value of all objects is 0 so objects are expressed solely in terms of x- and y-coordinates (see Figure 2.14).

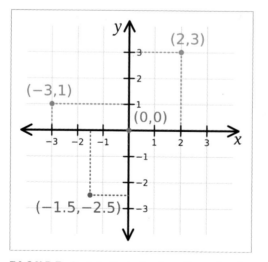

FIGURE 2.14 Cartesian two-dimensional coordinates

Using Absolute Coordinates

Coordinates can be *absolute* or *relative*, no matter which coordinate system is used. Let's first focus on drawing a line using absolute coordinates.

1. If it's not already open, open Ch2-A.dwg or Ch2-A-metric.dwg.

2. Click the Line tool on the Draw panel. The prompt in the Command window reads:

   Specify first point:

   Type **0,0** and press Enter. The origin point of Euclidean space has coordinates 0 in x and 0 in y, which is written as 0,0.

   Certification Objective

3. Now the prompt in the Command window reads

   Specify next point or [Undo]:

   Type **3´,0** (or **90,0** in metric) and press Enter. Right-click to finish the LINE command. You drew a line measuring 3´ (or 90 cm) horizontally along the x-axis.

Using Relative Coordinates

Calculating where every object is in relation to the origin point (which is what absolute coordinates require) would be far too cumbersome in practice. Therefore, relative coordinates are used more frequently. Let's explore how to use them:

1. Click the Line tool on the Draw panel. Click an arbitrary point in the middle of the living room. The coordinates of the point you clicked are unknown; thankfully you won't ever need to find out what they are.

   Certification Objective

2. Type **@3´,0** (or **@90,0** in metric) and press Enter twice. Another 3´ (or 90 cm) line has now been drawn horizontally. The @ symbol tells AutoCAD to consider the previous point as the origin point, relatively speaking.

3. Press Enter to repeat the last command. You'll see the prompt

   Specify first point:

4. Right-click in the drawing canvas and hold (for longer than 250 milliseconds) to open the context menu. Select the first coordinate value from the Recent Input menu (see Figure 2.15). You will use the last point entered as the first point in a new line. A rubberband connects the right end of the horizontal line to the cursor.

FIGURE 2.15 Drawing a new line
from the end of the previous line

5. Type **@0,6´** (or **@0,180** in metric) and press Enter. A line measuring 6´ (or 1.8m) is drawn vertically along the y-axis.

6. Type **@-3´,0** (or **@-90,0** in metric) and press Enter. Type **@0,-6´** (or **@0,-180** in metric) and press Enter twice to complete a rectangle.

7. Click the Erase tool on the Modify panel (of the Home tab); select all four lines you just drew and right-click.

8. It's very efficient to use RECTANGLE with Cartesian coordinates. Click the Rectangle tool on the Draw panel and then click an arbitrary point at the bottom of the living room. The prompt reads

   `Specify other corner point or [Area/Dimensions/Rotation]:`

9. Type **@3´,6´** (or **@90,180** in metric) and press Enter. The same rectangle that you more laboriously drew with lines is already done.

Using Polar Coordinates

Polar coordinates are another useful way of measuring Euclidean space. In polar coordinates, points are located using two measurements: the distance from the origin point and the angle from zero degrees (see Figure 2.16). East is the default direction of zero degrees.

Let's explore how to use polar coordinates:

1. Click the Line tool on the Draw panel. Click an arbitrary first point in the living room and then type **@3´<45** (or **@90<45** in metric) and press Enter to end the LINE command. You have drawn another 3´ (or 90 cm) line using relative polar coordinates.

2. Press Enter to repeat the last command. Click an arbitrary first point, move the cursor up and to the left, type **3´** (or **90** cm), and press Enter twice. A 3´ (or 90 cm) line is drawn at an arbitrary angle.

SPECIFYING ANGLES WITH THE CURSOR

Direct distance entry is the relative method of using the cursor to determine an angle, rather than typing in a specific number of degrees following the < symbol. Direct distance entry is most efficiently used with Ortho and/or Polar modes, which you'll learn about in Chapter 3.

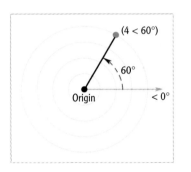

FIGURE 2.16 Polar coordinates

3. Press **L** and the spacebar. Click an arbitrary first point, type **@4´<180** (or **@120<180** in metric), and press Enter. The line is drawn to the left from the first point because 180 degrees is the same direction as angle zero but leads in the opposite direction.

4. Type **@3´** (or **@90<-90** in metric) **<−90** and press Enter. Negative angles are measured clockwise from angle zero by default. Press **C** and then Enter to close the 3:4:5 triangle you've just drawn.

5. Type **ucsicon** and press Enter. UCS stands for *user coordinate system*. You, the user, can change the coordinate system's orientation. Type on and press Enter. An icon indicating the directions of the positive x- and y-axes is displayed in the lower-left corner of the canvas (see Figure 2.17).

> AutoCAD LT has only one coordinate system that cannot be changed. LT users can skip ahead to the next section.

FIGURE 2.17 UCS icon in the default orientation

6. Type **UCS** and press Enter. The prompt in the Command window reads as follows:

    ```
    Specify origin of UCS or [Face/NAmed/Object/
    Previous/View/World/X/Y/Z/ZAxis] <World>:
    ```

    There is much you can do with the UCS, but here you will simply rotate the UCS about its z-axis (the axis coming out of the screen). Type **Z** and press Enter.

7. Type **90** and press Enter to rotate the coordinate system. Observe the UCS icon has changed to reflect the new orientation (see Figure 2.18).

FIGURE 2.18 Rotating the UCS about its z-axis

8. Type **PLAN** and press Enter. The prompt in the Command window reads

    ```
    Enter an option [Current ucs/Ucs/World] <Current>:
    ```

    The option in the angled brackets, <Current>, is what you want, so press Enter to make this selection. The house is reoriented with respect to the current UCS (see Figure 2.19). Notice that the ViewCube's compass directions are rotated (North is now to the right).

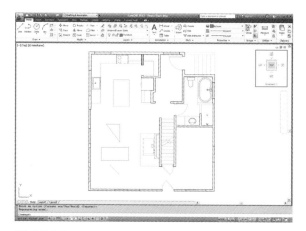

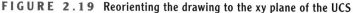

FIGURE 2.19 Reorienting the drawing to the xy plane of the UCS

ROTATING THE PLAN TO MATCH THE UCS

User coordinate systems are usually associated with 3D modeling, but there is one transformation especially useful for 2D drafting: rotation about the z-axis. If you are drawing a building wing or mechanical part that is at an angle with respect to horizontal (especially when the angle isn't an increment of 90 degrees), try rotating the UCS's z-axis and then use the PLAN command to reorient the drawing to the new horizontal.

9. Click the Line tool on the Draw panel. Click an arbitrary first point in the living room and then type @3´<45 (or @90<45 in metric) and press Enter to end the LINE command. You have drawn another 3´ (or 90 cm) line using relative polar coordinates (the same as step 1). However, this time the new line has a different orientation with respect to the original line and the rest of the house (see Figure 2.20).

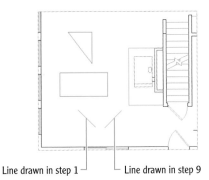

Line drawn in step 1 ⌐   ⌐ Line drawn in step 9

FIGURE 2.20 Angles are relative to the coordinate system in which they are drawn. Both lines were drawn at a 45 degree angle but in different coordinate systems.

10. To restore the current coordinate system to its original state, called the *world coordinate system* (WCS), type UCS and press Enter twice. Then type PLAN and press Enter twice more. The plan is oriented to the WCS as it was initially. Observe that North is up again in the ViewCube.

Drawing Circles, Arcs, and Polygons

Arcs are sections of circles. Polygons are regular figures made of straight segments such as a triangle, square, pentagon, or hexagon. A polygon with a large number of segments may look like a circle but is fundamentally different.

There are many options for creating circles, arcs, and polygons. AutoCAD provides these options to make it easier to create accurate shapes based on all the types of geometric situations that typically arise in drawings.

Creating Circles

Let's draw some circles on the kitchen stove to represent the burners:

1. Zoom into the stove in the kitchen. Two of the burner circles are missing and you will draw them.

2. On the Home tab, take a look at the Layer drop-down menu in the Layers panel and observe that Furniture is the current layer (because you see its name without having to open the drop-down). Open the Layer drop-down menu and select Equipment as the current layer (see Figure 2.21).

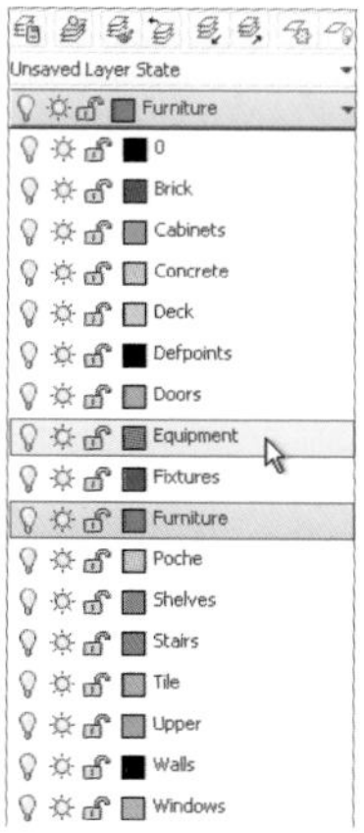

> ▶
>
> **Drawn objects appear on whichever layer is current.**

FIGURE 2.21 Making the Equipment layer current

3. You will use preexisting points as guides in drawing the burners. However, the points are difficult to see right now because they are represented as single pixels. Expand the Utilities panel on the Home tab and select Point Style. In the Point Style dialog box, select the X icon and click OK (see Figure 2.22).

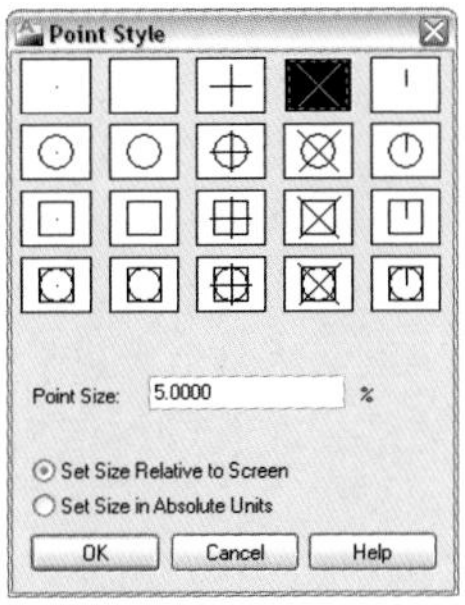
Point Style
Point Size: 5.0000 %
Set Size Relative to Screen
Set Size in Absolute Units
OK
Cancel
Help

FIGURE 2.22 Changing the point style so points are more visible

4. Click the Circle tool on the Draw panel. Before you click a center point, hold down Shift and right-click to open the Object Snap context menu (see Figure 2.23).

5. Select Node from the context menu and then click point A, as shown in Figure 2.24. The prompt in the Command window reads

```
Specify radius of circle or [Diameter] <0'-0">:
```

Type **3** (or **8** in metric) and press Enter to create a circle with a radius of 3″ (or 8 cm). Note that typing the inch symbol is not necessary. Never type m, cm, or mm to represent metric units.

Certification Objective

Drawing objects close by eye is not good enough in AutoCAD. Always use object snaps to connect objects precisely.

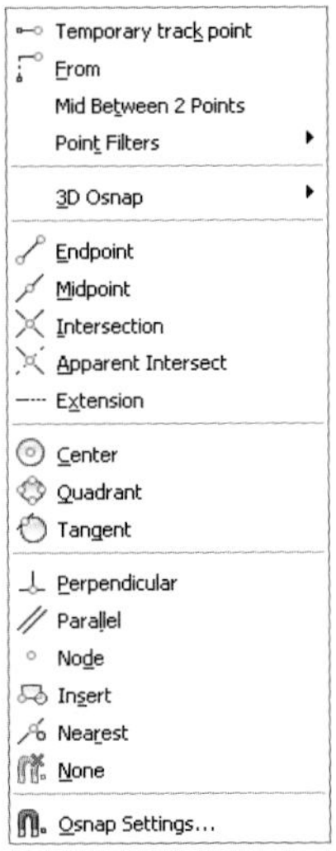
Temporary track point
From
Mid Between 2 Points
Point Filters
3D Osnap
Endpoint
Midpoint
Intersection
Apparent Intersect
Extension
Center
Quadrant
Tangent
Perpendicular
Parallel
Node
Insert
Nearest
None
Osnap Settings...

FIGURE 2.23 Object Snap context menu

6. Right-click to repeat the last command. The prompt in the Command window reads

```
Specify center point for circle or
[3P/2P/Ttr (tan tan radius)]:
```

Type **2P** to indicate the two point option and press Enter. Hold Shift and right-click to open the Object Snap context menu. Select Node and then click point B, as shown in Figure 2.24.

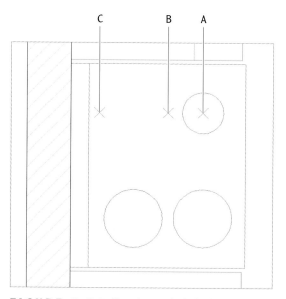

FIGURE 2.24 Drawing a circle by locating its center using node snap

Object snaps listed in the context menu must be selected each time they are used. You will learn how to set up running object snaps in Chapter 3.

7. Hold Shift again, right-click, and choose Node. Click point C, as shown in Figure 2.24, and the CIRCLE command is completed.

8. Click the arrow under the Circle tool in the Draw panel and select 3-Point. Shift+right-click and select Tangent. Click the circle you drew in the previous step.

9. Hold Shift and right-click again and type **G**. Notice that this letter is underlined in the word Tangent in the context menu (refer to Figure 2.23). Click the circle on the bottom left.

10. Type **tan**, press Enter to invoke the Tangent object snap, and click the circle on the lower right. You can type the first three letters

of any object snap as an alternative to using the context menu. AutoCAD draws a circle precisely tangent to the three others (see Figure 2.25).

11. Erase the three point objects and the last circle you drew to leave the four burners of the stove.

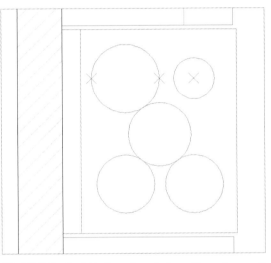

FIGURE 2.25 Drawing circles with various options

Creating Arcs

Arcs have more options than circles because of the complexities of the geometric situations arcs can be drawn in. In the next set of steps, you will use one such arc option to draw a door swing:

1. Zoom into the bathroom. The bathroom door needs an arc to represent the way it swings.

2. Select Doors from the Layer drop-down menu in the Layers panel.

3. Click the Arc tool's drop-down flyout menu in the Draw panel, which is indicated by the arrow under the word Arc. Select Center, Start, End. This is the sequence in which information must be entered.

4. Type **int**, press Enter to invoke the Intersection object snap, and click the center point A in Figure 2.26.

5. Hold Shift and right-click, select Endpoint from the context menu, and click the start point B (shown in Figure 2.26).

Arc

Certification
Objective

6. Hold Shift and right-click, type **E**, and click the arc endpoint C (shown in Figure 2.26). The arc appears and the command is completed.

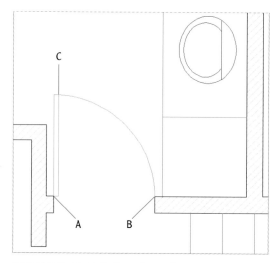

FIGURE 2.26 Drawing a door swing with an arc option

CONTROLLING ARC AND CIRCLE SMOOTHNESS

Arcs and circles are defined with perfect curvature in AutoCAD but sometimes they appear blocky on screen. The system variable VIEWRES controls how smoothly arcs and circles are drawn on screen. Adjust this on the View tab under the Visual Style panel's expansion menu. Set the resolution to the maximum VIEWRES value of 20000. Type **REGEN** and press Enter to make this change take effect on screen.

Drawing Polygons

When you want to draw triangles, squares, pentagons, or any figure having equally sized edges, use the POLYGON command. You can draw these shapes inside or outside a circle, or specify the edge length, as shown in the following steps:

1. Make the Furniture layer current by selecting it from the Layer drop-down menu in the Layers panel.

2. Zoom into the living room.

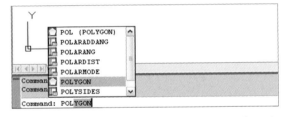

3. Select the Home tab if it's not already active. Click the Rectangle tool's drop-down flyout and select the Polygon tool. The prompt in the Command window reads

```
Enter number of sides <5>:
```

4. Type **4** and press Enter to draw a square.

5. The command prompt now reads

```
Specify center of polygon or [Edge]:
```

Type **E** and press Enter to specify an edge length and direction. Click a point somewhere in the living room as the first endpoint of the edge and type **@2´<0** (or **@60<0** in metric) to specify the second endpoint of the edge relative to the first one, using polar coordinates in this case. A 2´ (or 60 cm) square appears.

6. Type **POL** and observe that as you type, the AutoComplete menu appears above the command line suggesting commands and system variables (Figure 2.27). Press the down arrow until POLYGON is highlighted and press Enter.

Certification Objective

```
POL (POLYGON)
POLARADDANG
POLARANG
POLARDIST
POLARMODE
POLYGON
POLYSIDES
Command: POLYGON
```

FIGURE 2.27 Menu suggesting commands and system variables appears as you type

7. Type **6** and press Enter to draw a hexagon. Click a point in the living room where you want to center the hexagon. The prompt now reads

```
Enter an option [Inscribed in circle/
Circumscribed about circle] <I>:
```

8. Press Enter to accept the default Inscribed In Circle option.

9. Type **1´** (or **30** in metric) as the radius of the circle and press Enter. A hexagon fitting inside a 1´ (or 30 cm) radius circle appears.

Filleting and Chamfering Lines

Fillet and Chamfer are tools that create transitions between objects. Fillet creates arcs and Chamfer creates lines. Fillet is most commonly used for a purpose for which it probably wasn't designed—joining separate lines so they intersect at their endpoints, without creating arcs at all.

Joining Nonparallel Lines

Fillet and Chamfer can be used to join lines that are crossing as well as lines that don't meet. Chamfer doesn't work on parallel lines at all, but Fillet will create a half circle connecting the endpoints of parallel lines, regardless of the fillet radius. Let's explore the FILLET and CHAMFER commands:

1. Draw two lines. It doesn't matter what size they are or what angle is between them, as long as the lines aren't parallel.

2. Press the F12 key to toggle on *dynamic input*, an optional mode that displays command-line options on the canvas. Position the cursor on the canvas and type cha, the command alias for the CHAMFER command, and the AutoComplete window appears on the canvas rather than in the Command window.

3. Press Enter and then press the down arrow key to expand the command's options on screen.

4. Press the down arrow three more times and press Enter to select the Distance option in the Dynamic Input display (see Figure 2.28). Type **1´** (or **30** cm) and press Enter twice to input equal first and second distances equal to 1´.

Fillet and chamfer previewing works only if When A Command Is Active is selected on the Selection tab of the Options dialog box. This option should be selected by default.

FIGURE 2.28 Displaying a command-line option on the canvas with dynamic input

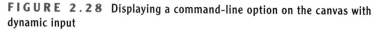

5. Click one line and then hover the cursor over the second line; you'll see a preview of the chamfer that will be created. Click the second line to perform the chamfer and complete the command (the chamfer is shown in the middle of Figure 2.29).

6. Draw two more noncrossing and nonparallel lines.

7. Type **F** and press Enter to execute the FILLET command. Press the down arrow and choose Radius from the Dynamic Input display. Type **1′** (or **30** cm) and press Enter.

8. Click the first line and then hover the cursor over the second line; the fillet preview shows on screen. Click the second line to commit to that particular radius (this fillet is shown at the right of Figure 2.29).

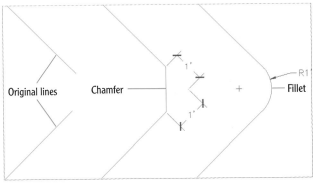

FIGURE 2.29 Chamfered and filleted lines

Joining Crossed Lines

When lines cross, there are multiple fillet and chamfer possibilities on different sides of the intersection. In the case of crossing lines, you must select the lines on the portions that you want to keep, as shown in these steps:

1. Draw two lines that cross.

2. Type **F** and press Enter. Press the down arrow to access the Dynamic Input display and select Radius. Type **0** and press Enter. Now Fillet will not create an arc at all.

3. Click the points A and B, as shown in Figure 2.30. The lines are joined at their endpoints and the remaining portions of the lines beyond their intersection point are trimmed away.

4. Click the Save As button on the Quick Access toolbar. Type **Ch2-B.dwg** or **Ch2-B-metric.dwg** as the filename. The end file is provided on Chapter 2's download page at **www.sybex.com/go/ autocad2012essentials** for your convenience.

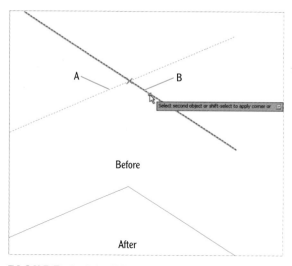

A   B

Select second object or shift-select to apply corner or

Before

After

FIGURE 2.30 Filleting lines with a zero radius joins them together precisely.

THE ESSENTIALS AND BEYOND

This chapter covered the mechanics of drawing many basic object types, including lines, circles, arcs, and polygons. You learned how to navigate 2D drawings in a variety of ways. By learning how to cancel, erase, and undo, you won't be afraid to make mistakes in AutoCAD. In addition, we explored how coordinate systems make accurate drawing possible. Finally, you altered existing lines with Fillet and Chamfer, and learned how to join lines by using a zero fillet radius.

ADDITIONAL EXERCISE

▶ Explore the Donut and Solid commands on your own. Unlike most AutoCAD drawing tools, these older commands produce objects that have two-dimensional solidity. Refer to AutoCAD's Help if you need further information.

CHAPTER 3

Using Drawing Aids

AutoCAD's drawing aids are like the triangles, compasses, and engineering scales of traditional drafting. Drawing aids are essential modes and methods of entering data that, once mastered, allow you to create measured drawings with ease. I highly recommend learning all the drawing aids because they will make you a more productive draftsperson. Most drawing aids can be toggled on or off from the application status bar. Additional settings and dialog boxes are accessible by right-clicking the individual status bar toggles.

▶ **Grid and snap**

▶ **Ortho and polar tracking**

▶ **PolarSnap**

▶ **Running object snaps**

▶ **From snap**

▶ **Object snap tracking**

Grid and Snap

Certification Objective

The most basic of drawing aids, *Grid* makes AutoCAD's canvas look like graph paper. You can adjust the grid's measured size and the spacing of its major lines to simulate many types of graph paper.

Snap constrains your ability to draw objects so that they automatically start and end precisely at grid intersections. Grid and Snap are most helpful when used together so that you can draw objects that snap to the grid. Figure 3.1 shows some of the status bar toggles that you'll be learning about in this chapter.

1. Click the New button on the Quick Access toolbar.

2. Choose the acad.dwt Imperial template (or acadiso.dwt metric template) from the Select Template dialog box (see Figure 3.2) and click Open.

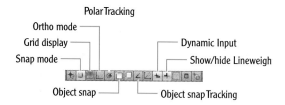

FIGURE 3.1 Various status bar toggles

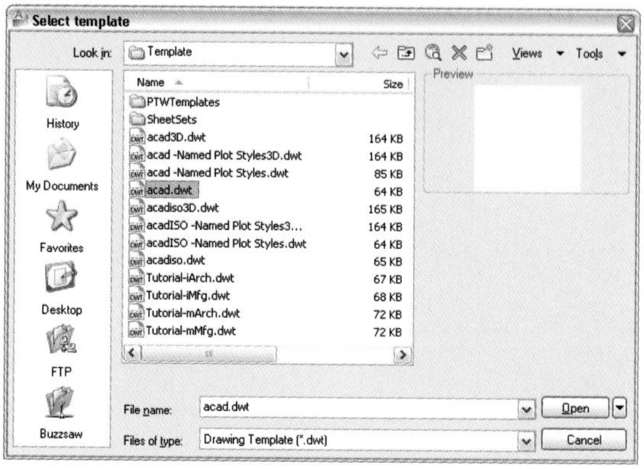

FIGURE 3.2 Choosing a template to begin drawing

Grid spacing is usually equal to or an increment of the snap interval.

3. Right-click the Grid Display toggle on the status bar and choose Settings from the context menu. Change Grid X spacing to 1″ (or 10mm) and press Tab; Grid Y spacing updates with the same value. Set Major Line Every to 12 for Imperial (or 10 for metric) so you'll see darker grid lines every foot. Notice that Snap spacing is set to ½″ (or 10mm) by default. Select Snap On and verify that the Grid Snap radio button is selected in the Snap Type area (see Figure 3.3). Click OK.

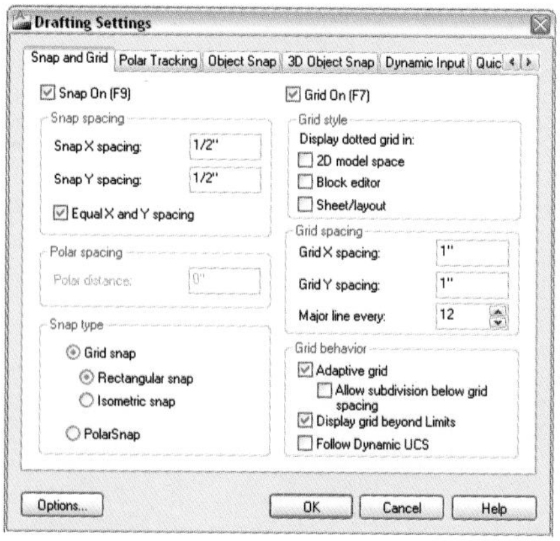

FIGURE 3.3 Setting up grid spacing and toggling on Snap

4. Click the Line tool in the Draw panel on the ribbon's Home tab. Click the first point near the lower-left corner of the canvas at the intersection of major grid lines (darker lines). Click the second point 2´ (or 600 mm) above the first point by clicking the second intersection (or sixth intersection in metric) of major grid lines. Right-click to end the LINE command. It's very difficult to see the line because the grid obscures it.

5. Click the Show/Hide Lineweight icon in the status bar so that the button is highlighted in blue. It's difficult to see the line because the default lineweight display is too thin.

6. Right-click the Show/Hide Lineweight icon and choose Settings from the context menu. Open the Default drop-down list and select 0.016˝ (or 0.40 mm) (see Figure 3.4) and click OK. The line you drew in step 4 is displayed thicker so it's more visible against the grid.

> **You'll learn how to control lineweight with layers in Chapter 6, "Controlling Visibility."**

FIGURE 3.4 Adjusting the default lineweight settings

7. Type **L** and press Enter twice to continue drawing from the last point clicked. Toggle Grid Display off and Dynamic Input on in the status bar. Move the cursor horizontally to the right from the point at which the rubberband is anchored. Notice that ½˝ (or 10 mm) increments are all that show up on screen; this is due to Snap. Snap can be used independently of the grid; the grid is merely a visual drawing aid. Click on the drawing canvas when dynamic input value reads 2´-0˝ (or 600 mm), as shown in Figure 3.5.

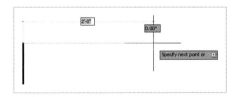

FIGURE 3.5 Using Snap with Dynamic Input to gauge distances without typing

TRANSPARENT COMMANDS

Status bar buttons can be toggled on or off and their settings adjusted while another command is running. Commands that operate while another command is running are called *transparent commands*. Typing a single quote before a command forces it to be run transparently. For example, while drawing a line, type 'z and press Enter. The ZOOM command is run transparently, and when it is done the LINE command resumes. The following transcript shows this command sequence:

```
Command: 1
LINE Specify first point: 'z
'ZOOM
>>Specify corner of window, enter a
scale factor (nX or nXP), or
[All/Center/Dynamic/Extents/Previous/
Scale/Window/Object] <real time>:
>>>>Specify opposite corner:
Resuming LINE command.
Specify first point:
```

Ortho and Polar Tracking

Ortho mode aids in drawing *orthogonal* (horizontal or vertical) lines. Polar Tracking is more flexible than Ortho mode, with the ability to constrain lines to increments of a set angle. A list of common angles is included on polar tracking toggle's context menu, such as 45°, 30°, 22.5°, 10°, and so on. The traditional square and a set of triangles from traditional drafting are analogues to AutoCAD's Ortho and Polar Tracking modes.

Let's try Ortho and Polar Tracking modes by drawing a series of line segments. You'll use Ortho when the segments are 90° apart and Polar Tracking when the segments are drawn at other angles.

▶

When Polar Tracking is set to 90°, it functions identically to Ortho mode.

1. If the file is not already open from performing the previous step, go to the book's companion web page at **www.sybex.com/go/ autocad2012essentials**, browse to Chapter 3, download the file Ch3-A.dwg (or Ch3-A-metric.dwg) and open it.

2. Type **L** and press Enter twice to continue drawing from the last point.

The dash is a necessary separator between whole and fractional inches.

◄

3. Toggle off Snap mode by pressing the F9 key.

4. Toggle on Ortho mode by pressing the F8 key.

5. Move the cursor down from the last point, type **10-3/4″** (or **240** mm), and press Enter. Ortho mode constrains the line vertically and typing in an explicit value obviates the need for Snap (see Figure 3.6). You don't have to use the comma from Cartesian coordinates or the angle symbol from polar coordinates with direct distance entry.

Certification
Objective

6. Toggle off Ortho mode by clicking its status bar button. Toggle on Polar Tracking by clicking the adjacent button on the right. Right-click the Polar Tracking button and choose 45.00 from the context menu.

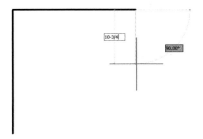

FIGURE 3.6 Drawing a line using Ortho mode and direct distance entry

7. Move the cursor around and observe that green dashed lines appear in eight locations around a circle (in 45° increments). Move the cursor to the right relative to the last point, and type **2′** (or **600** mm) and press Enter (see Figure 3.7). Press Esc to terminate the LINE command without deleting the last segment drawn.

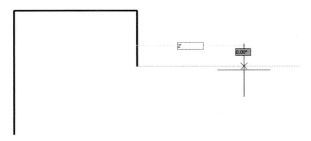

FIGURE 3.7 Drawing another line with Ortho mode and direct distance entry

8. Save your work as Ch3-B.dwg (or Ch3-B-metric.dwg).

Just like Ortho mode, Polar Tracking guarantees that the last line drawn was perfectly aligned to the set increment; you merely had to move the cursor in the general direction you wanted to direct the new line. Ortho and Polar Tracking save you from having to explicitly type in angles or coordinate values, or to even think about coordinate systems.

PolarSnap

PolarSnap includes a kind of Snap that is customized for Polar Tracking. Instead of being tied to a spatial grid (as with Snap), PolarSnap is appropriately based on relative polar coordinates. As you'll see in the steps that follow, PolarSnap is useful for drawing measured lines on angles other than horizontal or vertical.

1. If the file is not already open from the previous step, go to the book's web page at **www.sybex.com/go/autocad2012essentials**, browse to Chapter 3, download the file Ch3-B.dwg (or Ch3-B-metric.dwg), and open it.

2. Toggle on Snap by clicking its icon on the status bar. Right-click the same button and choose Settings from the context menu.

3. Select the PolarSnap radio button in the Drafting Settings dialog box. Type **1″** (or **10** mm) in the Polar Distance text box (see Figure 3.8). Click OK.

FIGURE 3.8 Choosing PolarSnap mode in the Drafting Settings dialog box

> The PolarSnap increment defaults to the Snap X spacing value unless a Polar Distance value is entered.

4. Type **L** and press Enter twice to continue drawing from the last point.

5. Move the cursor down at a 45° angle from East and observe the Snap values that appear with Dynamic Input on screen. Click when the value

is 6″ (or 150 mm) (see Figure 3.9). You avoided having to type anything with Polar Tracking and PolarSnap.

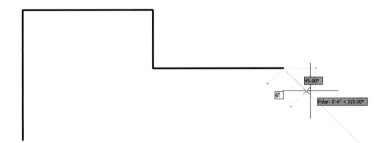

FIGURE 3.9 Drawing a line using Polar Tracking and PolarSnap

6. Move the cursor down and click to draw a line when the value reads 1′ (or 300 mm). Right-click to end the LINE command.

7. Press the spacebar to repeat the LINE command. Hold Shift and right-click to access the Snap context menu. Select Endpoint in the menu and click the lower endpoint of the first line you drew in this tutorial.

8. Toggle off Snap mode by clicking its icon on the status bar, thus disabling PolarSnap.

9. Move the cursor horizontally to the right until it overshoots the last line drawn in step 5. Click to draw the line without worrying about its length (see Figure 3.10). Right-click to complete the command.

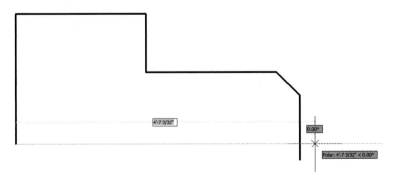

FIGURE 3.10 Drawing a horizontal line that overshoots the vertical line

10. Type **F** (for Fillet) and press Enter. Verify that Radius is set to 0 in the Command window and then click the vertical and horizontal lines

on the portions of the lines that you want to keep (marked A and B in Figure 3.11). The drawn shape forms a closed loop.

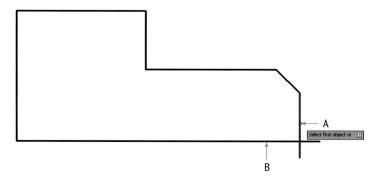

FIGURE 3.11 Filleting with a zero radius to form a corner

11. Save as Ch3-C.dwg (or Ch3-C-metric.dwg), which is available among the book's companion download files here:

   www.sybex.com/go/autocad2012essentials

Running Object Snaps

The lines you have drawn thus far are all precisely connected because they were chained together as they were drawn. In other words, the last point of one segment was reused as the first point of the next segment. Aside from this special circumstance, lines must be connected using object snap to ensure accuracy.

While you learned to use the Object Snap context menu in Chapter 2, we will now use that as a jumping-off point to learn a far more efficient method called *Running Object Snap*. As you will see in the steps that follow, with Running Object Snap, frequently used object snaps can be turned on continuously. That way you don't have to invoke them explicitly every time you want to use object snap.

1. If the file is not already open from performing the previous step, go to the book's Downloads page at **www.sybex.com/go/ autocad2012essentials**, browse to Chapter 3, download the file Ch3-C.dwg (or Ch3-C-metric.dwg), and open it.

2. Using Polar Tracking but without using Object Snap, draw a line using points A to B in Figure 3.12 as a guide. Click each point as accurately as you can because I want you to see that you can't make it perfect without using object snap.

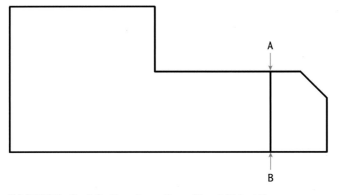

FIGURE 3.12 Drawing a line without Object Snap

3. Press **Z** and then Enter. Click two points to define a tightly cropped zoom window around point A. Zoom in again if necessary until you can see that the endpoint of the line you just drew is not on the horizontal line (see Figure 3.13). No matter how carefully you clicked point A in the previous step, the line you drew will not be on the edge (it will either fall short or overshoot).

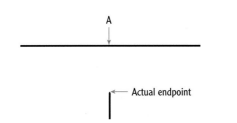

FIGURE 3.13 Zooming in reveals that the lines do not meet

4. Select Zoom Previous from the Navigation bar's Zoom menu. Click Zoom Previous again if necessary to return to the original view.

5. Click the line drawn in step 3 and press the Delete key.

6. Toggle on Object Snap on the status bar. Right-click the same icon and choose Settings from the context menu. Click the Clear All button and then select Endpoint, Midpoint, and Perpendicular (see Figure 3.14). Click OK.

7. Toggle off Polar Tracking and Dynamic Input modes on the status bar. Click the Line tool on the Draw panel. Move the cursor close to point A in Figure 3.15 and wait for the green endpoint marker to

> You can toggle on one object snap type at a time using the Object Snap icon's context menu. Choose Settings to make more extensive Snap selections.
>
> ◀
>
> Certification Objective

appear. When it does, click to precisely snap the first point of your line to this point.

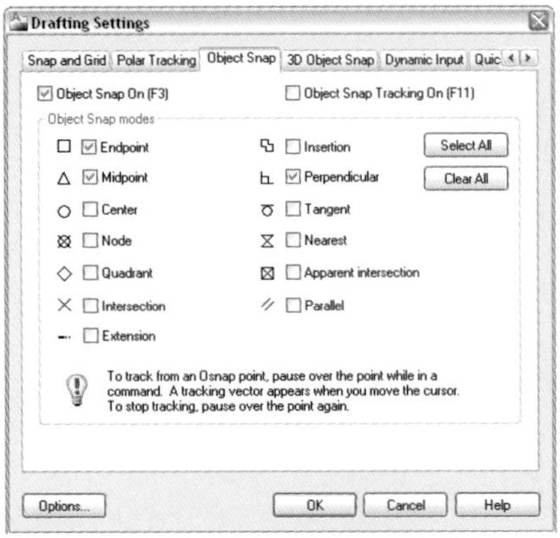

FIGURE 3.14 **Turning on a few Running Object Snap modes**

You don't have to try to position the cursor over the actual geometric perpendicular; as long as the perpendicular marker appears, AutoCAD will calculate the desired point exactly.

8. Move the cursor down to point B and wait until the green perpendicular marker appears. When it does, click the drawing canvas to select the second point. Press Esc to end the command. This line is connected precisely at both ends because object snap was used.

9. Zoom into point A or B in Figure 3.16 and verify that the lines are connected perfectly. Click Zoom Previous in the Navigation bar to return to the initial overall view.

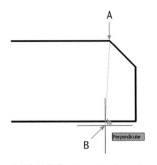

FIGURE 3.15 **Drawing a line using running object snaps**

Nearest should be used with caution as a running snap mode because it conflicts with other snap modes. Choosing None in the Snap context menu overrides any running snaps (with no snap).

10. Type **L** and press Enter. Hold Shift and right-click to open the Object Snap context menu and choose Nearest. Object snaps invoked from

the context menu override any running object snaps. Click point A, shown in Figure 3.16. Nearest ensures the new line is attached somewhere along the edge of the horizontal line.

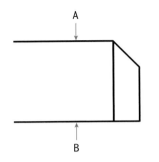

FIGURE 3.16 Overriding running snaps with Nearest snap

11. Move the cursor close to point B as shown in Figure 3.16 and click when the perpendicular marker appears. Press Esc to end the LINE command.

12. Save your work as Ch3-D.dwg (or Ch3-D-metric.dwg).

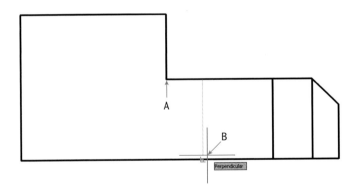

FIGURE 3.17 Drawing a line using the From object snap

From Snap

What happens if rather than snapping to an existing geometrical feature (such as an endpoint, midpoint, intersection, and so on), you want to snap a set distance and direction from one? Answer: Use the From snap, as shown in the following steps:

1. If Ch3-D.dwg (or Ch3-D-metric.dwg) is not still open from the previous section, go to the book's web page and open the document from the Chapter 3 file.

2. Type **L** and press Enter. Hold shift and right click to open the object snap context menu. Select From in the context menu.

3. Click point A shown in Figure 3.17. This is the point from which you will specify a displacement. Type **@6˝ <0** (or **@150<0** for metric) to specify the displacement to the first point of the line and press Enter.

4. Move the cursor to point B and wait for the running perpendicular snap marker to appear. When it does, click to specify the second point of the line. Press Esc to end the LINE command. You've drawn a line exactly 6˝ (or 150 mm) over from the corner.

5. Select the line you just drew and press the Delete key.

6. Save your work as Ch3-E.dwg (or Ch3-E-metric.dwg).

Object Snap Tracking

Object snap tracking is for situations where you want to snap to a point that has a geometric relationship with two or more snap points. As you'll see in the following steps, using object snap tracking saves time compared with drawing temporary construction lines that must later be deleted.

1. If Ch3-E.dwg (or Ch3-E-metric.dwg) is not still open from the previous section, go to the book's web page and open the document from the Chapter 3 folder.

2. Click the Circle tool on the Draw panel.

Certification Objective

3. Toggle on Object Snap Tracking by clicking its icon on the status bar. Verify that Ortho mode is on by looking at the status bar (if it isn't, press F8).

4. Move the cursor over point A, as shown in Figure 3.18. When the running midpoint snap marker appears, move the cursor horizontally to the right to establish the first tracking line. Do not click yet.

5. Move the cursor over point B in Figure 3.18 and wait for the Midpoint marker to appear. Move the cursor vertically down to establish the second tracking line. Again, do not click yet.

6. Move the cursor down until both tracking lines intersect. When they do, click to set the center point of the circle. Type **9** (or **220** for metric) and press Enter to create a circle with a radius of 9″ (or 220 mm).

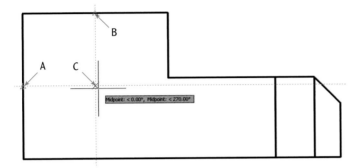

FIGURE 3.18 Locating a circle's center point with object snap tracking

7. Click the Rectangle tool on the Draw panel. Move the cursor over the endpoint marked A in Figure 3.19 and without clicking, move the cursor down to establish the first tracking line.

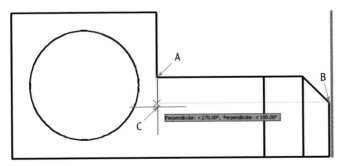

FIGURE 3.19 Drawing a rectangle by tracking its first corner

8. Move the cursor to point B in Figure 3.19 to track another endpoint. Move the cursor horizontally back to the intersection with the first tracking line and click to establish the first corner of the rectangle (point C).

9. Type **@1´,-6** (or **@280,-160** for metric) and press Enter. The rectangle and drawing is complete (see Figure 3.20).

10. Toggle off Show/Hide Lineweight.

11. Your drawing should now resemble Ch3-F.dwg (or Ch3-F-metric.dwg), which is available among the book's companion download files here:

www.sybex.com/go/autocad2012essentials

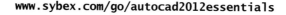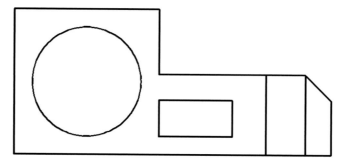

FIGURE 3.20 Completed mechanical part

THE ESSENTIALS AND BEYOND

You have learned how to draw accurately using a variety of drawing aids, including Grid and Snap, Ortho mode and Polar Tracking, PolarSnap, running object snaps, From snap, and object snap tracking. Each of these aids will become second nature to you, the more you practice drawing in AutoCAD. In time you will know which drawing aid most efficiently fits each geometric situation you encounter.

ADDITIONAL EXERCISES

▶ Draw the following diagram to the given dimensions. You will need to employ a variety of drawing aids learned in this chapter to draw the figure accurately.

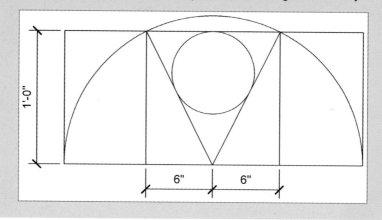

CHAPTER 4

Editing Entities

Drawing in AutoCAD is not just about creating lines, rectangles, circles, and other shapes. Most of your time will be spent editing entities. Although AutoCAD provides the basic tools for transforming shapes, such as Move, Copy, Rotate, and Scale, more complex editing tools are also available, such as Array, Trim, Extend, Lengthen, Stretch, Offset, Mirror, Break, Join, and Overkill.

► **Creating selection sets**

► **Move and Copy**

► **Rotate and Scale**

► **Arrays**

► **Trim and Extend**

► **Lengthen and Stretch**

► **Offset and Mirror**

► **Grip editing**

There is a distinction in AutoCAD Architecture (a program based on AutoCAD with additional architecture-specific functionality) between *entity* and *object*: entities are geometric (line, circle, and so on) and AEC (architecture, engineering, and construction) objects are parametric (wall, floor, and so on). However, these terms are used interchangeably in AutoCAD and in this book; entities/objects are lines, polylines, circles, arcs, splines, ellipses, and so on.

►

Creating Selection Sets

All editing commands operate on one or more drawing entities such as lines, polylines, circles, arcs, splines, ellipses, and so on. In complex drawings you have to plan how you will select only those entities you want to edit while leaving all other entities unaffected. You will learn a number of techniques for adding and removing entities from the *selection set*, which is the collection of entities your chosen editing command acts upon.

Creating a Selection Set at the *Select Objects:* Prompt

In order to edit objects, you must first select them. In complex drawings, selecting would be very tedious if you had to click one object at a time. In the following steps you will learn several efficient selection methods that you can use at any `Select objects:` prompt, which appears in every editing command.

1. Go to the book's web page at **www.sybex.com/go/ autocad2012essentials**, browse to Chapter 4, get the file `Ch4-A.dwg` (or `Ch4-A-metric.dwg`) (a fictitious office building), and open it (see Figure 4.1).

2. Zoom into Stair A in the building core.

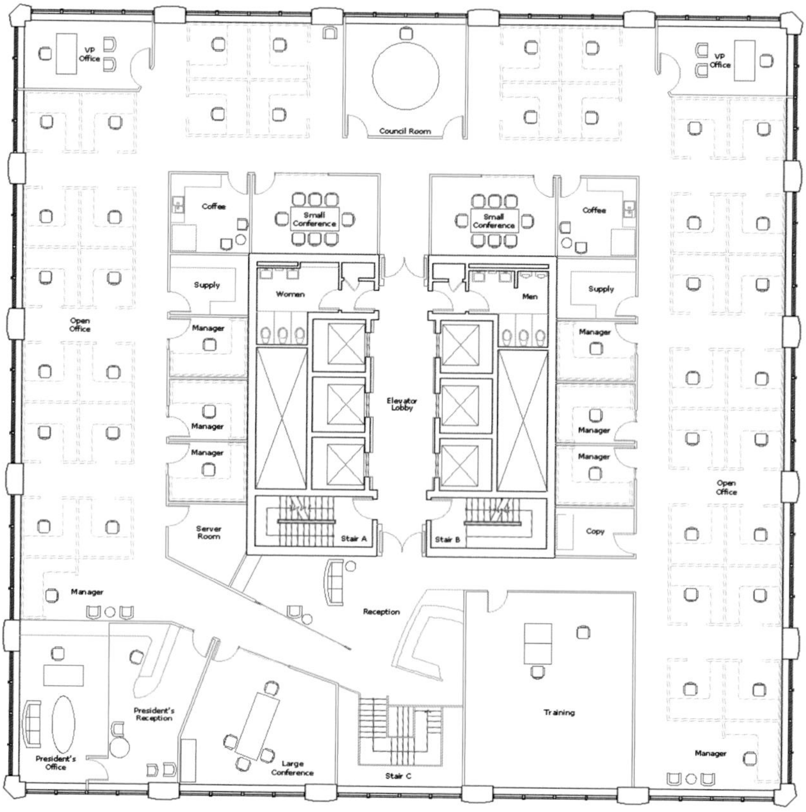

FIGURE 4.1 Office building start file

3. Click the Erase tool in the Modify panel on the Home tab of the ribbon. The prompt in the Command window reads as follows:

   `Select objects:`

   This is the same way almost every command begins: with the opportunity to create a selection set.

4. Click points A and then B, as shown in Figure 4.2. Observe that a transparent *implied window* appears between these points. The objects that are selected are only those completely contained within the borders of the blue window. This particular selection includes the stair arrows, handrails, and three lines representing stair treads near the break lines.

You can draw implied windows either with a click and a click, or a click and drag.

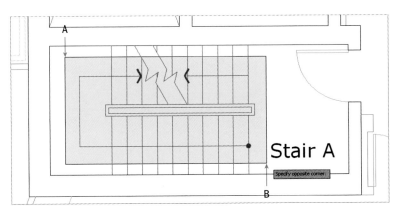

FIGURE 4.2 Drawing an implied window

5. Type **R** (for remove) and press Enter. The command prompt reads as follows:

    ```
    Remove objects:
    ```

6. Click points A and then B, as shown in Figure 4.3. When you click the first point on the right (A) and move the cursor to the left (at B), a transparent green *crossing window* appears between the points. Whatever the green window crosses is selected. The crossing selection removes the handrail and two of the stair treads because the selection was made at the `Remove objects:` prompt.

7. Click points A and then B, as shown in Figure 4.4. This implied window selects the short line segment trapped in the break line and removes it from the selection set.

8. Type **A** (for add) and press Enter. The command prompt again reads as follows:

    ```
    Select objects:
    ```

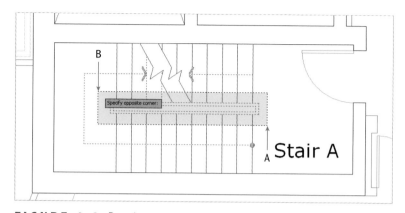

FIGURE 4.3 Drawing a crossing window to remove objects from the selection set

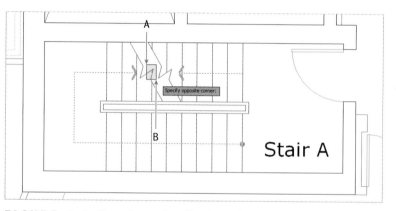

FIGURE 4.4 Removing a short line from the selection set with an implied window

9. Click each of the break lines to add them to the selection set. All of the break line segments are selected in two clicks because the break lines are polylines.

10. Hold Shift and click the break lines again. They are removed from the selection set without being at the Remove objects: prompt.

11. Press Esc to cancel the ERASE command.

Creating a Selection Set before Deciding upon a Command

In addition to creating a selection set at any Select objects: prompt, you can create a selection set first and then decide which command to use afterward. (Additional dynamic input prompts are available on screen when you select objects first.) Let's explore these additional selection methods.

1. If the file is not already open from performing the previous step, go to the book's web page, browse to Chapter 4, download the file Ch4-A.dwg (or Ch4-A-metric.dwg), and open it.

2. Toggle on Dynamic Input mode in the status bar.

3. Click point A, as shown in Figure 4.5. Press the down arrow key to expand the dynamic input menu on screen. Select WPolygon.

◄

The related CPolygon option creates a polygonal crossing window, shown in transparent green. The Fence option allows you to draw a multisegmented line that selects whatever it crosses.

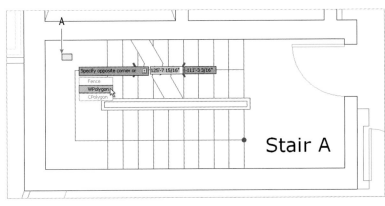

FIGURE 4.5 Selecting WPolygon selection mode from the dynamic input prompt

4. Click points B through H, as shown in Figure 4.6. The transparent blue polygon you are drawing functions the same as an implied rectangular window; the difference is the polygonal window offers more flexibility as you have the power to shape it. Only those objects completely contained within the borders of the blue window will be selected.

5. Press Enter to make the selection. Square blue dots appear on the selected objects—these are called *grips* and you will learn to use them later in this chapter. Press Esc to deselect.

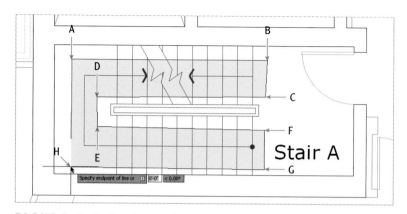

FIGURE 4.6 Drawing a polygonal implied window to create a selection set

6. Toggle on Ortho mode in the status bar. Without being concerned with measurements or accuracy, draw a line under the word Stair, a circle around the letter A, and a rectangle around the entire section, in that order (see Figure 4.7).

FIGURE 4.7 Drawing a few objects to learn about the selection buffer

7. Type **select** and press Enter. Select the circle and the line and press Enter. The SELECT command is used merely to make a selection. The grips for the circle and line appear; press Esc to deselect.

You can select the entire drawing by typing a11 at any Select objects: prompt.

8. Click the Erase icon on the Modify panel. At the Select objects: prompt, type **P** (for previous) and press Enter. The circle and line are selected because they comprise the set of objects that was selected previously. Press Enter again to delete these objects.

9. Press the spacebar to repeat the last command (ERASE). Type **L** (for last) and press Enter. The rectangle is selected because it was the last object you created. There can only ever be one last object. Press Enter again to delete the rectangle.

10. Toggle on Selection Cycling in the status bar.

11. Click the dot at the end of the stair direction line (shown in Figure 4.8). This dot is at the confluence of the horizontal stair direction line and the vertical tread line. When selection cycling is on, you are presented with the Selection dialog box whenever your selection is ambiguous. Hover the cursor over the items in the list and each one's grips are highlighted on the drawing canvas. Select the third item in the list (Line) and then press Esc.

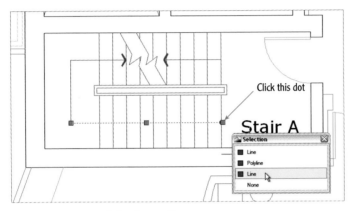

FIGURE 4.8 Selection cycling

12. Press Ctrl+W to toggle selection cycling off.

13. Select one of the vertical tread lines in Stair A by clicking on it. Right-click and choose Select Similar from the context menu that appears. All lines on the same layer are selected (see Figure 4.9). Other object types on the same layer remain unselected because they were not similar enough. Press Esc.

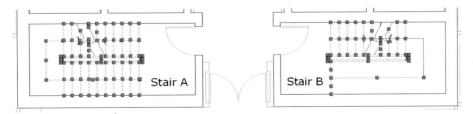

FIGURE 4.9 Selecting similar objects en masse

SELECTING SIMILAR OBJECTS

Type **SELECTSIMILAR**, press Enter, type **SE**, and press Enter again to open its settings dialog. Here you can select criteria to determine which object properties must match in order to be selected by this useful command.

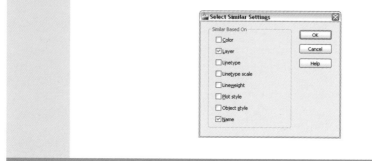

Move and Copy

MOVE and COPY are the most commonly used commands in AutoCAD. As you'll see in the following steps, they are very similar in that they both require a distance and a direction to indicate where you plan to displace the selected objects.

1. If the file is not already open from performing the previous step, go to the book's web page, browse to Chapter 4, download the file Ch4-A.dwg (or Ch4-A-metric.dwg), and open it.

2. Pan to the Training room, where there are two desks and two chairs.

3. Click the chair that is not in front of a desk to select it.

4. Position the cursor over the selected chair, but not over one of its grips. Drag the chair to move it closer to the upper desk as shown in Figure 4.10.

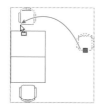

FIGURE 4.10 Moving a selected object by dragging

The disadvantage to moving by dragging is the displacement is unmeasured and you can't use object snap to maintain accuracy.

5. To position the chair more precisely, click the Move tool in the Modify panel. Select the chair you just moved in the previous step and press Enter. The command prompt reads as follows:

       `Specify base point or [Displacement] <Displacement>:`

6. Right-click the Object Snap toggle in the status bar and choose Midpoint from the context menu if it is not already selected. Click the base point at the midpoint of the front of the chair (point A in Figure 4.11).

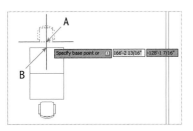

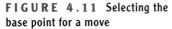

FIGURE 4.11 Selecting the base point for a move

7. Click the second point, B, as shown in Figure 4.12). The chair is moved precisely to the midpoint of the desk edge.

8. Press the spacebar to repeat MOVE. Type **P** and press Enter twice to select the same chair again. Press Enter once more to accept the default option <Displacement>. In Displacement mode, the first point is the origin point. Any coordinates you enter are relative to the origin, so typing the @ symbol is unnecessary. Type **4-1/8<90** (or **10<90** in metric) and press Enter. The chair is moved upward a distance equal to the gap between the lower desk and chair.

9. Click the Copy tool in the Modify panel. Click an implied window around both desks and chairs to select all four objects and press Enter. Toggle on Endpoint Running Object Snap mode if it's not already on.

10. Click point A, as shown in Figure 4.12, as the base point. Click points B, C, and D and press Enter to copy the selection set three times, creating a total of eight desks and chairs.

11. Type **CO** and press Enter. Select all eight desks and chairs with a crossing window and press Enter. Toggle Ortho mode on and move

the cursor down. Type **14'6** (or **440** cm) and press Enter twice. You now have two groups containing eight desks and chairs each.

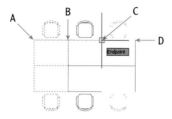

FIGURE 4.12 Copying multiple items with multiple clicks

12. Click the word Training to select the text object, which is obscured by the new seating group. Hold the Ctrl key and repeatedly press the arrow keys to nudge the selected object a few pixels at a time. Nudge the text into the center of the room (see Figure 4.13). Nudging, like dragging, isn't an accurate method to move objects but is convenient.

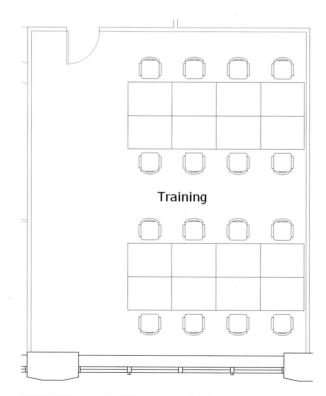

FIGURE 4.13 The completed training room

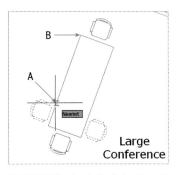

13. Pan over to the Large Conference room. Click the Copy icon in the Modify panel, select both chairs along the long edges of the table, and press Enter.

14. Hold Shift and right-click to open the Object Snap context menu. Select Nearest and click point A as the base point (see Figure 4.14).

FIGURE 4.14 Selecting the base point for a copy array

15. The command prompt reads as follows:

```
Specify second point or [Array]
<use first point as displacement>:
```

Type **A** (for array) and press Enter. Type **4** for the number of items and press Enter. Type **F** (for fit) and press Enter. Click point B in Figure 4.14 and press Enter to complete the array. Eight chairs are evenly spaced along both long sides of the large conference table.

16. Save your work as Ch4-B.dwg (or Ch4-B-metric.dwg).

Rotate and Scale

The ROTATE and SCALE commands are obviously essential to drawing; each requires a base point to indicate the center from which objects are transformed. Numerically speaking, you typically rotate by degrees or scale by percentages about base points. On the other hand, you can avoid using numbers entirely by choosing the Reference options, which let you rotate or scale selection sets in relation to other objects. Let's rotate and scale objects.

1. If the file is not already open from performing the previous step, go to the book's web page, browse to Chapter 4, download the file Ch4-B.dwg (or Ch4-B-metric.dwg), and open it.

2. Toggle off Ortho mode and copy a chair from the training room and place it behind the reception desk.

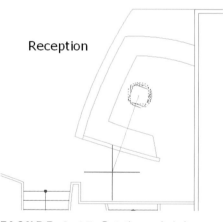

3. Click the Rotate tool on the Modify panel, select the new receptionist's chair, and press Enter. The command line reads

    Specify base point:

Click a point in the center of the chair; you don't need to snap this point because an approximation is good enough in this case.

4. Move the cursor around the base point and observe a rubberband line connects the base point to your cursor and a ghosted image of the chair is superimposed over the original chair representation. Move the cursor until the rubberband aligns more or less with the desk edge (see Figure 4.15) and click.

Reception

FIGURE 4.15 Rotating a chair by eye

5. Press the spacebar to repeat ROTATE. Select the sofa in Reception and press Enter. Click the upper-left endpoint of the sofa's top edge and press Enter; this will be the base point for rotation.

6. Toggle on Ortho mode and move the cursor down. The sofa pops into an orientation 90 degrees away from its initial position. Click to complete the turn.

7. Nudge the sofa down and to the right to place it next to the round side table (Figure 4.16).

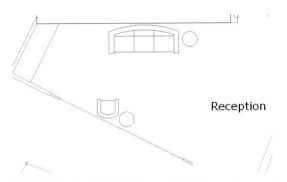

FIGURE 4.16 Rotating with Ortho mode on and nudging into position

8. Move the armchair in Reception so that the midpoint along the front edge of its seat aligns with the window glass as shown in Figure 4.17.

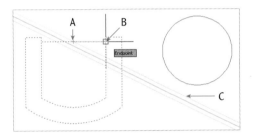

FIGURE 4.17 Rotating using the reference option

9. Type **RO** and press Enter. Select the armchair and press Enter. Click point A.

10. The command prompt reads

Certification Objective

```
Specify rotation angle or [Copy/Reference] <270.00>:
```

Type **R** (for reference) and press Enter. Click point A in Figure 4.17 again. Then click points B and C. Point C is at the midpoint of the glass framing. The chair matches the orientation of the line.

11. Move the armchair off the glass to be next to the round side table.

12. Navigate down to the President's Reception. Click the Scale tool on the Modify panel and select the large round table and press Enter. Hold Shift and right-click to access the Object Snap context menu. Choose Center and click the center point of the circle. Type **.75** and press Enter. The side table is scaled down by 75 percent.

13. One of the chairs in the President's Reception is slightly smaller than the other one. Type **SC** and press Enter. Select the small chair and press Enter again. Click point A in Figure 4.18 as the base point.

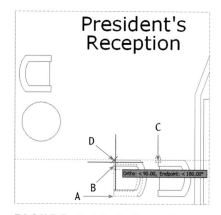

FIGURE 4.18 Scaling a chair up to match the size of another chair

14. The command line reads

    ```
    Specify scale factor or [Copy/Reference]:
    ```

    Type **R** (for reference) and press Enter. Click point A again and then point B to specify the reference length.

15. Toggle on Object Snap Tracking mode, hover the cursor over point C, and then move it toward point D. Click point D when the tracking line intersection appears. The chair has been scaled up to match the larger chair.

16. Save your work as Ch4-C.dwg (or Ch4-C-metric.dwg).

Arrays

The ARRAY command has been completely revamped in AutoCAD 2012. The command used to have a massive dialog box and now that's been replaced by onscreen commands and a contextual ribbon panel. The ARRAY command used to output individual objects that were not associated with the array after creation. Arrays now produce single associative objects, which you can edit at any time to alter the parameters of the array. You will learn how to create two types of arrays: rectangular and polar.

Rectangular Arrays

Rectangular arrays are arranged in a grid of rows (running horizontally) and columns (running vertically). Let's create a rectangular array:

1. If the file is not already open from performing the previous step, go to the book's web page, browse to Chapter 4, download the file Ch4-C.dwg (or Ch4-C-metric.dwg), and open it.

2. Navigate to Stair B and observe that one flight is missing.

3. Click the Rectangular Array tool on the Modify panel. Select both short line segments that are part of the otherwise missing flight and press Enter.

4. The command prompt reads

   ```
   Type = Rectangular  Associative = Yes
   Specify opposite corner for number of items or [Base point/
   Angle/Count]
   ```

   Type **B** (for base point) and press Enter. Click point A as shown in Figure 4.19 to specify the base point.

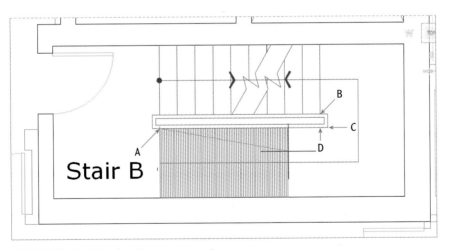

FIGURE 4.19 Creating a rectangular array

5. At the next prompt type **C** (for count) and press Enter. Type **1** (Row) and press Enter and then **12** (Columns) and press Enter again.

6. The command prompt now reads

   ```
   Specify opposite corner to space items or [Spacing]
   <Spacing>:
   ```

Track point D by hovering the cursor over B and C. Click point D when the intersection of both tracking lines appears. Press Enter to end the command.

7. Comparing the new flight with the flight above it, it is clear that the number of treads is wrong. Click the new flight to select it. A temporary green tab appears on the ribbon called Array (see Figure 4.20). Type **10** in the column box and then click the Reset Array button. Press Esc.

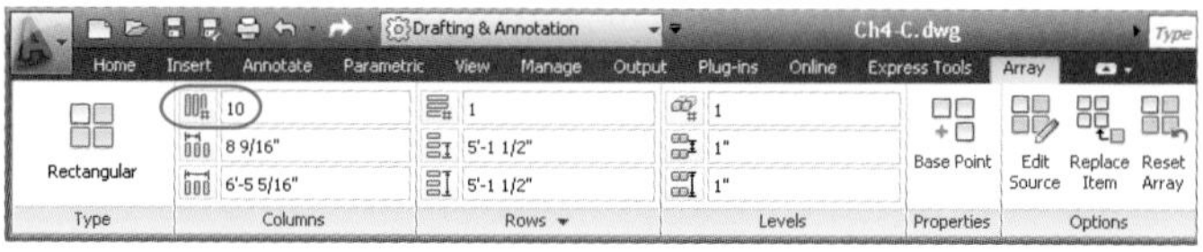

FIGURE 4.20 Array tab on the ribbon

8. The number of treads is correct but the spacing is off. Reselect the array and hover the cursor over the rightmost triangular grip. Select Total Column Spacing from the grip menu that appears. Track and snap to point D as shown in Figure 4.20. The array is now correct.

9. Type **X** and press Enter to issue the EXPLODE command. Select the stair you just arrayed and press Enter. The associativity is destroyed, leaving a series of lines that can no longer be edited as an array.

10. Save your work as Ch4-D.dwg (or Ch4-D-metric.dwg).

Polar Arrays

Polar arrays are used for rotating and copying objects around a common central point. Let's create a polar array:

1. If the file is not already open from performing the previous step, go to the book's web page, browse to Chapter 4, download the file Ch4-D.dwg (or Ch4-D-metric.dwg), and open it.

2. Navigate to the Council Room at the top of the plan (see Figure 4.21).

3. Type **AR** (for array) and press Enter. Select the chair at the top of the round table and press Enter.

4. The command prompt reads

```
Specify base point or enter array type
[Rect/PAth/POlar/Associative/Key point]<centroid>:
```

FIGURE 4.21 The Council Room

5. Type **PO** (for polar) and press Enter.

6. Hold Shift and right-click to open the Object Snap context menu. Choose Center and click the table's center to set the center point of the array.

7. Type **12** (for number of items) and press Enter. Press Enter to accept the default 360-degree angle to fill and press Enter again to end the ARRAY command.

8. The table is a bit too large. Click the circle to select the table. Click the circle's top blue quadrant grip and move the cursor down. Type **6"** (or **15** cm) to set a new radius. Press Enter and Esc.

9. Click any one of the chairs to select the polar array. Hover the cursor over the base point grip and choose Stretch Radius (see Figure 4.22). Type **5'9"** (or **175** cm), then press Enter and Esc. The chairs more closely wrap around the smaller table.

10. You can edit individual items in any array. Reselect the polar array and click the Replace Item button in the Options panel on the Array tab. Click the armchair in the corridor to the left of the War Room and press Enter.

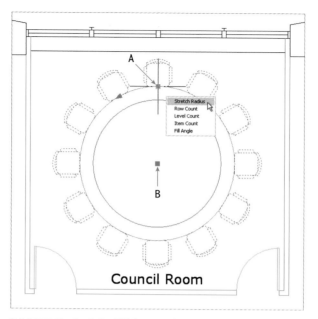

Council Room

FIGURE 4.22 Editing a polar array with its grips

11. The command prompt reads

    ```
    Select base point of replacement objects or
    [Key Point] <centroid>:
    ```

    Press Enter to accept the centroid (center of mass) option.

12. Click the top chair to replace it with the armchair. Press Enter twice to complete the replacement. The President's armchair is now located at the top of the table (see Figure 4.23).

13. Save your work as Ch4-E.dwg (or Ch4-E-metric.dwg).

DIVIDE AND MEASURE

The DIVIDE and MEASURE commands do not copy objects in a rectangular grid or around a center point like the ARRAY command does. Instead, these commands are used for arraying points. Divide splits up a path into any number of evenly spaced points. MEASURE lays out points at a set distance, often leaving a remainder at the end of a path. You'll use DIVIDE in Chapter 5.

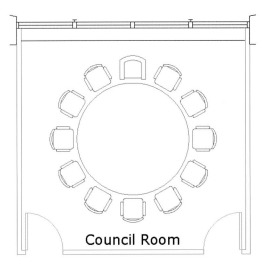

FIGURE 4.23 Replacing an item in an array

Trim and Extend

The TRIM and EXTEND commands are opposites. You can invoke the opposite command while running either by holding down Shift. This is especially helpful because TRIM and EXTEND are often used together:

1. If the file is not already open from performing the previous step, go to the book's web page, browse to Chapter 4, download the file Ch4-E.dwg (or Ch4-E-metric.dwg), and open it.

2. Navigate to Stair C at the bottom of the plan.

3. Click the Trim tool on the Modify panel. The command line reads

```
Current settings: Projection=UCS, Edge=None
Select cutting edges ...
Select objects or <select all>:
```

   Press Enter to select all edges as potential cutting edges.

EXTEND **works just the same as** TRIM **but yields opposite results.**

4. Create a crossing window by clicking points A and B in Figure 4.24. Three segments are trimmed. Hold down Shift and create another crossing window by clicking points C and D (also shown in Figure 4.24). Four lines are extended. Press Enter to end the TRIM command.

5. Type **TR** (for trim) and press Enter twice. Zoom in closer and click each one of the three stair tread lines that extend into the handrails to trim them off. Press Enter to complete the command.

6. Save your work as Ch4-F.dwg (or Ch4-F-metric.dwg).

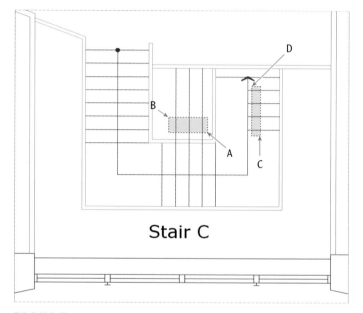

Stair C

FIGURE 4.24 Trimming and Extending at the same prompt

Lengthen and Stretch

The LENGTHEN and STRETCH commands are similar in how they can increase the length of objects. However, STRETCH is the more flexible of the two, allowing you to reposition interconnected objects. Let's lengthen a line and stretch a door within a wall:

1. If the file is not already open from performing the previous step, go to the book's web page, browse to Chapter 4, download the file Ch4-F.dwg (or Ch4-F-metric.dwg), and open it.

2. Navigate to the Copy room. Notice that there is a problem with the copy machine; the top line is drawn only half way. Although you

could use FILLET or EXTEND to fix it, type **len** (for Lengthen) and press Enter. The command prompt reads

```
Select an object or [DElta/Percent/Total/DYnamic]:
```

Type **P** (for percent) and press Enter.

3. Type **200** and press Enter. Click the line segment on the right side to lengthen it toward the right. The copy machine is fixed!

4. Click the Stretch tool on the Modify panel. The command prompt reads

```
Select objects to stretch by crossing-window
or crossing-polygon...
```

Implied windows won't work for stretch; only crossing windows or crossing polygons are acceptable. Click points A and B as shown in Figure 4.25 to select the objects to stretch and press Enter.

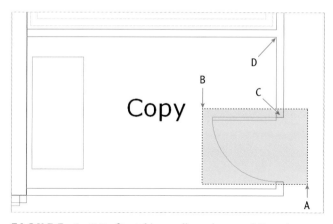

FIGURE 4.25 Stretching walls, a door, and its swing

5. Click point C as the base point. Hold Shift, right-click, and choose From in the context menu. Click point D and move the cursor downward. Type **4** (or **10** in metric) and press Enter to specify the second point. The wall, door, and swing end up 4 inches (or 10 cm) from the upper wall.

6. Save your work as Ch4-G.dwg (or Ch4-G-metric.dwg).

Offset and Mirror

The OFFSET and MIRROR commands are often used to create new objects. OFFSET creates an object a set distance on one side of the original object. MIRROR creates a reversed object at a distance from the original object determined by the position of a drawn reflection line. Let's explore these commands:

1. If the file is not already open from performing the previous step, go to the book's web page, browse to Chapter 4, download the file Ch4-G.dwg (or Ch4-G-metric.dwg), and open it.

2. Navigate to the President's Office. Observe that two of the walls have single line representations.

3. Click the Offset tool in the Modify panel. The command prompt reads

   ```
   Current settings: Erase source=No
   Layer=Source   OFFSETGAPTYPE=0
   Specify offset distance or [Through/Erase/Layer] <0'-0">:
   ```

   Instead of specifying an offset distance numerically, you can click two points and specify the distance graphically.

4. Click point A in Figure 4.26. Right-click the Object Snap toggle in the status bar and select Perpendicular if it is not already on. Click perpendicular to the horizontal red line at B. The distance from A to B specifies the offset distance.

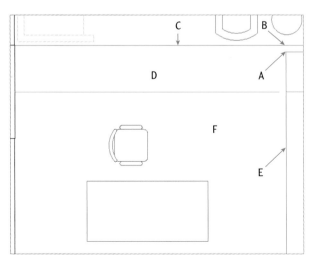

FIGURE 4.26 Offsetting walls a distance equal to the adjacent walls

5. Click the wall line at C to specify it as an object you wish to offset. The command line reads

```
Specify point on side to offset or
[Exit/Multiple/Undo] <Exit>:
```

Click at D to offset the horizontal red line downward. The OFFSET command automatically continues.

6. Click points E and F to offset the vertical line 4 inches (or 10 cm) to the left. Press Enter to end the command.

7. Click the Mirror tool in the Modify panel. Select the sofa in the President's Office and press Enter. The command prompt reads

```
Specify first point of mirror line:
```

You are asked to draw a mirror line through which the geometry will be reflected.

8. Hold Shift and right-click to open the Object Snap context menu. Choose Center and click the center of the coffee table. Press F8 to toggle on Ortho mode and move the cursor up or down to force a vertical mirror line centered on the table (see Figure 4.27).

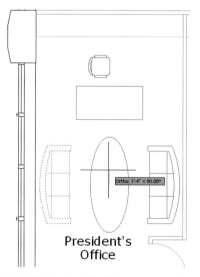

FIGURE 4.27 Mirroring a sofa

9. Click to reflect the sofa. The command prompt reads

    ```
    Erase source objects? [Yes/No] <N>:
    ```

    Press Enter to accept the default (No), so that you do not erase the source object, and retain the original sofa in addition to the newly reflected one.

10. Save your work as Ch4-H.dwg (or Ch4-H-metric.dwg).

Grip Editing

All objects have grips, the square blue symbols that appear in AutoCAD at significant points when objects are selected without issuing any command. Grips provide an alternative means of accessing a number of editing commands including stretch, move, rotate, scale, and mirror. Let's explore grip editing:

1. If the file is not already open from performing the previous step, go to the book's web page, browse to Chapter 4, download the file Ch4-H.dwg (or Ch4-H-metric.dwg), and open it.

2. In the President's Office, the president's chair is turned sideways in front of her desk. Click the chair to select it. A single blue grip appears on the chair because it is a *block* (see Chapter 7, "Organizing Objects" for more on blocks).

3. Click this single grip to activate it. The command prompt reads

    ```
    ** STRETCH **
    Specify stretch point or [Base point/Copy/Undo/eXit]:
    Press the spacebar. The command prompt changes
    ** MOVE **
    Specify move point or [Base point/Copy/Undo/eXit]:
    ```

4. Press the spacebar again. The command prompt says

    ```
    ** ROTATE **
    Specify rotation angle or
    [Base point/Copy/Undo/Reference/eXit]:
    ```

    Move the cursor downward, verify that Ortho mode is on so that the chair will move precisely 90 degrees, and click in the drawing canvas so the chair rotates to face the desk. Press Esc and Grip Editing mode ends.

5. Reselect the chair and click its grip. Press the spacebar to cycle to Move. Move the cursor down the screen and click to locate the chair closer to the desk.

6. Select the large oval table in the President's Office. Click its center grip and then cycle through the grip editing modes until you get to Scale. Type **.75** and press Enter to scale it down to 75 percent of its original size. Press Esc to exit Grip Editing mode. Figure 4.28 shows the completed drawing; compare this to Figure 4.1 to see how far you've come.

7. Your drawing should now resemble Ch4-Final.dwg (or Ch4-Final-metric.dwg)., which is available among the book's companion download files here: **www.sybex.com/go/autocad2012essentials**.

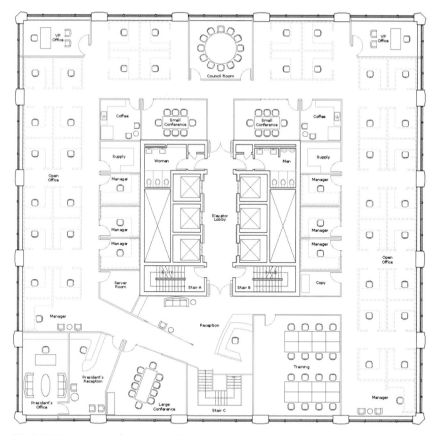

FIGURE 4.28 Completed office building drawing

THE ESSENTIALS AND BEYOND

In this chapter you have learned how to edit drawings by first making selections, and then by moving, copying, rotating, and scaling objects. You've created individual and associative rectangular and polar arrays; used Trim, Extend, Lengthen, Stretch, Offset, and Mirror; and edited with grips. In short you've learned how to draw in AutoCAD. Congratulations are in order!

ADDITIONAL EXERCISE

▶ Explore the BREAK, JOIN, and OVERKILL commands on your own. As the name suggests, the Break tool is used to interrupt an object at one or two points (leaving a gap). Join is used to connect two or more collinear lines into single segments. Overkill eliminates coincident lines. All three are used to clean up drawings.

Break   Join   Overkill

CHAPTER 5

Shaping Curves

For many years AutoCAD wasn't very sophisticated when it came to shaping curves. Sure, you could create circles, arcs, and ellipses, but shaping complex curves wasn't accurate compared to the capabilities of programs such as Maya or 3ds Max. In AutoCAD 2011 all this changed with the introduction of an all-new SPLINE command that offered much more flexibility in shaping true NURBS (nonuniform rational basis spline) curves using fit points or control vertices. AutoCAD 2012 now expands on this by giving you the ability to shape curves however you imagine and even use them to model surfaces, which you'll learn more about in Chapter 17, "Modeling in 3D."

▶ **Drawing and editing curved polylines**

▶ **Drawing ellipses**

▶ **Drawing and editing splines**

▶ **Blending between objects with splines**

Drawing and Editing Curved Polylines

The simplest curved objects are circles and arcs (which are just parts of circles), because they curve with a constant radius from a center point. In the following steps you will chain a series of arcs and/or lines together in a single *polyline* object, which not only streamlines editing and selection but also ensures smooth curvature between adjacent arcs.

1. Go to the book's web page at **www.sybex.com/go/ autocad2012essentials** and browse to Chapter 5 to get the files Ch5-A.dwg (or Ch5-A-metric.dwg) and Pond.jpg. Place them in the same folder on your hard drive and open the drawing file in AutoCAD (see Figure 5.1).

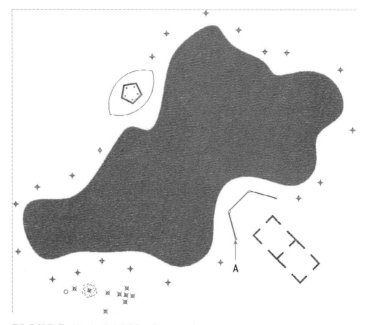

FIGURE 5.1 Initial landscape plan

2. You will begin by drawing curved pathways surrounding the lake. Click the Polyline tool on the Draw panel of the ribbon. Click the first point at point A as shown in Figure 5.1. Type **A** (for arc) and press Enter.

3. Toggle off Ortho mode if it is on. Observe that the arc you are in the process of drawing may curve the wrong way, against the curvature of the lake (see Figure 5.2). The command prompt reads

   ```
   Specify endpoint of arc or
   [Angle/CEnter/Direction/Halfwidth/Line/
   Radius/Second pt/Undo/Width]:
   ```

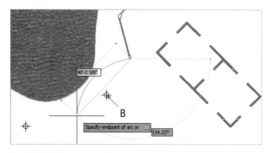

FIGURE 5.2 The direction of the default polyline arc opposes the curvature of the lake.

4. Type **S** (for second point), shown as B in Figure 5.2, and press Enter. Normally polyline arcs are defined by two points, and by using the second point option you are choosing the arc to be formed by three points so that you can determine its direction of curvature.

5. Right-click the Object Snap toggle in the status bar and select Node. By turning on Node running object snap, you will be able to snap arcs to all the point objects surrounding the lake. Turn on Endpoint running object snap if it is not already on. Click B as shown in Figure 5.2.

6. Click each subsequent node around the left half of the lake until you reach point C in Figure 5.3. Press Enter to end the PLINE command.

The point objects in the sample file are meant to guide you in the exercise; points typically aren't necessary when drawing curves on your own.

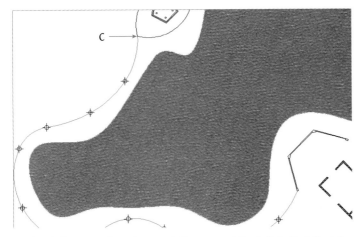

FIGURE 5.3 Drawing a polyline around the left half of the lake

7. Press the spacebar to repeat the last command. Click point D shown in Figure 5.4, type **A** (for arc), and press Enter.

8. Type **S** (for second point), press Enter, and snap to the node adjacent to point D.

9. Click each subsequent node around the right side of the lake until you reach point E in Figure 5.4. Press Enter.

10. Type **O** (for offset) and press Enter. Type **6´** (or **2 m**) and press Enter. Click the left polyline you drew around the lake in steps 1–6 and then click a point on the side of the polyline away from the lake. Click the right polyline and click outside the lake. Click the outer arc surrounding the pentagonal folly and then click outside the lake.

Certification Objective

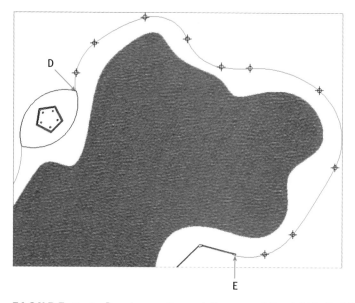

FIGURE 5.4 Drawing another polyline around the right half of the lake

11. Click the Trim tool in the Modify panel. Press Enter to select all objects as potential cutting edges and click the portions of the arcs that overlap in the top highlighted area in Figure 5.5. Zoom into the lower highlighted area and trim the arcs so that they meet at their endpoints. Press Esc to end the TRIM command.

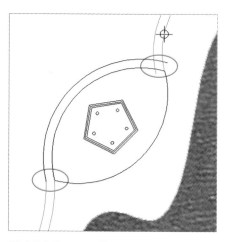

FIGURE 5.5 Trimming polylines and arcs

12. Pan over to the building at the bottom of the lake. We'd like the ends of the paths to open up to the building. Click the lower-left polyline to select it. Click the endpoint grip, move it down a short distance, and click again (see Figure 5.6). You can't get the end of the path to open up without distorting the path farther up because it's all part of the same arc segment.

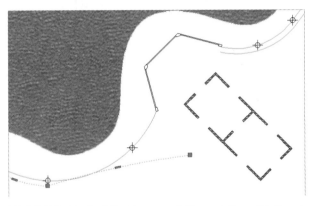

FIGURE 5.6 Adjusting an existing polyline with its grips

13. Press Esc and then click the Undo button in the Quick Access toolbar.

14. Click the Arc tool in the Draw panel, hold Shift and right-click, and choose Nearest from the context menu. Click points A, B, and C in Figure 5.7 to shape the arc as shown.

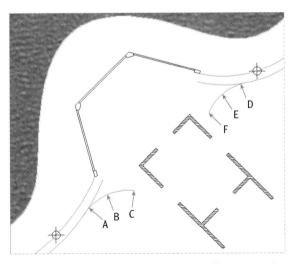

FIGURE 5.7 Drawing new short-radius arcs and snapping them along the longer existing arcs

15. Press Enter twice to end and restart the ARC command. Type **nea** (for nearest), press Enter, and click points D, E, and F in Figure 5.7.

16. Zoom in and trim away the portions of the original polylines that extend beyond the new arcs you've just drawn.

Certification Objective

17. Type **J** (for join) and press Enter. Select all five objects that comprise the outer path (three arcs and two polylines). Press Enter and the command line reads as follows:

    13 segments joined into 1 polyline

There are 13 segments if you include all the arcs that make up the two polylines. You are left with a single polyline marking the outer edge of the path.

18. Press the spacebar to repeat the JOIN command. Select the three objects along the inner edge of the path, which include two polylines and the arc above the pentagon. Press Enter and multiple segments are joined into one polyline (see Figure 5.8).

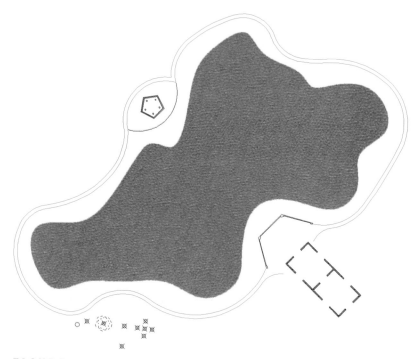

F I G U R E 5 . 8 The curving path around the lake joined into two objects

Should You Use *JOIN* or *PEDIT*?

In previous versions of AutoCAD, objects had to first be converted into polylines and then joined using the polyline editing command called PEDIT. The streamlined JOIN command makes the older workflow unnecessary. Use it on lines, 2D and 3D polylines, arcs, elliptical arcs (sections of ellipses), and/or helices. In AutoCAD 2012 multiple object types can be joined at once. The resulting object type depends on what was selected.

◀

Use JOIN to connect collinear lines even if there is a gap between them. JOIN is the antidote to BREAK.

Drawing Ellipses

AutoCAD can draw perfect ovals, which are mathematically known as ellipses. Instead of stretching a cord from two pins to a moving pencil point (which is how you draw an ellipse by hand), in AutoCAD you specify the lengths of its major and minor axes (see Figure 5.9).

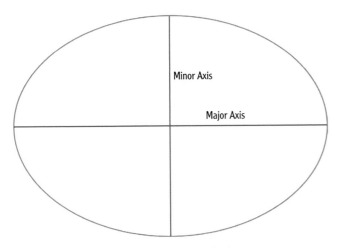

Minor Axis

Major Axis

FIGURE 5.9 An ellipse's major and minor axes

In this part of the exercise you will draw an ellipse and distribute shrubs along its edge:

1. Zoom into the area in the lower left where the remaining point objects are located.

2. Type **regen** (for regenerate) and press Enter. The size of point objects is recalculated when the drawing is regenerated.

3. Open the Ellipse menu in the Draw panel and choose the Center method. Click the center point, the end of the major axis, and the end of the minor axis, as shown in Figure 5.10.

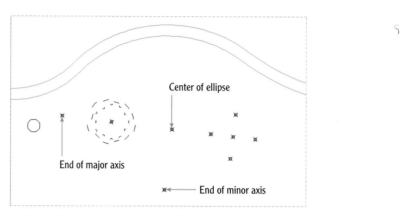

FIGURE 5.10 Drawing an ellipse

4. Type **br** (for break), press Enter, and select the ellipse. The command prompt reads

   ```
   Specify second break point or [First point]:
   ```

   Type **F** (for first point), right-click the Object Snap toggle in the status bar, and select Quadrant from the context menu. Click the quadrant point opposite the point object marking the end of the major axis (see Figure 5.10), and then click the aforementioned point object itself to break the ellipse in half. The lower half of the ellipse remains, leaving an *elliptical arc*.

5. Type **div** (for divide) and press Enter. Select the elliptical arc and press Enter. The command prompt reads

   ```
   Enter the number of segments or [Block]:
   ```

   Type **B** (for block) and press Enter. You'll learn more about blocks in Chapter 7, "Organizing Objects."

6. A block called Shrub is predefined, so at the next command prompt

   ```
   Enter name of block to insert:
   ```

   type **Shrub** and press Enter.

7. Press Enter to accept the default when asked if you want to align the block with the selected object (it doesn't matter in this case because the Shrub block is a circle).

8. Type **13** (for the number of segments) and press Enter. The DIVIDE command always creates one less point or block than the number of segments the object is divided into. Twelve "shrubs" appear along the elliptical arc (see Figure 5.11).

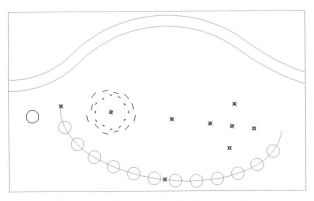

FIGURE 5.11 Dividing an elliptical arc with blocks

9. Delete the three points used in drawing the ellipse, the elliptical arc itself, and the black circle, which is the original Shrub block. You deleted the layout geometry and are now left with precisely positioned shrubs.

Drawing and Editing Splines

Splines are the equivalent of a French curve in traditional drafting, used for making curves of constantly changing radii. Splines have been part of AutoCAD for many releases, but the SPLINE command was completely overhauled in AutoCAD 2011. AutoCAD's new splines are NURBS-based curves (the same type used in Alias, Maya, 3ds Max, and many other high-end 3D programs). There are two types of NURBS curves:

▶ Those defined by control vertices (CVs), which don't lie on the curve except at its start and end points and endpoint

▶ Those defined by fit points, which lie on the curve itself

You have more control over shaping curves with CVs, but if you want the curve to pass through specific points, or want the curve to have sharp kinks, then Fit Points mode is preferable. Fortunately, it is easy to switch between CVs and Fit Points editing modes so you can make up your mind about which method to use to suit the situation.

Working with Control Vertices

CVs offer the most flexibility in terms of precisely shaping NURBS curves. A *control frame* connects CVs and represents the maximum possible curvature between adjacent CVs. You will now draw a CV spline around the lake:

Certification Objective

1. Type **spl** (for spline) and press Enter. The command prompt reads

   ```
   Current settings: Method=Fit    Knots=Chord
   Specify first point or [Method/Knots/Object]:
   ```

   Type **m** (for method) and press Enter.

2. The command prompt reads

   ```
   Enter spline creation method [Fit/CV] <Fit>:
   ```

   Type **cv** (for control vertices) and press Enter. Click the first point anywhere along the edge of the lake. Continue clicking points all the way around the lake. When you get close to the first point, type **C** (for close) and press Enter. Click the spline you just drew to reveal its CVs (see Figure 5.12).

3. Toggle off Object Snap, Ortho, and Polar Tracking modes on the status bar if any of them are on. Position the cursor over a CV and observe the multifunction grip menu. Select Stretch Vertex, move the cursor, and click to relocate that particular CV.

4. Try adding and removing vertices using the corresponding choices on the multifunction grip menu (see Figure 5.13).

5. Refining a vertex transforms one vertex into two adjacent vertices. Try refining vertices in areas where the curvature is changing rapidly.

6. Another way to affect the shape of a spline is to adjust the weights of individual CVs. Double-click the spline itself (rather than a CV or the control frame) to invoke the SPLINEDIT command. The prompt reads

> CV curves are typically roughed in initially and then immediately afterward refined in shape.

```
Enter an option [Open/Fit data/Edit vertex/convert to
Polyline/
Reverse/Undo/eXit] <eXit>:
```

Type **E** (for edit vertex) and press Enter.

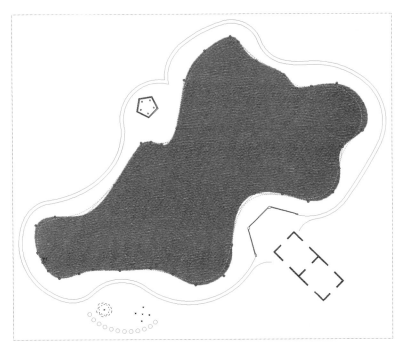

> ◀
>
> **Vertices with higher weights pull the curve toward the control frame and vertices with weights below 1 (but above zero) push the spline farther away.**

FIGURE 5.12 Drawing a rough CV spline around the lake

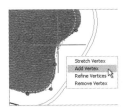

FIGURE 5.13 Adding and removing vertices from a CV spline using multifunction grips

7. The prompt now reads as follows:

```
Enter a vertex editing option [Add/Delete/Elevate order/
Move/Weight/eXit] <eXit>:
```

Type **w** (for weight) and press Enter. Before entering a weight value, you must select the vertex you're interested in. Press Enter repeatedly to enter the default option (Next) until your chosen vertex turns red.

8. Type **2** and press Enter (see Figure 5.14). The spline will get closer to the red CV and its control frame. Type **.5** and press Enter again; the curve moves farther away from the control frame. Type a value appropriate to your particular situation and press Enter. We set a weight of 0.75 for the CV shown in Figure 5.14 to push it away from the control frame and more closely match the shape of the lake. The weights you need to enter depend entirely on the exactly where you placed the CVs when creating the curve in step 2. Type **X** (for exit) and press Enter. Press **X** and Enter twice more to fully exit SPLINEDIT.

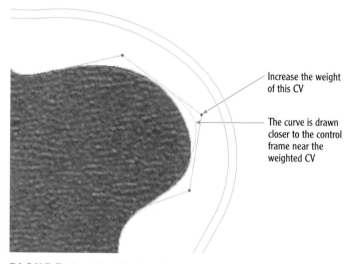

Increase the weight of this CV

The curve is drawn closer to the control frame near the weighted CV

FIGURE 5.14 Adjusting the weight of a CV

9. Continue adjusting the spline until it closely matches the outline of the lake.

10. Type **im** (for image) and press Enter. The External References palette appears (you'll learn more about this palette in Chapter 9, "Working with Blocks and Xrefs"). The lake that you have been tracing is an image that you will now detach.

11. Right-click Pond in the External References palette and choose Detach Image. Close the External References palette. Select the pond spline and change its color to Blue in the Properties panel (see Figure 5.15). The pond is now represented by a blue curve rather than a blue image.

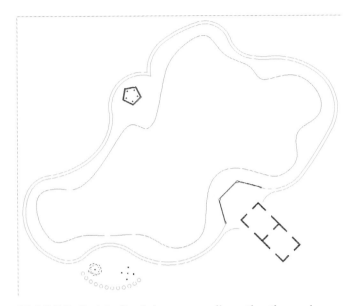

FIGURE 5.15 Pond shown as a spline rather than an image

SKETCH AND REBUILD CVS

Instead of stretching, adding, removing, refining, and/or adjusting CVs, you can sketch spline curves freehand. The SKETCH command is admittedly difficult with a mouse, so if you have one, try using a stylus on a drawing tablet for a more natural drawing feel. Unfortunately, sketching splines usually results in an uneven distribution of CVs, but this can be rectified using CVREBUILD. For an alternative natural drawing technique, draw splines on a tablet with SKETCH (using spline in its type option) and then redistribute the resulting CVs with CVREBUILD. The CVREBUILD command's Rebuild Curve dialog box is shown here.

Working with Fit Points

Fit point splines are straightforward in the sense that the fit points you click lie on (or very close to) the curve itself. Controlling the shape of a fit curve on the most basic level is a matter of adding more fit points in strategic locations. There are a few advanced options affecting the shape of a spline in between fit points (Tangent, Tolerance, Kink, and Knot Parameterization), and you will use Kink in this exercise to establish sharp points on the spline.

1. Zoom into the area at the bottom of the lake where you distributed the shrubs earlier in this chapter in an elliptical arc. More specifically, zoom into the grouping of five points.

2. Expand the Draw panel and click the Spline Fit tool. Toggle on Object Snap mode in the status bar (with Node snap on) and click the top point, the point on the right, the bottom, and then the one on the left. Type **C** (for close) and press Enter. The fit curve looks very much like a circle, although it is not perfectly round (see Figure 5.16). This will be the start of an abstract tree representation.

3. Toggle on Dynamic Input on the status bar. Select the spline you just drew, type **SPLINEDIT**, and press Enter. Choose Fit Data from the Dynamic Input menu. Then choose Add from the next Dynamic Input menu that appears.

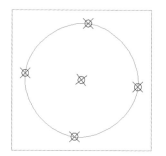

FIGURE 5.16 Snapping spline fit points to point objects

4. The prompt reads

    ```
    Specify existing fit point on spline <exit>:
    ```

    Click the top point.

5. The prompt now says

   ```
   Specify new fit point to add <exit>:
   ```

   This particular command requires that you snap the new fit point so type **nea** (for nearest) and press Enter. Click the curve in between the top and right points. Press Enter four times to fully exit SPLINEDIT.

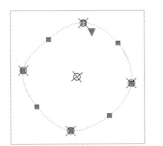

6. Another way to add fit points is with the multifunction grips, although this method doesn't work on the first point. To use this feature, click the spline to select it, hover the cursor over the right point, and choose Add Fit Point from the menu that appears. Hold Shift, right-click, and choose Nearest from the context menu. Click a point between the right and bottom points.

7. Repeat the previous step twice more, adding additional fit points between the bottom, left, and top points (see Figure 5.17).

8. Double-click the spline itself to invoke the SPLINEDIT command without typing. Type **F** (for fit data) and press Enter. The prompt reads

   ```
   Enter a fit data option
   [Add/Open/Delete/Kink/Move/Purge/Tangents/
   toLerance/eXit] <eXit>:
   ```

FIGURE 5.17 Adding additional fit points between the initial points

> There is no need to use Nearest snap with the Kink option in Fit Data mode of the SPLINEDIT command.

Type **K** (for kink) and click eight points in between all the existing fit points (see Figure 5.18). Press Enter three times to fully exit the command.

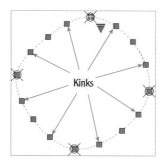

FIGURE 5.18 Adding kinks to the fit points spline

9. Click each kink grip and move it in toward the center to create an abstract representation of a tree. Delete the five point objects that helped you lay out the tree (see Figure 5.19).

FIGURE 5.19 Abstract tree created by stretching kinks in a fit point spline

Blending Between Objects with Splines

The BLEND command creates a CV spline in between two selected lines, circular or elliptical arcs, splines, or any combination of these object types. Blend curves join the endpoints of the two objects with a curve having either tangent or smooth continuity. There is a subtle difference between these types of blending.

A blend curve with tangent continuity has its control frame parallel to the control frame of the adjacent curve. A blend curve with curvature continuity not only has its control frame parallel to the control frame of the adjacent curve, but the control frames have equal lengths. In simpler terms, tangent continuity is smooth, and smooth continuity is "perfectly smooth." In the following steps you will create blend curves with two types of curvature:

1. Pan over to the other "tree" to the left of the tree you've drawn with kinks. Type **BLEND** and press Enter.

2. The prompt reads

   ```
   Continuity = Tangent
   Select first object or [CONtinuity]:
   ```

   Select a flat arc and a tight arc and the command is finished. A CV spline with tangent continuity blends between the two arcs.

3. Press the spacebar to repeat BLEND, type **con** (for continuity) press Enter, type **S** (for smooth), and press Enter again. Click two adjacent arcs to create another blend curve (see Figure 5.20).

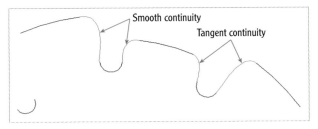

FIGURE 5.20 Blending between arcs with different types of continuity

4. Continue blending all the adjacent curves in the tree. Delete the point object at the center. Figure 5.21 shows the completed drawing.

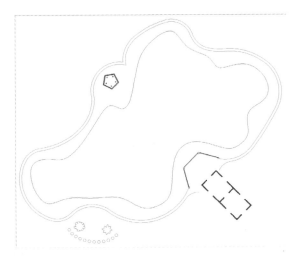

FIGURE 5.21 Completed landscape plan

5. Your drawing should now resemble Ch5-B.dwg (or Ch5-B-metric.dwg) which is available at this book's web page.

The Essentials and Beyond

You have learned how to shape many types of curvilinear objects in this chapter, including circular and elliptical arcs, polylines, ellipses, and CV and fit point NURBS-based splines. You've broken and joined objects, and blended smoothly between adjacent curves. In short, you now have the skills to shape just about any curve you can imagine with a fine degree of precision, which is what AutoCAD is all about.

Additional Exercises

▶ Explore the HELIX command on your own. The HELIX command creates spirals and helices. You are welcome to stick with two dimensions now and create spirals with this command. When you learn how to navigate and model in 3D (see Chapters 16 and 17), you can use this command to create springs, screw threads, or even DNA.

CHAPTER 6

Controlling Object Visibility and Appearance

Layers control objects whether they are visible or hidden. All objects have properties that control their appearance—properties such as color, linetype, lineweight, and so on. The layers that objects are assigned to usually control general object properties, but these properties can be set on a per-object basis as well. In this chapter we will discuss the many tools associated with layers that illustrate how important layers are in managing the complexity of design.

▶ **Changing object properties**

▶ **Setting the current layer**

▶ **Altering objects' layer assignments**

▶ **Controlling layer visibility**

▶ **Applying linetype**

▶ **Assigning properties by object or by layer**

▶ **Managing layer properties**

Changing Object Properties

All objects have properties controlling their appearance. When you draw a line, you are ultimately specifying its geometric properties (the start point and the endpoint). Likewise, when you draw a circle you are just specifying its center point and radius properties. Geometric properties are the most important factor governing how objects look and determining where the objects are in space.

In addition to geometric properties, all objects share a short list of general properties: layer, color, linetype, linetype scale, lineweight, transparency, and thickness. Although general properties are assigned on a per-object basis, they are usually controlled using layers.

Let's explore object properties in an existing drawing and learn how to change properties and merge layers to which objects are assigned:

1. Go to the book's web page at **www.sybex.com/go/ autocad2012essentials**, browse to Chapter 6, get the file Ch6-A. dwg (or Ch6-A-metric.dwg), and open it (see Figure 6.1). This is the architectural plan for a hypothetical small office.

FIGURE 6.1 Small office plan

2. Zoom into the reception desk at the center of the small office plan.

3. Toggle on Quick Properties mode in the status bar.

4. Click on the line of the desk immediately adjacent to the Reception text object; the Quick Properties palette appears to the top right of the selected object on the drawing canvas. Click the Desk-High layer name to activate the Layer drop-down menu (see Figure 6.2).

5. Select the Desk layer in the drop-down (see Figure 6.3) and press the Esc key to exit Quick Properties mode. Observe that the line whose layer property you changed now appears violet, like the other objects on the Desk layer.

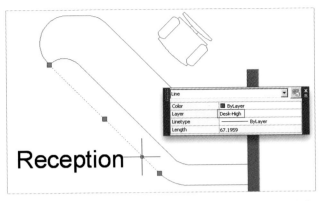

FIGURE 6.2 Targeting an object property using Quick Properties mode

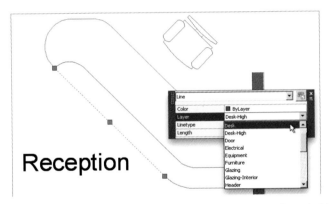

FIGURE 6.3 Assigning a different layer to the selected object

6. Expand the Layers panel on the Home tab of the ribbon.

Layers ▼

7. Click the Merge tool. The command prompt reads

```
Select object on layer to merge or [Name]:
```

8. Click one of the brown lines in the upper portion of the reception desk and press Enter.

9. Click the violet line you changed to the Desk layer in step 5 and press Enter. The command prompt reads:

```
Select object on target layer or [Name]:
******** WARNING ********
You are about to merge layer "Desk-High" into layer "Desk".
Do you wish to continue? [Yes/No] <No>:
```

List

10. Press Y (for Yes) and then press Enter to continue. The Desk-High layer is deleted and the objects that were on it have been reassigned to the Desk layer. The LAYMRG command is done.

11. Expand the Properties panel and click the List tool. Pan over and select the Business Development text object by clicking on it and pressing Enter. The AutoCAD Text window appears, displaying the following property information:

```
TEXT        Layer: "Title"
Space: Model space
Handle = 71e
Style = "Standard"
Annotative: No
Typeface = Arial
mid point, X= 193.8805  Y= 132.8080  Z= 0.0000
height    7.5000
text Business Development
rotation angle       0
width scale factor      1.0000
obliquing angle       0
generation normal
```

This list might be helpful if you were looking for a particular piece of information, but you can't edit any of the properties directly. Close the AutoCAD Text window.

Certification
Objective

Properties

12. Select the View tab on the ribbon and under Palettes click the Properties tool to open the Properties palette.

13. Select the Business Development text object you selected in step 11. Many of its properties appear in the palette (see Figure 6.4). Property values displayed on a white background are editable; those on a gray background are for your information only.

14. Select the words "Business Development" in the Contents property, type **Marketing**, and press Enter. Press Esc to deselect the text object. The department's name has been changed. You can now close the Properties palette.

Setting the Current Layer

Objects are always drawn on the current layer, and there is only one current layer at any given time. Every drawing has at least one layer, layer 0 (zero), which is current when you create a new drawing by default.

Text		
General		▲
Color	■ ByLayer	
Layer	Title	
Linetype	——— ByLayer	
Linetype scale	1.0000	
Plot style	ByColor	
Lineweight	——— ByLayer	
Transparency	ByLayer	
Hyperlink		
Thickness	0.0000	
3D Visualization		▲
Material	ByLayer	
Text		▲
Contents	Business Development	
Style	Standard	
Annotative	No	
Justify	Middle	
Height	7.5000	
Rotation	0	
Width Factor	1.0000	
Obliquing	0	
Text alignment X	193.8805	
Text alignment Y	132.8080	
Text alignment Z	0.0000	
Geometry		▲
Position X	140.3010	
Position Y	130.0991	
Position Z	0.0000	
Misc		▲
Upside down	No	
Backward	No	

F I G U R E   6 . 4   Editing a value in the Properties palette

AutoCAD has another special layer called Defpoints, which is automatically created when you add associative dimensions to a drawing (see Chapter 11, "Dimensioning").

Let's experiment with setting the current layer by drawing a few objects:

1. Using the Ch6-A.dwg (or Ch6-A-metric.dwg) file, zoom into the Manager's office. If this file is not open, find it on the book's web page.

2. Click the Rectangle tool on the Draw panel and click a point a few inches (no need to measure) from the lower-left corner of the room. Type @18˝,72˝ (or @45,180 cm) and press Enter to create a credenza in the Manager's office (see Figure 6.5).

> You cannot delete or rename layer 0 or Defpoints. It's okay to draw on layer 0 but not on Defpoints.

> Press Shift, right-click, and choose the None object snap to override any running object snap modes whenever necessary.

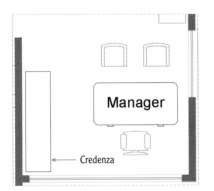

F I G U R E   6 . 5   Drawing furniture on layer 0

3. Select the rectangle you drew in the previous step and change its Layer assignment to Furniture in the Quick Properties window that appears. Press Esc to deselect.

4. If you plan on drawing more than one object, a more efficient approach is to set the current layer prior to drawing so that the new object will have the proper layer assignment automatically. Open the Layer drop-down menu in the Layers panel and click on or to the right of the word Furniture to set this layer current. Notice that Furniture appears "on top" when the drop-down is closed (see Figure 6.6); Furniture is now the current layer.

FIGURE 6.6 Setting Furniture as the current layer using the drop-down menu in the Layers panel

5. Pan over to the Marketing space.

6. Click the Rectangle tool on the Draw panel and click a point a few inches (without measuring) from the lower-right corner of the room. Type **@-18″,72″** (or **@-45,180 cm**) and press Enter to create a credenza in Marketing (see Figure 6.7).

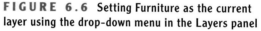

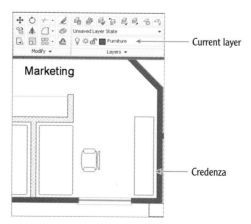

Current layer

Marketing

Credenza

FIGURE 6.7 Drawing another credenza on the Furniture layer

7. Select the rectangle you drew in the previous step and verify it is on the Furniture layer in the Quick Properties window that appears. Press Esc.

8. Pan over to the closet in Marketing. One of the lines representing shelves is missing. You will draw the missing line on the same layer as the existing shelf line.

9. Rather than selecting the existing shelf line by learning its layer name and then setting that layer current, there is a more efficient approach. In the Layers panel, click the Make Object's Layer Current tool. Click the existing shelf line in Marketing's closet. The layer appearing at the top of the Layer drop-down menu is Millwork, which shows that it's now the current layer.

10. Toggle on Endpoint and Perpendicular running object snap modes on the status bar.

11. Click the Line tool on the Draw panel and draw the line shown in Figure 6.8. Press Esc to end the LINE command.

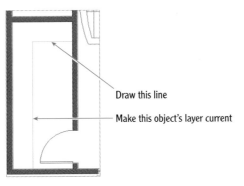

FIGURE 6.8 Drawing a line after using the Make Object's Layer Current tool

Altering Objects' Layer Assignments

Although you have already changed objects' layer assignments using Quick Properties, there are more efficient methods of doing this, some of which do not require you to remember a layer name. Let's explore several methods for changing existing objects' layer assignments:

1. Using the Ch6-A.dwg (or Ch6-A-metric.dwg) file, zoom into the Manager's office. If this file is not open, find it on the book's web page.

2. Toggle off Quick Properties mode on the status bar.

3. Select the coffee table in the Marketing space. Notice that the entry in the Layer drop-down in the Layers panel changes to layer 0: this does not mean that layer 0 is current (Millwork is), only that the selected item is on layer 0.

4. Open the Layer drop-down menu and click Furniture (see Figure 6.9) to change the layer assignment of the selected items. Press Esc to deselect.

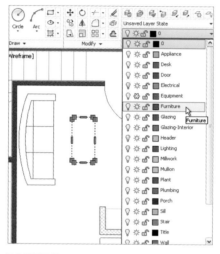

FIGURE 6.9 Changing layer assignment with the Layer drop-down menu

5. Pan over to the Lounge.

 6. Click the Match tool in the Layers panel, select the coffee table in the Lounge, and press Enter. The command prompt reads

```
Select object on destination layer or [Name]:
```

7. Click one of the sofas in the Lounge and press Enter; the LAYMCH command ends. The coffee table is now assigned to the same layer the sofas are on (Furniture).

8. Pan to the Manager's office.

Certification Objective

 9. Click the Match Properties tool in the Clipboard panel on the Home tab of the ribbon. Select the credenza in the Manager's office and press Enter. The command prompt reads

```
Select destination object(s) or [Settings]:
```

10. Type **S** (for Settings) and press Enter; the Property Settings dialog box appears. You can match many properties in addition to layers with this tool (see Figure 6.10). Click OK.

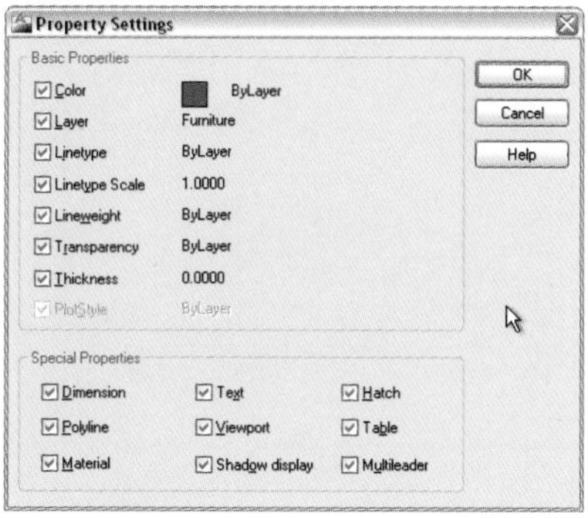

FIGURE 6.10 The Property Settings dialog box allows you to match much more than layers.

11. Click the desk in the Manager's office and press Enter; the desk turns green because it is now on the Furniture layer. Press Esc to exit the MATCHPROP command.

Controlling Layer Visibility

In traditional drafting, separate drawings would have to be made for the floor plan and the reflected ceiling plan to represent the floor and ceiling of the same space. In AutoCAD, simply displaying some layers while hiding others allows you to create some of the drawings required to graphically describe the space.

To better understand how to do this, you need to learn how to toggle layer status, isolate layers to work without distraction, and save layer states to quickly recall the layer status of multiple layers.

Toggling Layer Status

In addition to having properties such as color, linetype, lineweight, and so on, layers have states that can be toggled, including On/Off, Thaw/Freeze, and Lock/Unlock. As you'll see in the following steps, layer states control the visibility and editability of the objects assigned to layers:

1. Using the Ch6-A.dwg (or Ch6-A-metric.dwg) file, zoom into the Manager's office. If this file is not open, find it on the book's web page.

2. Expand the Layers panel and click the Turn All Layers On tool. You now see the switches ($ symbols), downlights, and header layers. Figure 6.11 shows the result.

FIGURE 6.11 The Small Office plan with all layers on

3. Open the Layer drop-down menu in the Layers panel and click the Appliance layer's lightbulb icon to toggle it off. Toggle off the Desk layer as well. Click outside the Layer drop-down menu to close it.

4. Another approach to turning layers off doesn't require that you know layer names. Click the Off tool in the Layers panel and click the following objects: sink, door, chair, plant, stairs, low wall, low wall's pattern fill, text, and the porch. Click a kitchen cabinet and the command prompt reads

```
Layer "Millwork" is current, do you want to
turn it off? [Yes/No] <No>:
```

If you turn the current layer off, then anything you draw subsequently will be hidden.

5. Type **Y** (for Yes) and press Enter. Press Esc to end the LAYOFF command. Figure 6.12 shows the result.

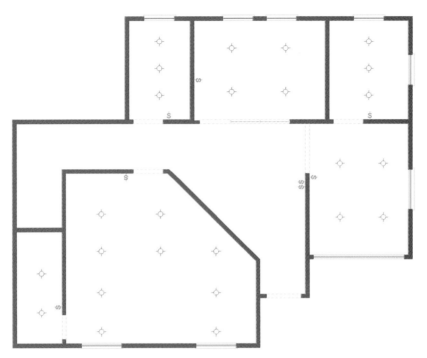

FIGURE 6.12 Reflected ceiling plan created by toggling layers off

6. Open the Layer drop-down menu in the Layers panel and set layer 0 current.

7. Click Zoom Extents in the Navigation bar. Notice that there is a gap between the bottom wall of the building and the lower edge of the drawing canvas. Even though it is off, the Porch layer is still defining the extents of the drawing.

8. Open the Layer drop-down menu in the Layers panel and freeze the Porch layer. Press Esc to close the drop-down menu.

9. Click Zoom Extents in the Navigation bar again. The gap disappears as the Porch layer is no longer calculated when it is frozen and therefore is no longer part of the drawing extents.

10. Expand the Layers panel and click the Lock tool. Select one of the lights. The Lighting layer is now locked.

11. Type **E** (for Erase) and press Enter. Click on a different light and observe a tiny padlock appear near the object (see Figure 6.13). You can't select the object because it is locked.

> **Locking layers doesn't provide security other than disallowing selection. You can unlock layers as easily as you lock them. Dragging the Locked Layer Fading slider in the expanded Layers panel visually differentiates locked from unlocked layers.**
>
> ◀

FIGURE 6.13 Objects on locked layers cannot be selected.

In order to see the padlock, you must select When A Command Is Active in the Selection Preview area on the Selection tab in the Options dialog box (OPTIONS command).

Isolating Layers

You can quickly isolate one or more layers to work on them without the visual clutter of all the other layers. Let's try out Isolation mode:

1. Using the Ch6-A.dwg (or Ch6-A-metric.dwg) file, zoom into the Manager's office. If this file is not open, find it on the book's web page.

2. Click the Isolate tool on the Layers panel and then make a crossing selection through one of the windows. Press Enter and all the other layers disappear (see Figure 6.14).

FIGURE 6.14 Isolating a couple of layers for focused work

3. Expand the Layers panel and click the Copy Objects To New Layer tool. Select each one of the nine sill lines on the inside of the building and press Enter. The command prompt reads

   ```
   Select object on destination layer or [Name] <Name>:
   ```

4. Type **N** (for Name) and press Enter. The Copy To Layer dialog box appears (see Figure 6.15). Select Header from the Destination Layer list and click OK. There are now nine lines on the Sill layer and nine duplicate lines on the Header layer.

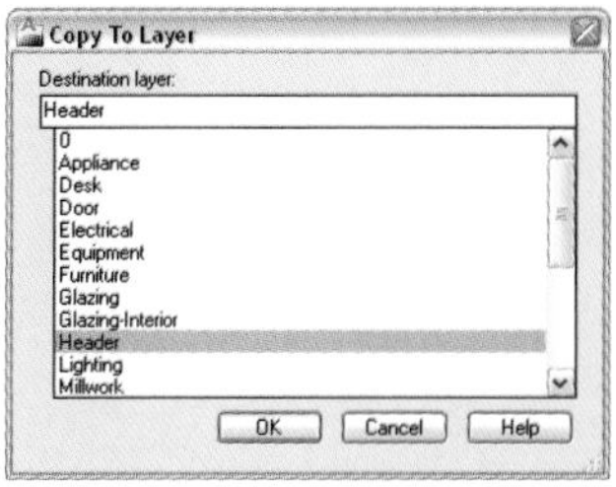

FIGURE 6.15 Selecting a layer in the Copy To Layer dialog box

5. Click the Unisolate tool on the Layers panel. The layers return to their states as they were prior to using the Isolate tool.

6. Type **LAYOFF** and press Enter. Click one of sills on the outside of the building to turn off the Sill layer and press Enter.

7. Zoom into one of the lower windows and click the Distance tool in the Utilities panel. Click points A and B in Figure 6.16 to measure the wall thickness. The command prompt reads

```
Distance = 5.0000,  Angle in XY Plane = 270,
Angle from XY Plane = 0
Delta X = 0.0000,  Delta Y = -5.0000,  Delta Z = 0.0000
```

8. Press Esc to cancel the DISTANCE command.

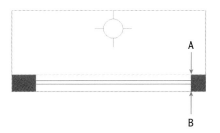

FIGURE 6.16 Measuring the wall thickness with DISTANCE

9. Type **O** (for Offset), press Enter, type **5˝** (or **12.7 cm**) and press Enter again. Click the header line in the window opening and then click below it to offset a line on the outer edge of the wall.

10. Continue clicking each header and a point outside the building to offset a second header line in each window opening. Press Enter to end the OFFSET command when done. The reflected ceiling plan is complete.

Saving Layer States

In this section you will learn how to save collections of layer states for later recall. In this chapter you have already created a reflected ceiling plan; you will now save it as a layer state so you won't have to repeat all the work of toggling layer states in the future.

1. Using the Ch6-A.dwg (or Ch6-A-metric.dwg) file, zoom into the Manager's office. If this file is not open, find it on the book's web page.

2. Open the drop-down menu directly above the Layer drop-down (it says Unsaved Layer State by default). Select New Layer State in the drop-down menu (see Figure 6.17).

FIGURE 6.17 Saving a new layer state

3. Type **Reflected Ceiling Plan** in the New Layer State To Save dialog box and click OK. The closed drop-down now says Reflected Ceiling Plan.

4. Expand the Layers panel and click the Turn All Layers On tool.

5. Expand the Layers panel again and click the adjacent Thaw All Layers tool.

6. Click the Freeze tool in the Layers panel and select the following objects: light, switch, header, and computer. The layers Lighting, Electrical, Header, and Equipment are frozen. Press Enter to end the LAYFRZ command.

7. Open the Layer State drop-down menu in the Layers panel and click New Layer State. Type **Furniture Plan** in the New Layer State To Save dialog box and click OK.

8. Open the Layer State drop-down menu and select Reflected Ceiling Plan (see Figure 6.18). All the layer states associated with the Reflected Ceiling Plan are immediately toggled. Switch back to the Furniture Plan state and you'll see the value in saving layer states (it saves lots of time).

> **Using** LAYERP **(layer previous) undoes the last set of changes to layers. This is different from** UNDO, **which affects more than layers.**

FIGURE 6.18 Accessing saved layer states from the drop-down in the Layers panel

Applying Linetype

In traditional drafting you draw short interrupted line segments when you want to indicate what is called a *hidden line*. Hidden lines represent objects that are above the section plane. Examples, including upper cabinets, high shelves, or a roof edge, are shown as hidden because they are above an imaginary section line cutting the building horizontally.

In AutoCAD, lines are not interrupted (broken into multiple little pieces) to indicate hidden lines. Instead, continuous lines are assigned a *linetype* and this style makes lines appear as if they are interrupted. One advantage to this is that you can adjust the scale of the line breaks without having to redraw myriad little lines. Let's explore linetype and linetype scale:

1. Using the Ch6-A.dwg (or Ch6-A-metric.dwg) file, zoom into the Manager's office. If this file is not open, find it on the book's web page.

2. Open the Linetype drop-down menu in the Properties panel and select Other at the bottom of the menu (see Figure 6.19).

Certification Objective

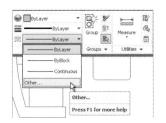

FIGURE 6.19 Accessing other linetypes

3. In the Linetype Manager dialog box that appears, click the Load button. Scroll down in the Load Or Reload Linetypes dialog box that appears and select Hidden in the list (see Figure 6.20); then click OK. Hidden

now appears in the Linetype Manager dialog box because this particular linetype style has been loaded in the drawing file; click OK to close the Linetype Manager dialog box.

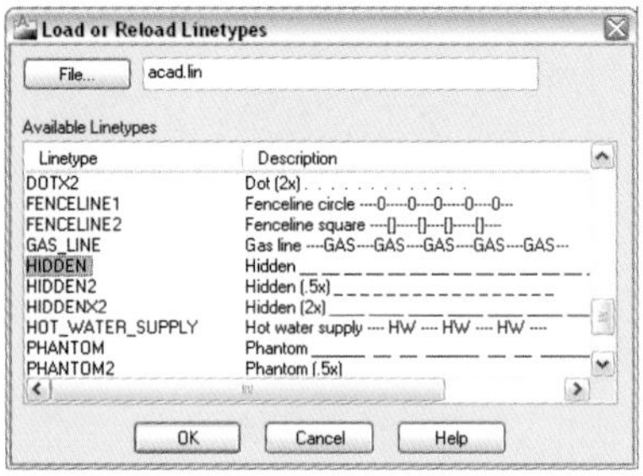

FIGURE 6.20 Loading the Hidden linetype

4. Zoom into the closet in the Marketing space and select both lines on the Millwork layer, representing a high shelf.

5. Open the Linetype drop-down menu in the Properties panel and select Hidden from the menu. Now the two selected lines have the hidden linetype assigned.

6. You still don't see breaks in the lines because the linetype scale is too small by default. Type **LTSCALE** (for linetype scale) and press Enter. The command prompt reads

```
LTSCALE Enter new linetype scale factor <1.0000>:
```

> **The factor 50 is appropriate for 1:50 metric drawings.**

> ▶

7. Type **48** (or **50** for metric) and press Enter. The lines appear with breaks indicating that the shelf is above the section plane (see Figure 6.21).

8. Select the horizontal shelf line, right-click, and choose Properties from the context menu.

> ▶

> **Use LTSCALE to set the linetype scale affecting the entire drawing. Higher values of LTSCALE scale linetypes smaller.**

9. Change Linetype Scale to **0.5** in the General section of the Properties palette (see Figure 6.22).

10. Press Esc to deselect the horizontal shelf line. The breaks in the horizontal line are half as large as those in the vertical segment (see Figure 6.23). Close the Properties palette.

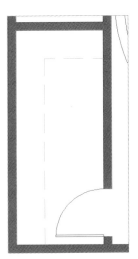

FIGURE 6.21 Hidden lines representing a high shelf in the closet

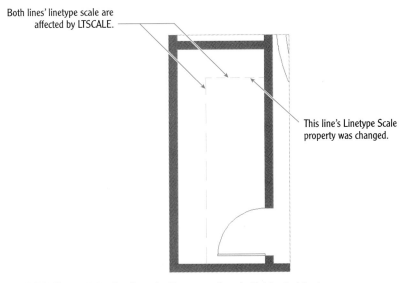

General		
Color	☐ ByLayer	
Layer	Millwork	
Linetype	– – – – – HIDDEN	
Linetype scale	0.5000	🔲
Plot style	ByColor	
Lineweight	——— ByLayer	
Hyperlink		
Transparency	ByLayer	
Thickness	0.0000	

FIGURE 6.22 Adjusting the Linetype Scale property

Alter the linetype scale of specific objects by adjusting the Linetype Scale property in the Properties palette. Lower Linetype Scale values scale linetypes smaller.

Both lines' linetype scale are affected by LTSCALE.

This line's Linetype Scale property was changed.

FIGURE 6.23 Scaling the linetype of an individual object

Assigning Properties by Object or by Layer

Properties such as color, linetype, and lineweight are typically assigned by layer rather than by object. There is a special property value called *ByLayer* that passes control over specific properties to the properties managed by the layer to which the objects are assigned. As you'll see in these steps, using the ByLayer property is a lot easier than it sounds:

1. Using the Ch6-A.dwg (or Ch6-A-metric.dwg) file, zoom into the Manager's office. If this file is not open, find it on the book's web page.

2. Open the Linetype drop-down menu on the Properties panel and select Hidden (see Figure 6.24). Draw a line of arbitrary length anywhere on the canvas.

FIGURE 6.24 The Properties panel settings affect all the objects you create.

3. Open the Linetype drop-down menu on the Properties panel and select ByLayer.

4. Draw another line and observe that it has continuous linetype.

5. If you want to change the property of a specific object, use Quick Properties instead of the drop-down menus in the Properties panel. Toggle on Quick Properties mode on the status bar.

6. Select the continuous line drawn in step 2 and change its Linetype property to Hidden (see Figure 6.25).

Objects should be assigned specific colors, linetypes, or lineweights only in exceptional circumstances.

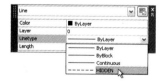

FIGURE 6.25 Changing a specific object property

7. Draw another line and verify that it has continuous linetype.

8. Delete all three arbitrary lines you've just drawn.

Managing Layer Properties

The Layer Properties Manager is where you create layers and manage the properties that are assigned to them. Let's explore the Layer Properties Manager with a practical example:

1. Using the Ch6-A.dwg (or Ch6-A-metric.dwg) file, zoom into the Manager's office. If this file is not open, find it on the book's web page.

2. Click the Layer Properties tool in the Layers panel. The Layer Properties Manager appears (see Figure 6.26).

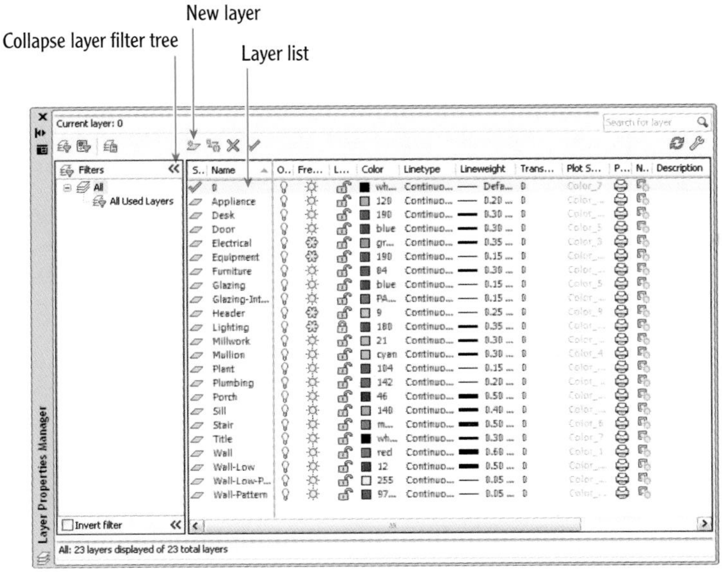

FIGURE 6.26 Layer Properties Manager

3. Click Collapse The Layer Filter Tree to save some space in the palette.

4. Click the New Layer button, type **Millwork-Upper** as the new layer's name, and press Enter.

5. Double-click the blue parallelogram next to the new layer to set it current. Now there is a green check mark next to the Millwork-Upper layer.

6. Right-click any one of the column headers to access a context menu. Choose Maximize All Columns from this menu. Figure 6.27 shows the result: The columns are all readable.

7. Click the Freeze column header to sort the column by that criterion (frozen state). Click the Freeze column header again to reverse the sort order. All columns are sortable.

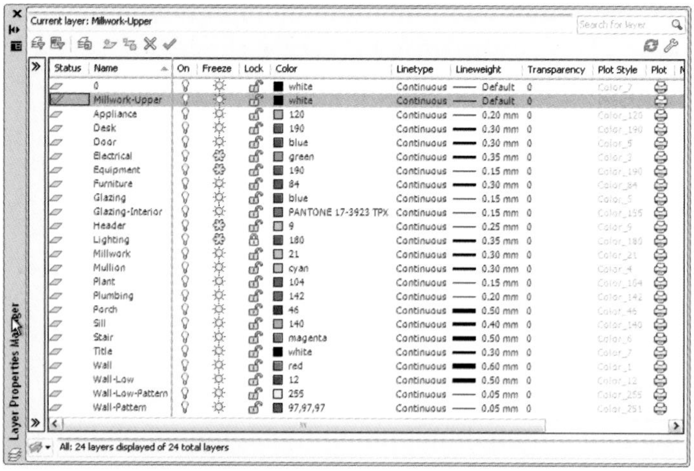

Sorting columns is a quick way to find layers having common properties. Drag the vertical bars between columns to resize them.

FIGURE 6.27 Maximizing the columns in the Layer Properties Manager makes them easier to read.

8. Click the word Continuous in the Linetype column in the Millwork-Upper layer. In the Select Linetype dialog box that appears, choose Hidden and click OK.

9. Click Millwork-Upper's color swatch to open the Select Color dialog box. Click the larger red swatch where indicated (see Figure 6.28) and click OK.

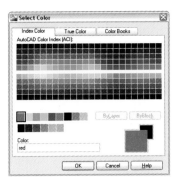

FIGURE 6.28 Selecting a layer color

10. Zoom into the closet in the Marketing space and select both shelf
    lines. Change Layer to Millwork-Upper and Linetype to ByLayer in
    the Quick Properties window (see Figure 6.29). The two lines appear
    red with hidden linetype. Close the Layer Properties Manager.

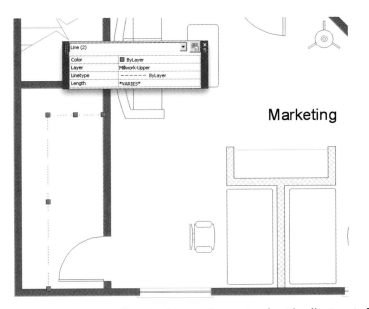

FIGURE 6.29 Changing layer assignment and setting linetype to ByLayer

11. Your drawing should now resemble Ch6-B.dwg (or Ch6-B-metric.dwg),
    which is available among the book's download files.

THE ESSENTIALS AND BEYOND

In this chapter you have learned how to control object visibility and how to modify object appearance with layers and properties. You learned many ways to change object properties, set the current layer, alter objects' layer assignments, control layer visibility, apply linetypes, use the ByLayer property, and manage properties with layers. You now have a greater ability to manage design complexity.

ADDITIONAL EXERCISES

Explore layer property and group filters on your own by opening one of the sample files that ship with AutoCAD, such as

```
C:\Program Files\Autodesk\AutoCAD 2012\Sample\
Sheet Sets\Architectural\A-01.dwg
```

Layer filters are especially useful in complex drawings where you need to manage dozens, or even hundreds, of layers.

CHAPTER 7

Organizing Objects

AutoCAD's fundamental entities are lines, polylines, circles, arcs, and text. By combining these entities into blocks and/or groups, you can manipulate more complex objects, such as chairs, mechanical assemblies, trees, or any other organizational designation appropriate to your industry.

Manipulating blocks is an efficient means of working not only because it reduces the number of items requiring selection, but also because blocks can potentially control numerous references from a single definition. In this chapter you will learn how groups are a flexible means of organizing collections of objects, which often include blocks as members. You will also learn how to select and manipulate a group as a whole or access the members of the group individually whenever needed.

▶ **Defining blocks**

▶ **Inserting blocks**

▶ **Editing blocks**

▶ **Redefining blocks**

▶ **Working with groups**

Defining Blocks

Before drawing and copying a series of repetitive elements, you should first define them as a block. This is because you have a higher level of organizational control over blocks than you do over individual entities. In this section, you will draw a chair and a door and then define them as blocks.

Drawing a Chair and Defining It as a Block

In the following steps you will use the drawing skills you've learned in previous chapters to draw a chair. Then you will convert the chair into a block definition.

1. Go to the book's web page at **www.sybex.com/go/ autocad2012essentials**, browse to Chapter 7, get the file Ch7-A.dwg, (or Ch7-A-metric.dwg) and open it (see Figure 7.1).

FIGURE 7.1 Three rooms

2. Zoom into the leftmost room above the desk.

 3. Click the Rectangle tool on the Modify panel and then click an arbitrary point above the desk (which is represented as the blue rectangle) as the first corner point. The command prompt reads

    Specify other corner point or [Area/Dimensions/Rotation]:

    Type **@18˝,18˝** (or **@45,45 cm**) and press Enter.

4. Click the Explode tool on the Modify panel, select the rectangle you just drew, and press Enter. The single polyline is converted into four independent line objects.

5. Click the Fillet tool on the Modify panel, type **R** (for radius) and press Enter. Type **3˝** (or **7 cm**) and press Enter to set the fillet radius and then click the left and bottom edges to create an arc.

6. Press the spacebar to repeat the FILLET command. Click the bottom and right edges to create another arc. Figure 7.2 shows the result.

FIGURE 7.2 Using Fillet
to round two corners

7. Expand the Modify panel, click the Join tool, select all the objects making up the chair you are drawing, and press Enter. Four lines and two arcs have now been converted into a single polyline.

8. Toggle on Ortho mode on the status bar.

9. Select the polyline you joined in step 7. Hover the cursor over the top middle grip and select Convert To Arc from the multifunction grip menu that appears (see Figure 7.3).

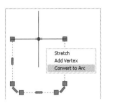

FIGURE 7.3 Converting a straight
polyline segment into an arc

10. Move the cursor upward, type **3″** (or **7 cm**), press Enter, and then press
    Esc to clear the selection. You've created the curve of the backrest.

11. Type **X** (for explode), press Enter, select the chair, and press Enter
    again. The polyline is converted into three lines and three arcs.

12. Click the Offset tool in the Modify panel, type **2″** (or **5 cm**) and press
    Enter. Select the arc you created in step 9 and then click a point above
    it on the drawing canvas to offset a new arc 2″ (or 5 cm) above.

13. Type **BLEND**, press Enter, and select the two arcs making up the back-
    rest near their left endpoints. A spline object smoothly joins the arcs.

14. Press Enter to repeat the BLEND command and select the two arcs near
    the right endpoints; another spline object is created (see Figure 7.4).

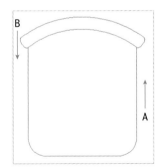

FIGURE 7.4 Blending between concentric arcs

15. Click the Stretch tool in the Modify panel, click points A and B shown
    in Figure 7.4 to create a crossing window, and press Enter. Click an
    arbitrary point on the drawing canvas as the first point of the Stretch
    operation. Move the cursor downward on the drawing canvas, type 3″
    (or **7 cm**) and press Enter. The seat depth is reduced.

16. Select the entire chair with an implied window. Click the Create tool
    in the Block panel on the ribbon's Home tab and the Block Definition

A preview image of
the chair appears to
the right of the Name
field because you
selected its constitu-
ent objects prior to
opening the Block
Definition dialog box.

◀

Certification
Objective

dialog box appears. Type **Chair** in the Name field. Every block must have a name.

17. Every block has a *base point*, which should be related to its geometry. Click the Pick Point button in the Base Point section; the Block Definition dialog box disappears. Hold Shift and right-click to open the context menu; select Midpoint. Click the midpoint of the chair's front edge. The Block Definition dialog box reappears, showing the coordinates of the point you snapped to (see Figure 7.5).

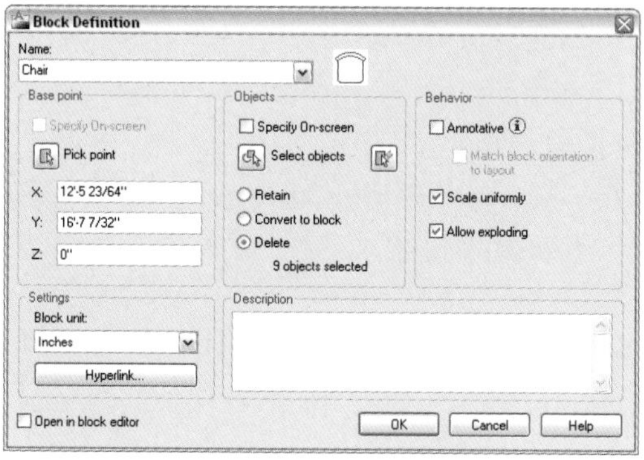

FIGURE 7.5 Defining a chair block

18. Choose the Delete radio button in the Objects section of the Block Definition dialog box. Select Scale Uniformly and Allow Exploding. Deselect Annotative and Open In Block Editor. Set the Block Unit drop-down to Inches (or Centimeters) and click OK. The chair disappears; don't worry, you will insert it later.

UNDERSTANDING THE BLOCK TABLE

When the chair disappeared from the drawing canvas it was defined in the drawing's *block table*. Although every drawing has a block table, you can't see it. Blocks defined there can be inserted into the drawing as block references. Changes made to block definitions (stored in the block table) affect all block references in the drawing.

Drawing a Door and Defining It as a Block

In the following steps, you will draw a door and the representation of its swing (an arc) and define it as a block:

1. If the file Ch7-A.dwg (or Ch7-A-metric.dwg) is not already open, go to the book's web page, browse to Chapter 7, and open the file.

2. Pan over to the middle room. Zoom into the door opening along the bottom edge of this room.

3. Toggle on running object snap mode on the status bar. Right-click this button and turn on Endpoint snap if it's not already highlighted in the context menu.

4. Click the Rectangle tool in the Draw panel. Snap the first corner at point A, as shown in Figure 7.6. Type @1.5,2´6 (or @4,75 cm) and press Enter to complete the door.

▲

**All door openings
in the sample file
measure 2´6˝
(75 cm) in width.**

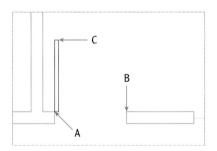

F I G U R E 7 . 6 Drawing a door

5. Click to open the Arc menu on the Draw panel and select the Center, Start, End tool. Click points A, B, and C as shown in Figure 7.6 to create the swing.

6. Type **B** (for block) and press Enter. The Block Definition dialog box appears.

7. Type **Door** in the Name field and click the Select Objects button. Select the rectangle and the arc and press Enter. Select the Pick point button, click the door hinge, and press Enter. Select the Convert To Block radio button and click OK.

▲

**The Convert To
Block option both
creates a block defi-
nition and inserts it
into the drawing as a
block reference.**

8. Select the door and observe that it has only one grip because it is now a block reference (see Figure 7.7). Press Esc to deselect.

9. Save your work as Ch7-B.dwg (or Ch7-B-metric.dwg).

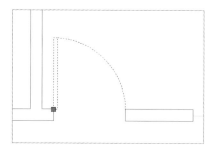

FIGURE 7.7 The door has only one grip because it is a block reference.

Inserting Blocks

After you create a block definition, you can insert *local block references* (from the current drawing's block table) into the drawing. In Chapter 9, "Working with Blocks and Xrefs," you will learn how to create and insert *global blocks*, which are blocks that exist outside the current drawing file. In this section, however, we will simply focus on inserting the local chair and door blocks you defined in the previous section.

1. If the file is not already open, go to the book's web page, browse to Chapter 7, get the file Ch7-B.dwg (or Ch7-A-metric.dwg), and open it.

2. Type **UN** (for units) and press Enter. Open the Insertion Scale drop-down menu and select Inches (or Centimeters) if it is not already selected (see Figure 7.8). Click OK to close the Drawing Units dialog box.

> The units you use in the Block Definition dialog box should match the Insertion Scale units; otherwise, AutoCAD will scale blocks when you insert them into the drawing.

Drawing Units

Length
Type: Architectural
Precision: 0'-0 1/16"

Angle
Type: Decimal Degrees
Precision: 0
☐ Clockwise

Insertion scale
Units to scale inserted content:
Inches

Sample Output
1 1/2",2",0"
3"<45,0"

Lighting
Units for specifying the intensity of lighting:
International

OK   Cancel   Direction...   Help

FIGURE 7.8 Setting Insertion Scale in the Drawing Units dialog box

3. Zoom into the room with the table on the left. Verify that Dynamic Input is off.

4. Right-click the object snap toggle on the status bar and turn on Midpoint snap if it's not already highlighted in the context menu.

5. Click the Insert tool on the Block panel on the ribbon's Home tab. Open the Name drop-down list in the Insert dialog box and select Chair. If it's not already selected, choose Specify On-Screen in the Insertion Point section of the Insert dialog box (see Figure 7.9). Click OK.

Certification
Objective

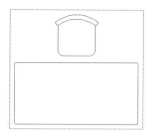

Insert dialog box showing:

Name: Chair   Browse...
Path:
Locate using Geographic Data

Insertion point
☑ Specify On-screen
X 0"
Y 0"
Z 0"

Scale
☐ Specify On-screen
X 1
Y 1
Z 1
☑ Uniform Scale

Rotation
☐ Specify On-screen
Angle: 0

Block Unit
Unit: Inches
Factor: 1

☐ Explode   OK   Cancel   Help

F I G U R E 7 . 9 Selecting the Chair block definition in the Insert dialog box

6. Hold Shift, right-click, and choose From in the context menu. Click the midpoint of the upper desk edge, type **@0,3**, (or **@0,7 cm**) and press Enter. The Chair block reference appears 3″ (or 7 cm) up from the center of the desk (see Figure 7.10).

F I G U R E 7 . 1 0 Chair block inserted 3″ from the desk

7. Click the Move tool in the Modify panel, select the Chair block, and press Enter. Click an arbitrary point on the drawing canvas, type **@1´3<180**, (or **@40<180** in metric) and press Enter to move the chair to the left.

8. Click the Copy tool in the Modify panel, type **L** (for last), and press Enter twice. Click an arbitrary point on the drawing canvas, type **@2´6˝<0**, (or **@80<0** in metric) and press Enter to copy a chair to the right (see Figure 7.11). Press Esc to end the COPY command.

FIGURE 7.11 Copying a block reference

9. Type **I** (for insert) and press Enter. Type **180** in the Angle text box in the Rotation section of the Insert dialog box and click OK.

10. Hold Shift, right-click, and choose From in the context menu. Click the midpoint of the lower desk edge and type @0,-3˝ (or **@0,-7 cm**) **@0,-3**, and press Enter. The Chair block reference appears 3˝ (or 7 cm) down from the center of the desk.

11. Press Enter to repeat the last command (Insert) and select Door from the Name drop-down list in the Insert dialog box. Select Specify On-Screen in the Rotation section and click OK.

12. Click point A in the leftmost room, as shown in Figure 7.12. Verify that Ortho mode is on in the status bar; if not, toggle it on. Move the cursor to the left to rotate the door into the proper orientation (see Figure 7.12). Click on the drawing canvas to insert the door.

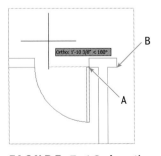

FIGURE 7.12 Inserting a door and rotating it on screen

13. Press the spacebar to repeat the INSERT command. Select Specify On-Screen in the Scale and Rotation sections of the Insert dialog box (see Figure 7.13) and click OK.

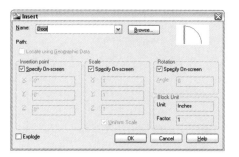

FIGURE 7.13 Specifying everything on screen when inserting a block

14. Click point B, as shown in Figure 7.12. The command prompt reads

```
Specify insertion point or [Basepoint/Scale/Rotate]:
Specify scale factor <1>:
```

Type **-1** and press Enter.

15. The command prompt now says

```
Specify rotation angle <0>: 180
```

Type **180** and press Enter. The door is inserted properly in the middle room.

16. Click the Copy tool in the Modify panel, select the door at the bottom of the middle room, and press Enter. Click points A and B shown in Figure 7.14 to copy a door block into the room on the right. Press Esc to end the COPY command.

Specifying a negative scale factor mirrors the block about its base point.

Copying a block has the same effect as inserting a block: a new block reference is added to the drawing.

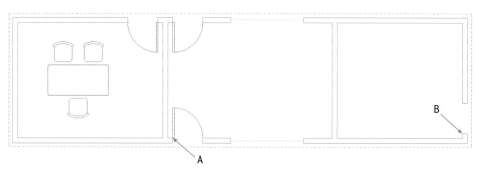

FIGURE 7.14 Copying a block

17. Select the new door in the rightmost room. Click its single blue grip to activate Grip Editing mode. Press the spacebar twice so that the command prompt reads as follows:

```
** ROTATE **
Specify rotation angle or
[Base point/Copy/Undo/Reference/eXit]:
```

Type **90** and press Enter to rotate the door block around its base point.

18. Save your work as Ch7-C.dwg (or Ch7-C-metric.dwg).

Editing Blocks

You can edit blocks after they have been defined and inserted into the drawing as block references. In addition to editing geometry, you can assign floating properties to control property inheritance, nest blocks within blocks, or explode blocks entirely. We'll explore each of these topics in this section.

Editing Block Definition Geometry

Blocks definitions are not frozen in stone; you can redraw them after block references have been inserted multiple times in a drawing. In fact, this is one of the reasons to use blocks: efficient control over multiple objects from a single editable definition. In the following steps you will alter the door block and see all its references update automatically.

1. If the file is not already open, go to the book's web page, browse to Chapter 7, get the file Ch7-C.dwg (or Ch7-C-metric.dwg), and open it.

2. Zoom in on the lower door in the middle room.

3. Select the door, right-click, and choose Edit Block In-Place from the context menu. Click OK in the Reference Edit dialog box that appears (see Figure 7.15).

4. Click the Rotate tool on the Modify panel, select the door itself (not its swing), and press Enter. Click the hinge point and the command prompt reads

```
Specify rotation angle or [Copy/Reference] <0>:
```

Type **-45** and press Enter.

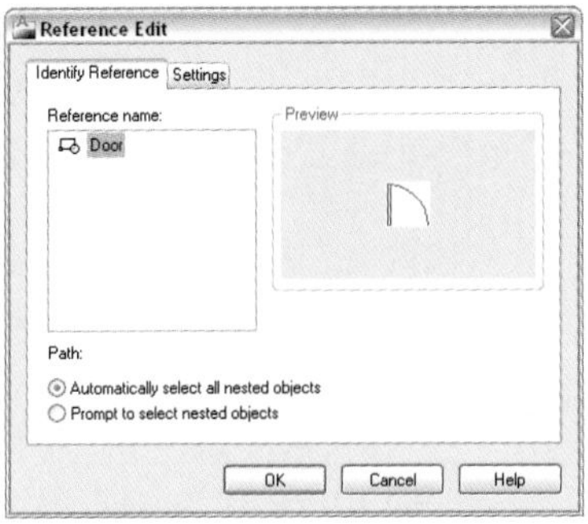

FIGURE 7.15 Editing a block reference in place

5. Click the Trim tool in the Modify panel and press Enter. Click the portion of the wing that extends beyond the door to trim it off and press Esc to end the TRIM command.

6. Expand the temporary Edit Reference panel on the ribbon's Home tab and click the Save Changes button. Click OK in the AutoCAD warning dialog box that appears, which says, "All reference edits will be saved." Figure 7.16 shows the result: All door references have been automatically updated with the new door geometry.

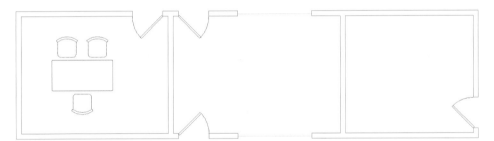

FIGURE 7.16 All doors have been updated by editing the door block in place.

7. Save your work as Ch7-D.dwg (or Ch7-D-metric.dwg).

Assigning Floating Properties

When you set objects' color, linetype, or lineweight to specific values such as Red, Hidden, or 0.5mm, you are setting those properties explicitly. Explicit object properties assigned to objects in block definitions are retained when those blocks are inserted onto different layers in the drawing.

It is often advantageous to assign floating properties—either *ByLayer* or *ByBlock*—to the objects in block definitions. Floating properties allow block references to inherit properties from the layer on which they are inserted. Or you can override these inherited properties with explicit properties by assigning them to the block reference.

The Door layer has been current throughout this chapter, so the objects you drew to define the chair and door blocks reside on this layer. In the following steps, you will assign floating properties to the chair and door blocks.

1. If the file is not already open, go to the book's web page, browse to Chapter 7, get the file Ch7-D.dwg (or Ch7-D-metric.dwg), and open it.

2. Click on each of the three chair block references to select them. Type **qp** (for Quick Properties) and press Enter. Select Furniture from the Layer drop-down menu (see Figure 7.17). Notice that the chairs are still green, even though the Furniture layer is blue. Click the close box in the upper-right corner to close the Quick Properties palette and press Esc to deselect.

> You can use the QP command as an alternative to toggling on Quick Properties mode on the status bar.

FIGURE 7.17 Assigning the Furniture layer to the chair block references

3. Select one of the chairs (it doesn't matter which one), right-click, and choose Edit Block In-Place from the context menu. Click OK in the Reference Edit dialog box that appears.

4. Create an implied window to select all nine objects making up the chair.

5. Type **qp** (for Quick Properties) and press Enter. Open the Color drop-down menu and select ByBlock. Click the Quick Properties palette's close box and press Esc to deselect.

6. Expand the Edit Reference panel and click the Save Changes button. Click OK in the AutoCAD warning dialog box. The chairs turn blue because the ByBlock floating property allows them to inherit the Furniture layer's blue color.

7. Select the lower chair by clicking on it. Open the Color drop-down menu in the Properties panel, select Magenta, and press Esc. The

chair turns magenta because ByBlock allows explicit properties assigned to the block reference to override inherited layer properties.

8. Open the Layer drop-down menu in the Layers panel and set Layer 0 current.

9. Open the Layer drop-down menu again and toggle off the Door layer. All the chairs and doors disappear because the geometry in the chair and door block definitions is on the Door layer. Toggle on the Door layer and click outside the Layer drop-down menu to close it.

10. Select the lower chair, right-click, and choose Edit Block In-Place from the context menu. Click OK in the Reference Edit dialog box that appears.

11. Create an implied window to select all nine objects making up the chair.

12. Open the Layer drop-down menu and select layer 0 to assign this layer to the selection. Press Esc to deselect the layer.

BLOCKS AND LAYER 0

I recommend that you always draw objects within block definitions on layer 0 so that block references will inherit the layer they are inserted on. Layer 0 is the only layer that works like this for block definitions. In addition, you should assign floating properties for the color, linetype, and/or lineweight of the objects in the block definition.

13. Expand the Edit Reference panel and click the Save Changes button. Click OK in the AutoCAD warning dialog box.

14. Open the Layer drop-down menu in the Layers panel and toggle off the Door layer. The doors disappear but the chairs remain because the chair references have inherited the Furniture layer (see Figure 7.18).

◀

Toggling off layer 0 does not hide block definition geometry referenced onto other layers.

FIGURE 7.18 Turning off the Door layer hides the doors but not the chairs when the chair block definition geometry is on layer 0.

15. Toggle on the Door layer.

16. Save your work as Ch7-E.dwg (or Ch7-E-metric.dwg).

Nesting Blocks

You can *nest* blocks within other blocks to simplify complex block definitions. However, you can't create circular references where blocks reference themselves or you'd create an infinite loop. In the following steps, you'll nest a phone block reference inside the desk block definition so that every desk you insert will have a phone on it.

1. If the file is not already open, go to the book's web page, browse to Chapter 7, get the file Ch7-E.dwg (or Ch7-E-metric.dwg), and open it.

2. Type **BEDIT** (for Block Editor) and press Enter. Select Desk in the Edit Block Definition dialog box that appears (see Figure 7.19). Click OK.

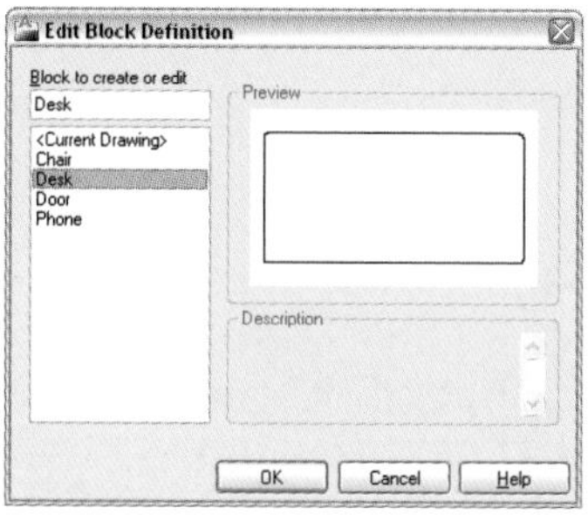

FIGURE 7.19 Selecting a block definition to edit

3. A temporary tab called Block Editor appears on the ribbon and the selected block (desk) fills the drawing canvas. Click the Authoring Palettes tool on the Manage panel to toggle them off because they are not needed for this exercise (see Figure 7.20).

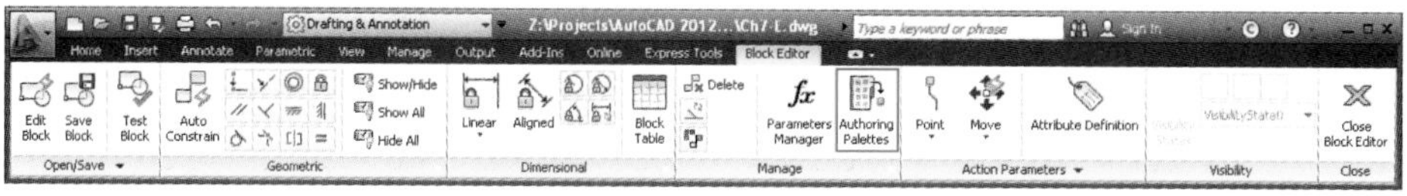

FIGURE 7.20 The Block Editor ribbon

The Block Editor is an alternative to editing blocks in place.

4. Type **I** (for insert) and press Enter. Select Phone in the Name drop-down list. Deselect Specify On-Screen in the Scale and Rotation sections of the Insert dialog box and click OK.

5. Click an arbitrary point on the right side of the desk to insert the phone block reference there.

6. Select the phone block, type **qp** (for Quick Properties), and press Enter. Change Layer Assignment to Equipment, click the close box to exit Quick Properties, and press Esc to deselect (see Figure 7.21).

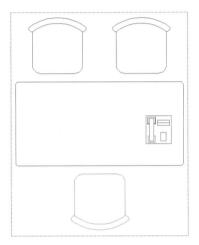

FIGURE 7.21 A phone nested within the desk block and surrounding chair blocks

> The phone is magenta because the objects in the phone block definition have floating properties that allow the Equipment layer's magenta color to be inherited.

7. Click the Close Block Editor button on the Close panel. Click Save Changes To Desk in the Block – Changes Not Saved dialog box that appears.

8. Save your work as Ch7-F.dwg (or Ch7-F-metric.dwg).

Exploding Blocks

There are two commands that blow away blocks, leaving you only with their defining geometry: EXPLODE and XPLODE. The former has no options whatsoever; the latter offers many options dealing with what happens to object properties after the block is disassembled. Let's explode a block using both methods:

> Use the PURGE command to delete unused block definitions to make the drawing file smaller.

1. If the file is not already open, go to the book's web page, browse to Chapter 7, get the file Ch7-F.dwg (or Ch7-F-metric.dwg), and open it.

2. Type **X** (for explode) and press Enter. Select the magenta chair and press Enter.

3. Select the parts of the chair and observe in the Layers panel that the objects are on layer 0 and in the Properties panel their color is set to ByBlock (see Figure 7.22). Press Esc to deselect.

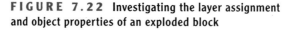

FIGURE 7.22 Investigating the layer assignment and object properties of an exploded block

4. Click the Undo button on the Quick Access toolbar. The block is re-created.

5. Type **xp** (for Xplode) and press Enter. Select the magenta chair and press Enter. The command prompt reads

```
[All/Color/LAyer/LType/LWeight/
Inherit from parent block/Explode]
 <Explode>:
```

Type **I** (for inherit from parent block) and press Enter.

6. Select all the parts of the chair and observe that the objects are on the blue Furniture layer and their color is explicitly set to magenta. This time the disassembled objects received the layer assignment and object properties of the block reference.

7. Expand the Modify panel and click the Set To ByLayer tool. The command prompt reads

```
Change ByBlock to ByLayer? [Yes/No] <Yes>:
```
Press Enter to accept the default Yes. Now the prompt says
```
Include blocks? [Yes/No] <Yes>:
```

Type **N** (for no) and press Enter. The SETBYLAYER command ends and the chair is blue now because its color has been set to ByLayer.

8. Save your work as Ch7-G.dwg (or Ch7-G-metric.dwg).

Redefining Blocks

You already know that block definitions have names, and that blocks are inserted by name. So what do you suppose happens if you define a new block using a name that's already been used in the drawing?

In the following steps, you are presented with just such a situation where you will have the opportunity to redefine a block definition. Any block references in the drawing will be automatically updated with the new definition.

1. If the file is not already open, go to the book's web page, browse to Chapter 7, get the file Ch7-G.dwg (or Ch7-G-metric.dwg), and open it.

2. Zoom into the lower chair you exploded in the previous section.

3. Click the Rectangle tool on the Draw panel. The command prompt reads

   ```
   Specify first corner point or [Chamfer/Elevation/
   Fillet/Thickness/Width]:
   ```
   Type **F** (for fillet) and press Enter. The prompt now says
   ```
   Specify fillet radius for rectangles <0'-0">:
   ```

   Type **1″** (or **3 cm**)and press Enter. The rectangle will have rounded corners.

4. For the first corner, click point A, as shown in Figure 7.23. Then type **@3,-10** (or **@7,-25** in metric) and press Enter to complete the RECTANGLE command.

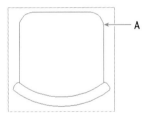

FIGURE 7.23 Drawing an armrest

5. Click the Mirror tool in the Modify panel. Type **L** (for last) and press Enter twice. The command prompt reads

   ```
   Specify first point of mirror line:
   ```

   Snap to the midpoint of the chair's front edge, move the cursor downward, and click on the drawing canvas to specify the second point of the mirror line. Press Enter twice to complete the MIRROR command (see Figure 7.24).

6. Select all objects in the chair and its armrests. Open the Layer drop-down menu and select layer 0 to change the assignment of the selected objects.

FIGURE 7.24 Mirroring an armrest

7. Type **B** (for block) and press Enter. Type **Chair** in the Name field in the Block Definition dialog box. Click the Pick Point button and then snap to the midpoint of the chair's front edge.

8. Select the Convert To Block radio button in the Objects section of the Block Definition dialog box and click OK. Click Redefine Block in the Block – Redefine Block dialog box that appears. Figure 7.25 shows the result: All three chair block references are updated.

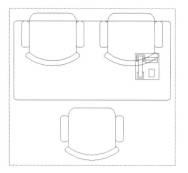

FIGURE 7.25 Redefining the chair block causes the chairs to lose their original orientation.

9. Unfortunately the redefined chair block references didn't preserve their original orientations. No matter; click the Mirror tool on the Modify panel, select the top two chairs, and press Enter. Snap to the front edge of one of the seats, move the cursor to the right, and click on the drawing canvas. The command prompt reads

```
Erase source objects? [Yes/No] <N>:
```

Type **Y** (for yes) and press Enter. The chairs are now oriented correctly (see Figure 7.26).

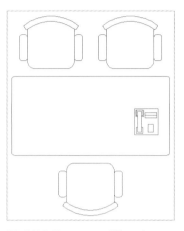

FIGURE 7.26 Mirroring two chair blocks

10. Save your work as Ch7-H.dwg (or Ch7-G-metric.dwg).

Working with Groups

Groups are a means of organizing objects that is less formal than blocks. Groups don't need to be named, nor do they require base points as blocks do. You can toggle group selection on and off so you can manipulate the entire group as a unit or access individual members of the group at will. You can't redefine the many with the few as you can with blocks, however. That said, it's certainly convenient to be able to manipulate many blocks with a few groups. In the following steps, you will group the desk and chairs, copy this group into adjacent rooms, and make adjustments to various blocks within the groups.

1. If the file is not already open, go to the book's web page, browse to Chapter 7, get the file Ch7-H.dwg, (or Ch7-G-metric.dwg) and open it.

2. Click the Group tool on the Groups panel on the ribbon's Home tab. Select the desk and the three chairs surrounding it, and then press Enter.

3. Click the Copy tool on the Modify panel, click the group to select it, and press Enter. Click an arbitrary point inside the desk and then

click in the middle and right rooms to copy the group twice. Press Esc to end the COPY command.

4. Click the Rotate tool on the Modify panel, select the group in the room on the right, and press Enter. Click an arbitrary point inside the desk, type **-90**, and press Enter (see Figure 7.27).

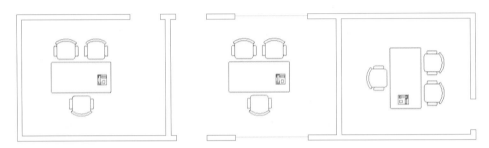

FIGURE 7.27 Copying and rotating groups in rooms

5. Click the Group Selection On/Off toggle in the Groups panel (turning it off).

6. Select the lower chair in the middle room and press the Delete key.

7. Click the Copy tool on the Modify panel, select the chair on the right, and press Enter. Snap to the midpoints at points A and B in Figure 7.28 and press Enter. A third chair is copied so all three are equidistant.

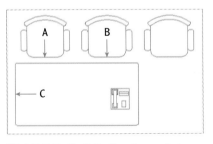

FIGURE 7.28 Copying a chair

8. Click the Mirror tool on the Modify panel, select the three chairs in the middle room, and press Enter. Click point C in Figure 7.28, move the cursor to the right, and click in the drawing canvas to complete the mirror line. Press Enter to mirror three more chairs on the opposite side of the desk.

9. Type **xp** (for Xplode) and press Enter, select the desk, and press Enter. Type **I** (for inherit from parent block) and press Enter.

10. Click the Stretch tool on the Modify panel, select the right edge of the desk with a crossing window, and press Enter. Click an arbitrary point inside the desk, move the cursor to the right and type **2'6** (or **80 cm**) and press Enter. The desk is enlarged.

11. Select the phone block on the desk and press the Delete key.

12. Click the Group Edit tool on the Groups panel, select the upper-left chair in the middle room, and press Enter. The command prompt reads

        Enter an option [Add objects/Remove objects/REName]:

    Type **A** (for add objects) and press Enter. Select all six chairs and the desk, and then press Enter.

13. Click the Group Selection On/Off toggle in the Groups panel (turning it on). Hover the cursor over the desk and observe that the entire group highlights (see Figure 7.29).

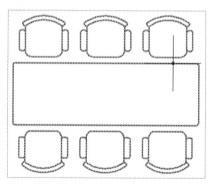

FIGURE 7.29 Reconstituted group after its constituent objects have been deleted, added, and stretched

14. Open the Layer drop-down menu and toggle on the Door layer. Figure 7.30 shows the final result.

15. Your drawing should now resemble Ch7-Final.dwg (or Ch7-Final-metric.dwg), which is available among the book's companion download files at **www.sybex.com/go/autocad2012essentials**

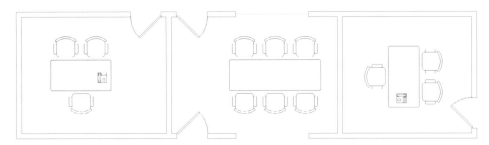

FIGURE 7.30 Final organized plan containing blocks and groups

THE ESSENTIALS AND BEYOND

In this chapter you learned how to organize objects into blocks and groups. More specifically, you defined, inserted, edited, nested, exploded, and redefined blocks. You saw how floating properties and layer 0 affect property inheritance when block references are inserted into a drawing. Finally, you worked with groups, manipulated them as whole units, accessed their individual members, and added objects to an existing group. In short, you now have the skills to organize objects for efficient drafting.

ADDITIONAL EXERCISE

Explore the BCONSTRUCTION command on your own. It is used to convert geometry into construction geometry that is only visible within the Block Editor for layout purposes. For example, try drawing a mirror line down the center line of the chair block and converting it to construction geometry with the BCONSTRUCTION command. The mirror line serves as a helpful visual reference while in the Block Editor but the construction geometry will not be displayed in the block reference.

CHAPTER 8

Hatching and Gradients

The term hatching refers to filling bounded areas with solids, patterns, and/or gradients. You will create hatching to indicate transitions between materials and to improve the readability of drawings in general. Hatching with solid fill, patterns, and/or tonal gradients can transform staid line drawings into attractive illustrations. This chapter will cover the basics of hatching so you can use it in your own drawings.

▶ **Specifying hatch areas**

▶ **Associating hatches with boundaries**

▶ **Hatching with patterns**

▶ **Hatching with gradients**

Specifying Hatch Areas

Every hatch area is defined by a boundary containing the solid fill, pattern, or gradient. The boundary can be determined either by picking a point on the drawing canvas or by selecting an object or set of objects.

Picking Points to Determine Boundaries

When a boundary is picked, AutoCAD uses a raycasting algorithm to determine the precise extents of the area bounded by the objects on screen. In the following steps you will pick points to determine the boundaries of multiple hatch objects:

1. Go to the book's web page at **www.sybex.com/go/ autocad2012essentials**, browse to Chapter 8, get the file Ch8-A.dwg, and open it. The drawing (see Figure 8.1) is based on a 100-year-old patent for fluid propulsion (CA 135174) by Nikola Tesla. Tesla is best known for inventing alternating electrical current that powers the modern age.

FIGURE 8.1 Initial line drawing based on Tesla's patent for fluid propulsion

2. Zoom into the center of the rotor in the drawing on the left.

  3. Click the Hatch tool in the Draw panel on the ribbon's Home tab. Click point A in Figure 8.2.

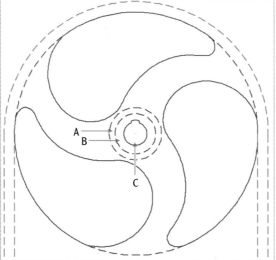

FIGURE 8.2 Picking a point to detect a boundary

4. A temporary contextual tab called Hatch Creation appears on the ribbon. This tab will remain active while you configure the hatch object that you are creating. Click Solid in the Pattern panel and turn off Associative mode if it is on (you'll learn about associative hatches in the next section) by clicking its button in the Options panel (see Figure 8.3).

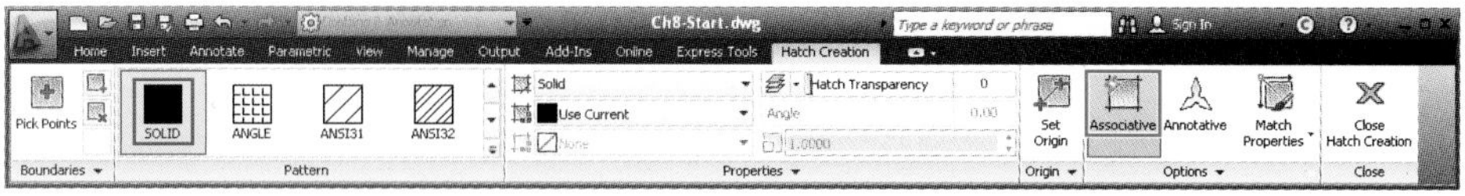

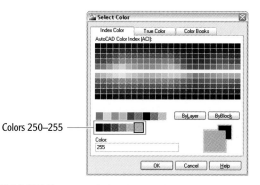

FIGURE 8.3 Using ribbon controls when creating a hatch

5. Expand the Options panel, open the Island Detection menu, and select Outer Island Detection. The thumbnails indicate different ways of treating nested boundaries, called *islands*. In this case you want only the outer island filled with a solid hatch.

6. Open the Hatch Color drop-down in the Properties panel and choose Select Colors at the bottom of the list of standard colors. Choose color 255 (see Figure 8.4) from the Select Color dialog box and click OK.

> You can over-ride hatch objects default color, transparency, and layer assignment on the Hatch Creation tab's Properties panel.

Colors 250–255 ——

FIGURE 8.4 Selecting a color override for the hatch object

7. Expand the Properties panel, open the Hatch Layer Override drop-down, and select the Solid layer (see Figure 8.5).

8. Click the Close Hatch Creation icon in the Close panel at the extreme right edge of the ribbon's Hatch Editor tab. The HATCH command ends.

9. Type **H** (for hatch) and press Enter. Click point B in Figure 8.2.

FIGURE 8.5 Using Hatch Layer Override

> **All the settings and overrides in the Hatch Creation tab are "sticky," meaning they remain the same the next time you create a hatch object.**

10. Open the Hatch Color drop-down in the Properties panel and choose Select Colors at the bottom of the list of standard colors. Choose color 253 from the Select Color dialog box and click OK.

11. Click the Close Hatch Creation icon in the Close panel.

12. Press the spacebar to repeat the last command. Click point C in Figure 8.2.

13. Open the Hatch Color drop-down in the Properties panel and choose Select Colors at the bottom of the list of standard colors. Choose color 250 from the Select Color dialog box and click OK.

14. Click the Close Hatch Creation icon in the Close panel. The Hatch Editor tab disappears.

15. Click the Isolate tool on the Layers panel of the ribbon's Home tab, drag a crossing selection over the hub of the rotor, and select a dashed blue line at the edges of the spokes. Press Enter and all the other layers are hidden, leaving the entire rotor.

> **Use the BOUNDARY command to create a polyline or region object from a picked point. BOUNDARY uses the same ray-casting algorithm that the HATCH commands use.**

16. Click the Hatch tool on the Draw panel and then click point A in Figure 8.6.

17. Open the Hatch Color drop-down in the Properties panel and choose Select Colors at the bottom of the list of standard colors. Choose color 255 from the Select Color dialog box and click OK.

18. Drag the Hatch Transparency slider to the right until the value is approximately 50 (see Figure 8.7).

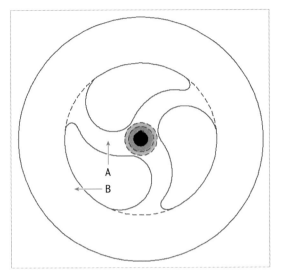

F I G U R E   8 . 6 Picking points on the rotor

F I G U R E   8 . 7 Overriding layer transparency
within the HATCH command

19. Toggle on the Show/Hide Transparency button on the status bar. The
hatch pattern you just created appears lighter.

20. Type **H** (for hatch) and press Enter. Click point B in Figure 8.6. The
command prompt reads

    Selecting everything...

AutoCAD can't find this particular area; press Esc before the program crashes.

21. Save your work as Ch8-B.dwg.

Selecting Objects to Define Boundaries

In complex drawings, picking points to determine boundaries sometimes
doesn't work. Fortunately you can always successfully define boundaries using

> The raycasting
> algorithm has a ten-
> dency to crash when
> analyzing complex
> areas, such as arcs,
> splines, and a circle
> forming the bound-
> ary of the outer por-
> tion of the rotor.
> ◀

closed objects. In the following steps you will select two closed objects to define a hatch boundary.

1. If the file is not already open from performing the previous step, go to the book's web page, browse to Chapter 8, get the file Ch8-B.dwg, and open it.

2. In the previous section, the raycasting algorithm probably had trouble with the inner part of the rotor where arcs and splines meet. To simplify the boundary, you will draw a circle. Click the Circle tool on the Draw panel.

▶

Don't worry about which layer the circle you are drawing is on; you will delete the circle later.

3. Shift+right-click and choose Node from the context menu. Click point A shown in Figure 8.8 as the center point. Type **qua** (for quadrant) and press Enter. Click point B in Figure 8.8 to set the inner circle's radius. The CIRCLE command ends.

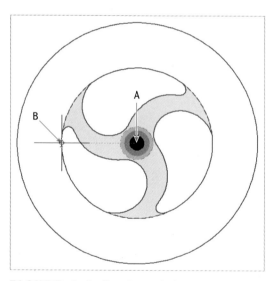

FIGURE 8.8 Drawing a circle

4. Type **H** (for hatch) and press Enter. Click the Select Boundary Objects tool in the Boundaries panel of the ribbon's Hatch Editor tab. Select the six arcs making up the inner circle of the rotor and then select the single outer circle. Select Solid in the Pattern panel and press Enter. The hatch appears correctly (see Figure 8.9); click the Close Hatch Editor icon in the Close panel at the extreme right edge of the Hatch Editor tab.

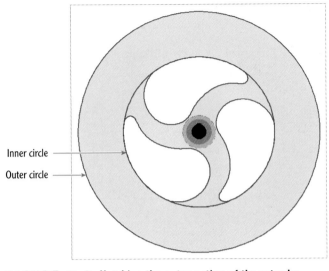

Inner circle

Outer circle

FIGURE 8.9 Hatching the outer potion of the rotor by
selecting objects

5. Click the Erase tool on the Home tab's Modify panel. Select the
inner circle you drew in step 3 and press Enter. The dashed arcs
are again visible.

6. Save your work as Ch8-C.dwg.

Associating Hatches with Boundaries

When hatches are associated with their boundary objects, the boundary objects
themselves define the extents of the hatch fill, pattern, or gradient. Altering the
shape of any of the boundary objects necessarily changes the extents of an associated hatch object. For example, the rotor needs to have a larger diameter and
by associating the hatch with the outer circle you will be able to get the hatch to
expand to fill the larger rotor simply by changing the diameter of the circle.

When hatches are not associated with their boundary objects, altering the
boundary objects does not change the shape of the hatch.

In the following steps you will re-create the boundary objects from the last
hatch pattern created in the previous section. Then you will alter the shape of
one of the boundary objects to change the extents of the solid hatch.

1. If the file is not already open from performing the previous step, go
to the book's web page, browse to Chapter 8, get the file Ch8-C.dwg,
and open it.

2. Click the outer portion of the rotor to select the hatch object; the Hatch Editor tab appears on the ribbon.

 3. Click the Recreate Boundary tool on the Boundaries panel. The command prompt reads

```
Enter type of boundary object [Region/Polyline] <Polyline>:
```

Press Enter to accept Polyline as the default option. Now the prompt says

```
Associate hatch with new boundary? [Yes/No] <Y>:
```

Press Enter again to accept the default, Yes. Two new circles are created and associated with the hatch.

 4. Click the Close Hatch Editor icon in the Close panel.

5. Toggle on Object Snap on the status bar. Right-click this toggle button and turn on Center, Quadrant, and Endpoint running object snap modes in the context menu if they are not already on.

6. Toggle on Ortho mode on the status bar.

7. Toggle on Object Snap Tracking on the status bar.

8. Click the Scale tool on the Modify panel, select the rotor's outer circle, and press Enter. Select the center of the rotor (point A in Figure 8.10) as the base point. The command prompt reads

```
Specify scale factor or [Copy/Reference]:
```

Type **R** (for reference) and press Enter. Pick the reference length by clicking points A and B in Figure 8.10.

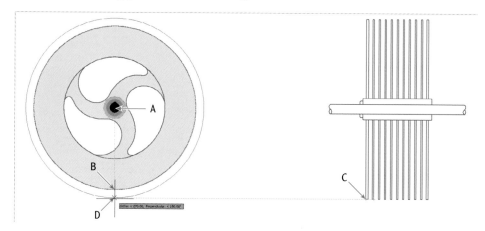

FIGURE 8.10 Scaling up the outer circle of the rotor enlarges its associative hatch.

9. Hover the cursor over point C as shown in Figure 8.10. Then bring the cursor back toward point D. When the tracking X appears on the drawing canvas, click point D. When the SCALE command ends, the rotor matches its depiction in the drawing on the right and the solid associative hatch fills the new boundary.

10. Click the outer portion of the rotor to select the hatch object; the Hatch Editor tab appears on the ribbon.

11. Convert the object into a nonassociative hatch by clicking to toggle off the Associative button in the Options panel and then click the Close Hatch Editor icon.

12. Click the Erase tool on the Modify panel, select the two re-created boundaries as shown in Figure 8.11, and press Enter.

ACCESSING THE HATCH EDIT DIALOG BOX

You can access all the hatching tools that you see on the ribbon in a dialog box interface by selecting a hatch object using the HATCHEDIT command. You'll see this dialog box when using the HATCH command if you are using a workspace that doesn't have the ribbon (such as AutoCAD Classic).

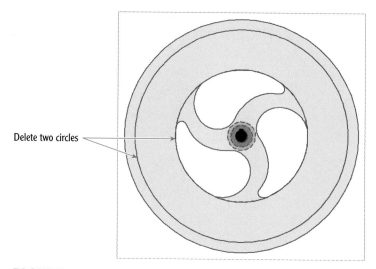

Delete two circles

FIGURE 8.11 Deleting the re-created boundary objects

13. Click the Unisolate tool on the Layers panel.

14. Save your work as Ch8-D.dwg.

Hatching with Patterns

Hatch patterns are repeating arrangements of lines and/or dots used to identify a material or a cutting plane, or to visually highlight an area. You'll learn how to specify pattern properties, separate hatch areas, and set the origin point of the pattern.

Specifying Properties

Hatch patterns have a few additional properties as compared to solid hatch objects. In the following steps you will select a pattern, set its scale, and adjust the pattern angle.

1. If the file is not already open from performing the previous step, go to the book's web page, browse to Chapter 8, get the file Ch8-D.dwg, and open it.

2. Pan over to the drawing on the right.

3. Click the Hatch tool on the Draw panel.

4. Click points A through F inside the red housing as shown in Figure 8.12. A solid hatch appears within the red boundaries.

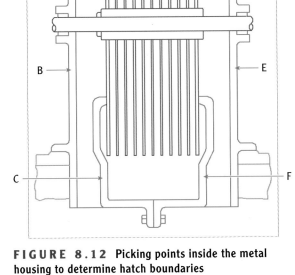

FIGURE 8.12 Picking points inside the metal housing to determine hatch boundaries

Increase Gap
Tolerance in the
Options panel (try
a value of 0.1) if
AutoCAD says a
boundary is not
closed.

5. Select the pattern called ANSI31 in the Pattern panel. Select Red in the Color drop-down in the Properties panel. Select Color 255 in the Background Color drop-down. Repeatedly click Scale's up arrow to increase the value to 2.000. Expand the Properties panel and select Pattern from the Hatch Layer Override drop-down (see Figure 8.13).

6. Click Close Hatch Editor in the Close panel.

7. Save your work as Ch8-E.dwg.

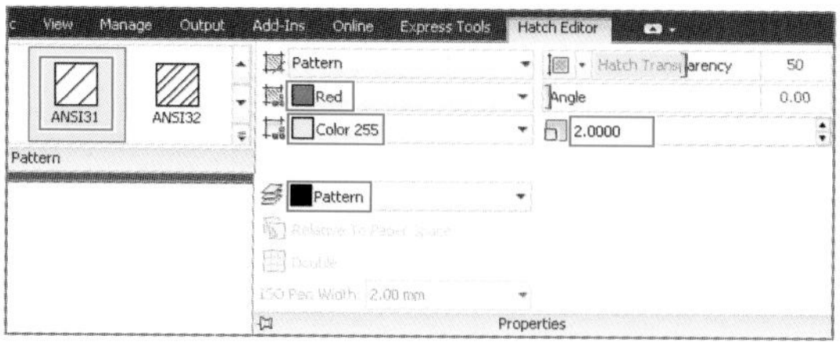

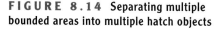

FIGURE 8.13 Configuring hatch properties

Separating Hatch Areas

When you picked points within multiple boundaries in the previous section, it formed a single hatch object. The properties you specified were assigned to this object. However, at this point we want to rotate the cross-sectional pattern 90° on the right side to better illustrate the separate pieces of metal that are bolted together. In the following steps you will separate the multiple bounded areas of a single object into individual hatch objects and then rotate patterns on half of them:

1. If the file is not already open from performing the previous step, go to the book's web page, browse to Chapter 8, get the file Ch8-E.dwg, and open it.

2. Select the hatch object you created in the previous section.

3. Expand the Options panel and click Separate Hatches (see Figure 8.14).

FIGURE 8.14 Separating multiple bounded areas into multiple hatch objects

4. Click Close Hatch Editor in the Close panel.

5. Select the upper-right hatch pattern, type **90** in the Angle text box, and press the Tab key. Click the Set Origin button and then click point A shown in Figure 8.15. Press Esc to exit the ribbon's Hatch Editor tab.

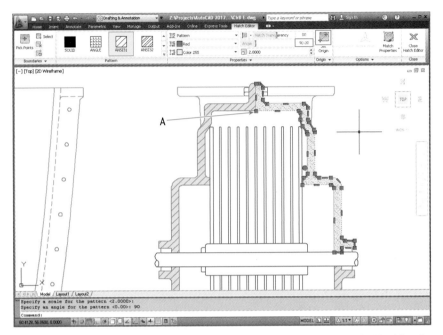

FIGURE 8.15 Changing the angle and setting the origin of an individual hatch pattern object

Exploding hatch patterns removes their associativity (if any). Exploding them again converts the hatch pattern into its constituent lines; background color fill is lost in the process.

6. Select the hatch pattern on the left side, click the Set Origin button, click point A as shown in Figure 8.15, and press Esc. The outer patterns on left and right both meet symmetrically at point A.

7. Select the pattern on the lower right, click the Match Properties tool in the Options panel, and select the upper-right pattern. Press Esc to deselect; the lower pattern matches the upper pattern's angle.

8. Select the inner pattern on the right. Click the Match Properties tool in the Options panel and select the lower-right pattern.

9. Click the Set Origin button and click point B in Figure 8.16. Press Esc to deselect.

10. Select the inner pattern on the left. Click the Set Origin button and click point B in Figure 8.16. Press Esc to deselect. The inner patterns on left and right both meet symmetrically at point B. Figure 8.17 shows the result.

11. Save your work as Ch8-F.dwg.

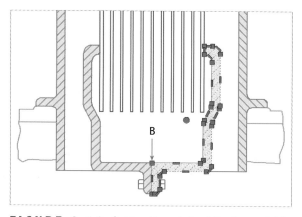

FIGURE 8.16 Setting the origin of the inner-right pattern

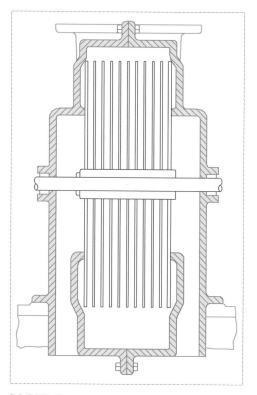

FIGURE 8.17 Symmetrical crosshatching highlights separate metal castings.

Hatching with Gradients

In addition to hatching with solid fill and line patterns, you can hatch with one- and two-color *gradients* to vary tonality in a smooth fashion. Gradients can subtly hint at an extra dimension that helps make drawings more readable. In the following steps you will create gradient hatches that give depth to metal parts in the drawings.

1. If the file is not already open from performing the previous step, go to the book's web page, browse to Chapter 8, get the file Ch8-F.dwg, and open it.

2. Open the flyout next to the Hatch tool on the Draw panel and select Gradient from the menu. Click points A through F shown in Figure 8.18.

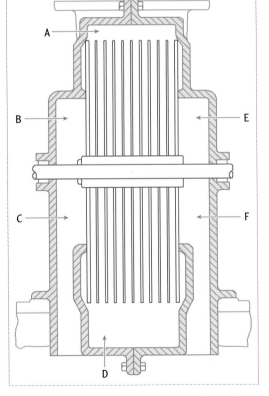

FIGURE 8.18 Picking points to determine boundaries for gradient hatch

3. Scroll down in the Pattern panel and select the GR_CURVED gradient. Select Color 253 in the Gradient Color 1 drop-down. Click the Gradient Tint And Shade button (if it is not already highlighted in blue) to create a one-color gradient. Drag the Hatch Transparency slider all the way to the left until its value reads 0. Expand the Properties panel and select Gradient in the Hatch Layer Override drop-down (see Figure 8.19). Click the Close Hatch Creation icon at the right edge of the ribbon.

> **Click the Gradient Tint And Shade button to toggle one- or two-color gradients. You can select both colors in two-color gradients whereas one-color gradients fade to white.**

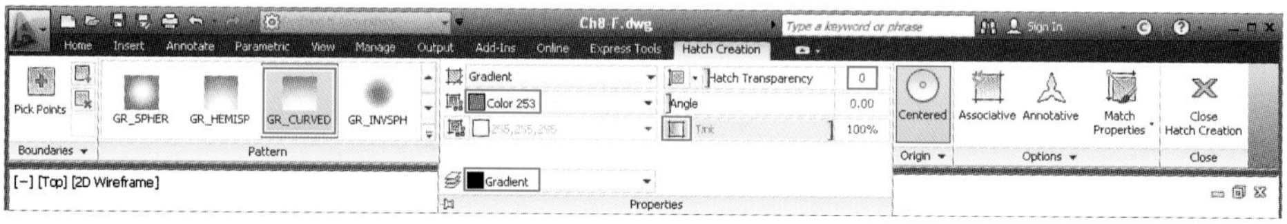

FIGURE 8.19 Configuring a gradient hatch

4. Zoom in on the rotor shaft.

5. Type **GRADIENT** and press Enter. Click a point in the center of the shaft to determine the boundary for a new gradient hatch. Select the GR_CYLIN pattern, set Angle to 90, and select Color 250 in the Gradient Color 1 drop-down. Click the Close Hatch Creation icon. Figure 8.20 shows the result.

> **Use the DRAWORDER command to change the display behavior of individual overlapping objects.**

6. Objects typically overlap objects drawn earlier. Type **HATCHTOBACK** and press Enter. All hatch objects (solid fills, patterns, and/or gradients) are sent to the back of the *draw order* stack so they don't overlap any of the other objects in the drawing.

7. Your drawing should now resemble Ch8-G.dwg, which is available for download at the book's web page.

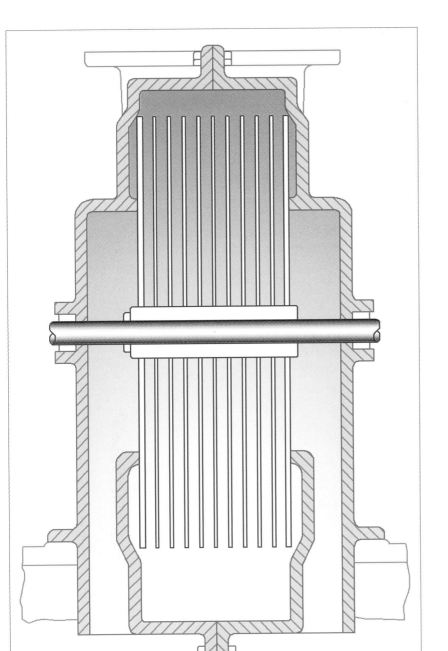

FIGURE 8.20 Adding a cylindrical gradient to the shaft

THE ESSENTIALS AND BEYOND

In this chapter you have learned how to create hatch objects that are filled with sold color, line patterns, and/or gradients. You now have the tools to improve the readability of your drawings by graphically indicating transitions between materials and section cutting planes, and by adding depth to parts with variable shading.

ADDITIONAL EXERCISE

Explore the WIPEOUT command on your own. Think of wipeouts as solid hatches that completely obscure what they cover with the current canvas background color. They can be useful in complex drawings when you want to wipe out areas to make room for notes. Try creating a wipeout object that obscures a portion of the upper rotor blades in the cross-sectional drawing on the right of Ch8-G.dwg.

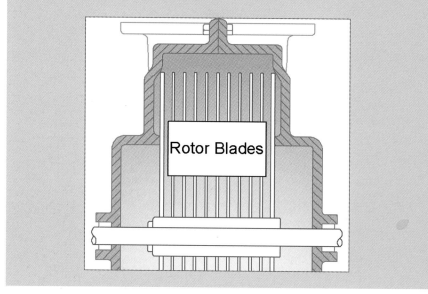

CHAPTER 9

Working with Blocks and Xrefs

In Chapter 7, "Organizing Objects," you learned how to define and reference blocks within a single drawing. In this chapter you will create and insert *global blocks* from outside the current drawing. Harnessing the power of a search engine, you'll cast a net across multiple drawings to locate specific blocks and a variety of other content. Once key content is found, you will place it on tool palettes for quick access in the future. In addition, you will make external references (*Xrefs*) to drawings outside the current file.

▶ **Working with global blocks**

▶ **Searching for content across multiple drawings**

▶ **Storing content on tool palettes**

▶ **Referencing external drawings and images**

Working with Global Blocks

Global blocks are drawing files that you will later insert as blocks into another drawing. In this section, you will learn how to write local blocks to files, insert a drawing file as a local block, and redefine local blocks with global blocks.

Writing a Local Block Definition to a File

In the following steps you will export one of the current drawing's block definitions to an individual drawing file. In addition you will open the newly created file and alter its contents.

1. Go to the book's web page at **www.sybex.com/go/ autocad2012essentials**, browse to Chapter 9, get the file Ch9-A.dwg, and open it.

2. Type **W** (for write block) and press Enter. Select the Block radio button in the Source area of the Write Block dialog box. Select Sofa from the Block drop-down. Select Inches from the Insert Units drop-down in the Destination area (see Figure 9.1). Click OK and the geometry within the Sofa block definition is written to Sofa.dwg.

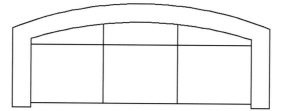

The Sofa block that was written to Sofa.dwg does not itself have a Sofa block definition; only the geometry was transferred to the new file.

FIGURE 9.1 Writing a block to a file

 3. Click the Open tool on the Quick Access toolbar. Browse to the following folder:

    C:\Documents and Settings\<your user name>\My Documents

    Open Sofa.dwg (see Figure 9.2).

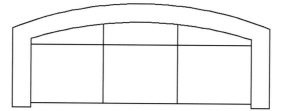

FIGURE 9.2 Open the Sofa.dwg file.

4. Click Zoom Extents on the Navigation bar.

5. Click the Erase tool on the Modify panel, select the two arcs in the sofa's backrest, and press Enter.

6. Toggle on Ortho mode on the status bar.

7. Toggle on Object Snap on the status bar. Right-click the Object Snap toggle and select Endpoint if it is not already selected.

8. Click the Line tool on the Draw panel. Snap the first point of the line to the endpoint shown in Figure 9.3. Move the cursor to the right and click an arbitrary second point. Press Esc to end the LINE command.

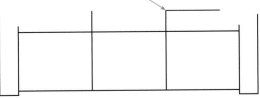

Snap the first point to this endpoint

FIGURE 9.3 Drawing a straight-backed sofa

9. Click the Fillet tool on the Modify panel. Verify that the command prompt says the following:

```
Current settings: Mode = TRIM, Radius = 0'-0"
```

If the radius is not 0, type **R** (for radius), press Enter, type **0**, and press Enter again. Select the line you just drew and then click the inner line on the right arm of the sofa.

10. Press the spacebar to repeat the FILLET command. Click the inner line on the left arm of the sofa and then click the back line. Figure 9.4 shows the result.

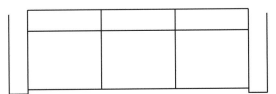

FIGURE 9.4 Filleting lines to meet at sharp corners

11. Click the Offset tool on the Modify panel. Click points A and B in Figure 9.5 to set the offset distance. Select the back line of the sofa and then click above it to offset another line.

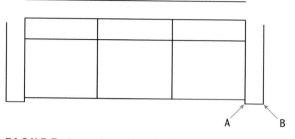

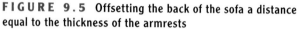

A   B

FIGURE 9.5 Offsetting the back of the sofa a distance equal to the thickness of the armrests

12. Click the Fillet tool on the Modify panel. Select the line you just offset and then click the outer line on the right arm of the sofa.

13. Press the spacebar to repeat the FILLET command. Click the outer line on the left arm of the sofa and then click the top back line. The sofa redesign is complete (see Figure 9.6).

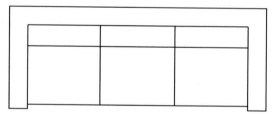

FIGURE 9.6 Redesigned sofa drawing

14. Click the Save As tool on the Quick Access toolbar. Type **Sofa2.dwg** in the File Name text box and then click the Save button.

15. Type **close** and press Enter to close the file you just saved.

Inserting a Drawing as a Local Block

When you insert a DWG file (having global scope) into the current drawing, it comes in as a block. In the following steps, you will twice insert the new sofa block into the same file in which you started this chapter:

1. If the file is not already open, go to the book's web page, browse to Chapter 9, get the file Ch9-A.dwg, and open it.

2. Zoom into the Manager's office directly above the President's office, select the two armchairs and side table, and press the Delete key (see Figure 9.7).

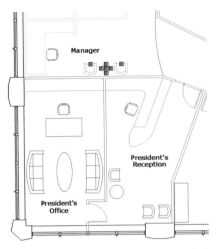

FIGURE 9.7 Deleting two armchairs and
a side table to make way for a new sofa

3. Toggle off Object Snap on the status bar.

4. Click the Make Object's Layer Current tool in the Layers panel. Click
the Manager's chair and A-furn becomes the current layer.

5. Click the Insert tool on the Block panel. The Sofa2 block is not yet
defined in this drawing's block table, so you won't find it in the Name
drop-down. Click the Browse button and locate the Sofa2.dwg file
you saved in the previous exercise, or use the Sofa2.dwg file provided
in the Samples folder for Chapter 9. Type **180** for Angle in the Insert
dialog box (see Figure 9.8) and click OK.

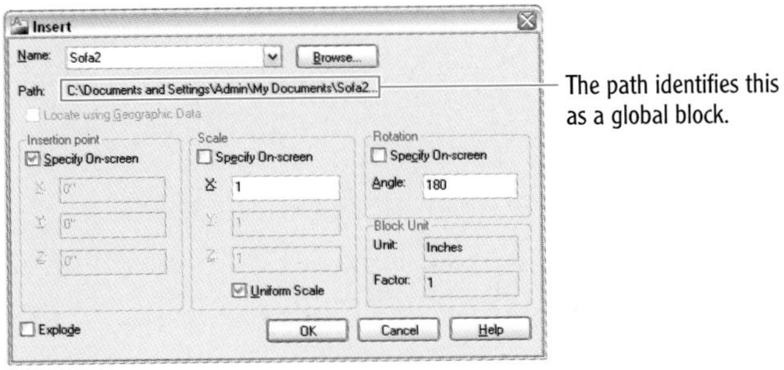

FIGURE 9.8 Configuring a global block in the Insert dialog box

6. Click approximately where you deleted the armchairs and side table
to insert a Sofa2 block reference in the drawing (see Figure 9.9).

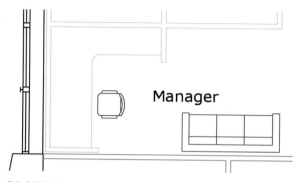

FIGURE 9.9 Inserting the new sofa

7. Pan over to the lower-right corner of the building. Delete the two armchairs and side table in the corner Manager's office.

8. Type **I** (for Insert) and press Enter. Sofa2 is already selected in the Name drop-down. No path is listed in the Insert dialog box this time because Sofa2 was defined as a local block when you inserted it in step 5. Type **180** for Angle and click OK.

9. Click approximately where you deleted the armchairs and side table to insert a Sofa2 block reference in the drawing (see Figure 9.10).

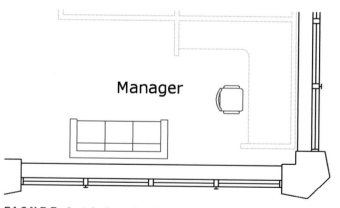

FIGURE 9.10 Inserting Sofa2 again as a local block

10. Save your work as Ch9-B.dwg.

Searching for Content Across Multiple Drawings

The Content Explorer is new in AutoCAD 2012; it allows you to search for—and insert—content from *within* other drawings. Using the Content Explorer to locate and insert blocks is much more efficient than writing blocks to files and then inserting the resulting files into drawings, as you learned in the previous section.

The reasons for the increased efficiency of the Content Explorer are twofold:

▶ You can access all the blocks within every file in *your search path.*

▶ Harnessing the power of a search engine gets you to what you are looking for much faster than a manual search.

In the following steps, you will use the Content Explorer to search for blocks and other types of content among numerous drawing files:

1. If the file is not already open, go to the book's web page, browse to Chapter 9, get the file Ch9-C.dwg, and open it.

2. Click the Add-Ins tab on the ribbon and click the Explore tool on the Content panel; the Content Explorer appears (see Figure 9.15).

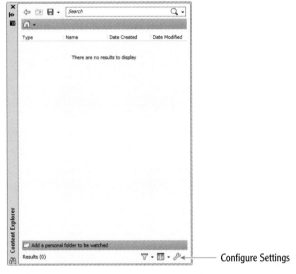

FIGURE 9.15 An empty Content Explorer

3. Click the Configure Settings button in the Content Explorer.

4. Click the Add Watched Folder in the Configure Settings dialog box. Add the following path (if it's not already there):

```
C:\Program Files\Autodesk\AutoCAD 2012\Sample
```

AutoCAD goes to work indexing the watched folder (see Figure 9.16). Click the Close button in the Configure Settings dialog box.

Your computer name will appear here.

Your CAD manager can add additional content sources (workstations and servers).

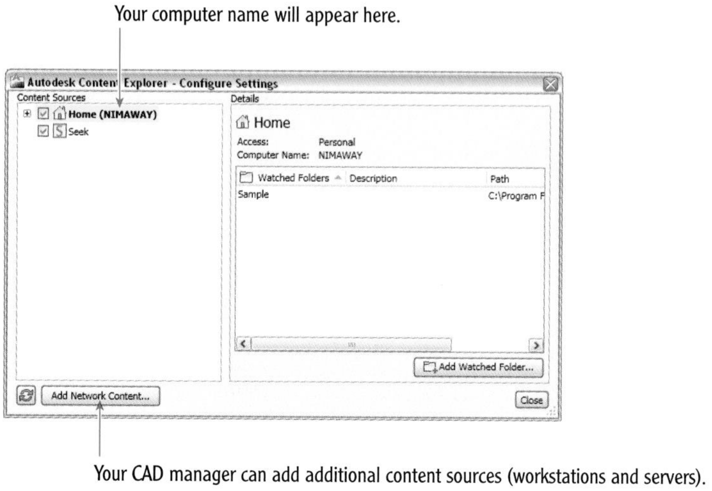

FIGURE 9.16 Configuring a watched folder

> **The Content Explorer's search engine indexes files as they are added to Watched Folders list. This process can take a few minutes when folders are first added, but after that search time is negligible.**

5. Double-click the Sample folder that appears in the Content Explorer. Then double-click Sheets Sets, Architectural, and A-03.dwg. The Content Explorer shows all the block references, block definitions, layers, layouts, and styles present in the drawing (see Figure 9.17).

6. You can click on any of the *breadcrumbs* to go to specific folders in the path. A more efficient means of using the Content Explorer is to harness the power of its search technology. Type sofa in the search field at the top of the Content Explorer and press Enter; the results are instantaneous. Hover the cursor over individual block thumbnails to learn which drawings they are stored in. Figure 9.18 shows the result.

7. Open the Content Sources drop-down menu near the top of the Content Explorer and select Autodesk Seek. Select the sofa folder and a variety of sofas are displayed from the manufacturers that participate in Autodesk's Seek program. Any of these could be inserted into the current drawing. Double-click the second thumbnail marked Castelli.

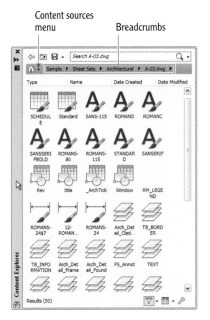

FIGURE 9.17 Content Explorer showing content within the specific drawing

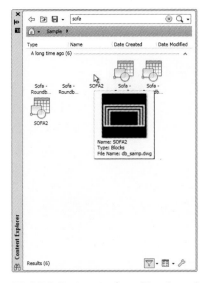

FIGURE 9.18 Searching for sofas in the Sample folder

8. The selected sofa is sold through Haworth (see Figure 9.19). Click Available Files; right-click SLMS-FD03, 2D; and choose Insert.

FIGURE 9.19 Getting detailed information about products through the Content Explorer

9. Type **Sofa3** and click OK in the Substitute Block Name dialog box that appears. Click a point on the drawing canvas to insert the new sofa. Press Enter until the command is done; you must press 13 times in this case because of this block's attributes, something you'll learn more about in Chapter 15, "Storing, Presenting, and Extracting Data."

10. Delete the sofas in the President's office and replace them with two new Haworth sofas. Figure 9.20 shows the result.

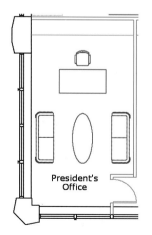

FIGURE 9.20 Replaced sofas in the President's office with Haworth sofas from Autodesk Seek

11. Save your work as Ch9-D.dwg.

12. Close the Content Explorer.

Storing Content on Tool Palettes

Tool palettes are used for storing just about any type of content for quick reuse. You create tools on a palette by dragging objects—including blocks, hatches, images, dimensions, tables, lights, cameras, materials, visual styles, and Xrefs—onto the palette from any saved drawing.

In the following steps, you'll create a new palette and drag a sofa onto it, and then use the tool to add another sofa:

1. If the file is not already open, go to the book's web page, browse to Chapter 9, get the file Ch9-D.dwg, and open it.

2. Select the ribbon's View tab and click the Tool Palettes button on the Palettes panel (see Figure 9.21).

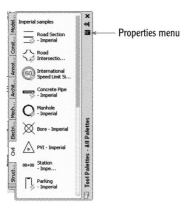

FIGURE 9.21 Click the Tool Palettes button.

3. Open the Properties menu on the Tool Palettes panel and select Architectural. The items listed at the bottom of the menu are palette groups. The Architectural palette group contains one palette, which is also called Architectural.

4. Reopen the Tool Palettes panel's Properties menu and select New Palette. Type **Furniture** and press Enter. A second palette appears under Architectural.

5. Select one of the Haworth sofas in the President's office. Drag the sofa (not using a grip) onto the Furniture palette. Sofa3 appears with a preview icon (see Figure 9.22).

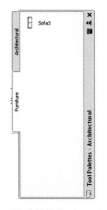

FIGURE 9.22 Creating a tool on a new palette by dragging a sofa block onto it

Blocks dragged to tool palettes are global blocks that can be inserted into any drawing.

6. Right-click the Sofa3 tool in the Furniture palette and choose Properties from the context menu. Change Prompt For Rotation to Yes in the Tool Properties dialog box that appears (see Figure 9.23). Click OK.

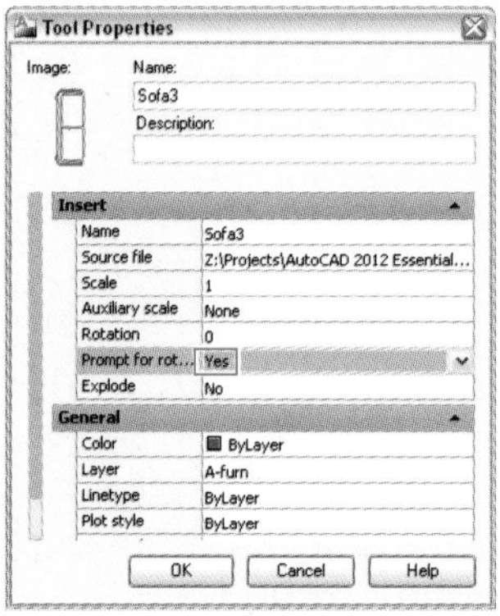

FIGURE 9.23 Adjusting tool properties to prompt for rotation

7. Select the sofa in Reception and press the Delete key. Click the Sofa3 tool in the Furniture palette and then click a point in Reception to insert the new sofa. Move the cursor down and, if Ortho mode is not

on, press F8. Click on the drawing canvas to accept the rotation value and then click OK in the Edit Attributes dialog box that appears. Figure 9.24 shows the result.

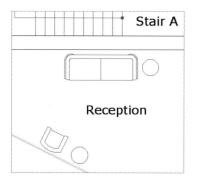

FIGURE 9.24 Inserting a sofa from the tool palette

8. Close the Tool Palettes tool.

9. Save your work as Ch9-E.dwg.

Referencing External Drawings and Images

External references (called *Xrefs*) are a more dynamic alternative to blocks. Xrefs linked to the current drawing are automatically updated every time the current drawing is opened. Blocks, on the other hand, must be edited in place or redefined when they are changed. The real efficiency with Xrefs comes when you link one file into multiple drawing files because changes made to the linked file are automatically reloaded in all the files that have the Xref attached.

In the following steps, you will externally reference a *core* (elevators, stairs, shafts) and *shell* (exterior envelope) drawing into the drawing containing items owned by the building tenant (walls, doors, furniture, and so on). The advantage of working this way is that the core and shell generally do not change from floor to floor, whereas the tenant improvement drawings are typically unique on each floor. Changes made to the core and/or shell can be made in one drawing that is linked to all the individual tenant drawings.

1. Go to the book's web page, browse to Chapter 9, get the file Ch9-CoreShell.dwg, and open it. Figure 9.25 shows the building core and shell.

This is just one example of using Xrefs in the case of a high-rise building. Xrefs can be used in every discipline whenever you want the advantages they provide.

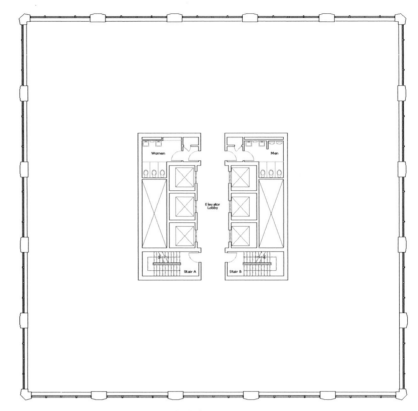

FIGURE 9.25 Core and shell drawing

2. Return to the book's web page, browse to Chapter 9, get the file Ch9-F.dwg, and open it. Figure 9.26 shows the objects owned by the tenant.

3. Select the ribbon's View tab and click the External References Palette button in the Palettes panel. Open the Attach menu, as shown in Figure 9.27.

4. Select Attach DWG from the menu. Select the file Ch9-CoreShell. dwg and click Open in the Select Reference dialog box.

5. In the Attach External Reference dialog box that appears, deselect Specify On-Screen in the Insertion Point area. Change Path Type to Relative Path (see Figure 9.28). Click OK.

▶

You can Xref DWG, DWF, DGN, PDF, and a variety of image file formats.

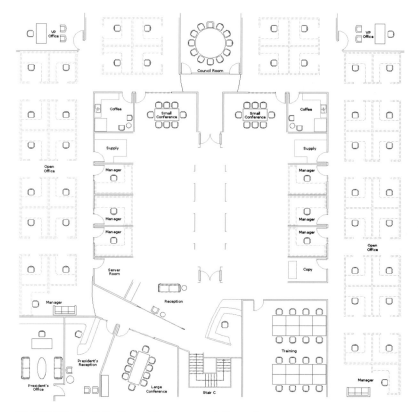

FIGURE 9.26 Tenant improvement floor plan

Attach menu

FIGURE 9.27 Attaching a DWG
file in the External References palette

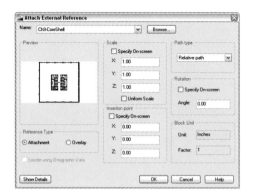

FIGURE 9.28 Attaching an external reference

You can adjust the amount of fading the Xref displays in the OPTIONS command on the Display tab within the Options dialog box.

6. The core and shell appear faded with respect to the tenant drawing (see Figure 9.29).

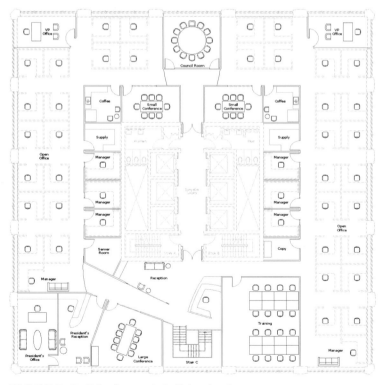

FIGURE 9.29 Core and shell drawing is externally referenced into the tenant drawing.

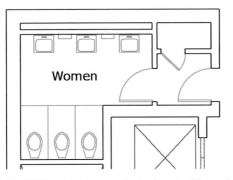

7. Select the core or shell to select the single Xref object. Click the Open Reference tool on the Edit panel of the External Reference tab that appears on the ribbon.

8. Redesign the Women's washroom so that it has three sinks, as shown in Figure 9.30.

Women

FIGURE 9.30 Redesigning the Women's washroom for three sinks

9. Type **close** and press Enter twice to close and save Ch9-CoreShell.dwg.

10. A balloon appears in the drawing status bar informing you that an external reference has changed (see Figure 9.31). Click the hyperlinked blue text to reload the Ch9-CoreShell Xref. The changes made to the Women's washroom are now visible in the tenant drawing.

FIGURE 9.31 Balloon notification that an Xref has changed

11. Save your work as Ch9-G.dwg.

THE ESSENTIALS AND BEYOND

In this chapter you learned how to work with global blocks, the Content Explorer, tool palettes, and Xrefs. You learned how to increase drawing and editing efficiency by using blocks and Xrefs. You can now access and work with content beyond the current drawing. This is the key to working in a team because team members regularly need to share content with one another. Global blocks and Xrefs are the means for exchanging design data within a team. The Content Explorer and the Tool Palettes feature make finding and using design data much easier.

ADDITIONAL EXERCISE

Certification Objective

Explore the Autodesk Design Center using the ADC command. The Design Center is similar to the Content Explorer but without the search engine functionality. Reopen Ch9-G.dwg if it's not still open. Expand the folder list in the DesignCenter palette and navigate to the Chapter 06 folder on your hard drive; then expand Ch6-Final.dwg. Select Blocks and then drag the Phone-Desk block into the drawing canvas of Ch9-G.dwg. Move this phone to the President's desk.

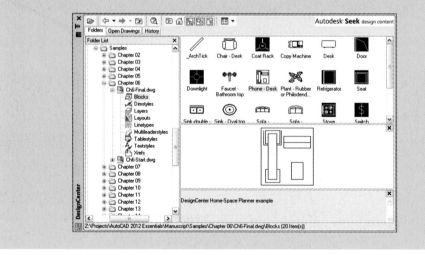

CHAPTER 10

Creating and Editing Text

Text is an essential part of every drawing. You use the written word to clarify graphical depictions and delineate your design intent with specific language. It's good to remember that drawings can be used as part of legal construction documents and you typically need to clarify your design intent with text that appears on the drawings themselves. In this chapter you'll learn how to style text, how to write both lines and paragraphs of text using specialized commands, and how to edit existing text.

▶ **Creating text styles**

▶ **Writing lines of text**

▶ **Writing and formatting paragraphs of text using MTEXT**

▶ **Editing text**

Creating Text Styles

AutoCAD can't help you with your grammar or linguistic style, but it can style the appearance of text. Text styles associate specific fonts, optional text heights, and special effects with text objects. In the following steps, you will create text styles that you will use in the next section when creating text objects.

1. Go to the book's web page at **www.sybex.com/go/ autocad2012essentials**, browse to Chapter 10, get the file Ch10-A.dwg or Ch10-A-metric.dwg, and open it.

Certification Objective

2. On the ribbon's Home tab, expand the Annotation panel and open the first drop-down menu (for text styles). Every drawing has both an Annotative and Standard style by default. Select Manage Text Styles at the bottom of the panel (see Figure 10.1).

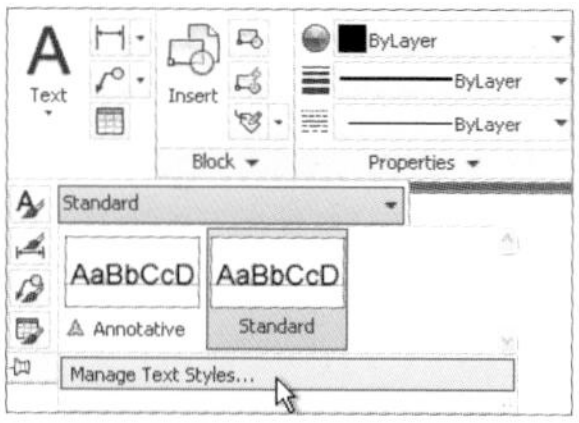

FIGURE 10.1 Managing text styles

3. Click the New button in the Text Style dialog box that appears. Type **Title** in the New Style dialog box (see Figure 10.2) and click OK.

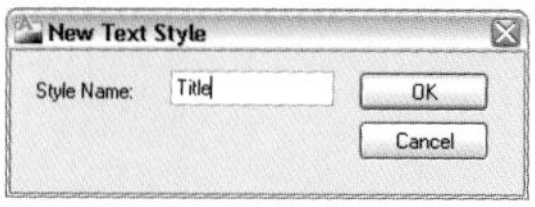

FIGURE 10.2 Naming a new text style

4. Open the Font Name drop-down and select Garamond. The symbol next to the font name indicates this is a TrueType font. Set Font Style to Bold and deselect Annotative (see Figure 10.3). Click the Apply button.

TrueType is the most common format for fonts on both Mac OS and Windows. The names that appear in the Font Name drop-down reflect the fonts installed on your operating system.

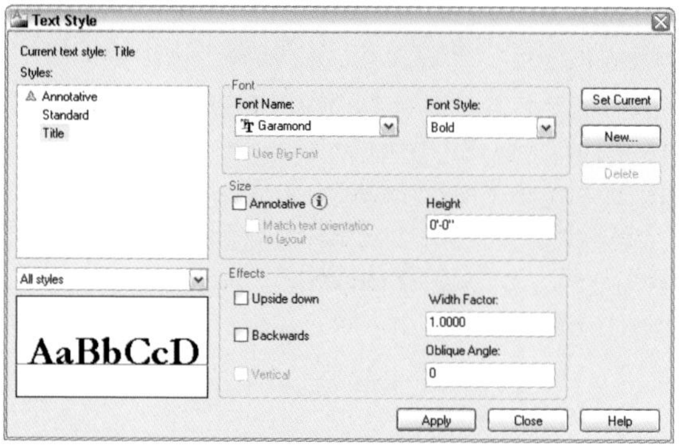

FIGURE 10.3 Configuring the Title style

5. Select Standard in the Styles list on the left side of the Text Style dialog box. Open the Font Name drop-down and select simplex.shx. The symbol next to the font name indicates this is a shape-based font that is specific to AutoCAD. Type **1'-0"** (or **30** cm) in the Height text box.

Type **0.8000** as the Width Factor value in the Effects area so that this style will be 20 percent narrower than the default (see Figure 10.4). Click the Apply, Set Current, and Close buttons (in that order).

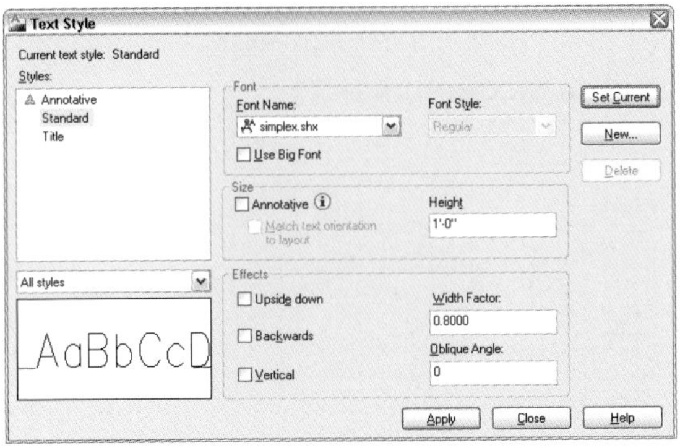

FIGURE 10.4 **Configuring the Standard style**

AutoCAD SHX fonts were designed to optimize motion in pen plotters (now obsolete) but are still commonly used today as simple fonts suitable for architectural and engineering lettering.

6. Save your work as Ch10-B.dwg or Ch10-B-metric.dwg. The styles you created are saved within the drawing even though you can't see them on the drawing canvas.

Writing Lines of Text

You will use the TEXT command when you want to create a single line of text. TEXT creates independent objects on every line so these objects are suitable for use in symbols or labels on drawings. You will learn how to create text that fits within a specified linear distance so that the text fits within a rectangle or circle, for example. In addition, you will justify text so that it can be easily reused and its content changed without having to reposition the text every time to maintain alignment with surrounding geometry. You will also discover that text objects can be manipulated and duplicated using many of the commands you already know.

Creating Text to Fit

There are many situations where you will want to fit text within geometric objects. For example, you might employ a rectangular symbol in which a number of room names might be displayed in each case where the symbol is to be used. If a text object were to always fit perfectly within the given rectangle, it would simplify having to create rectangles of different widths for each room the symbol is to be used in. In the following steps, you will create single-line text, justified to fit within just such a rectangular symbol:

1. If the file is not already open from performing the previous step, go to the book's web page, browse to Chapter 10, get the file Ch10-B.dwg or Ch10-B-metric.dwg, and open it.

2. Zoom in on the small rectangle in the upper-left corner of the drawing canvas.

3. Click the Offset tool in the Modify panel, type **4**" (or **10** cm) to set the offset distance, and press Enter. Select the small rectangle and then click a point inside the rectangle to offset another smaller rectangle inside.

4. Toggle on Object Snap on the status bar. Right-click the same button and select both Endpoint and Center running object snap modes if they are not already selected.

5. Open the menu under the Text tool on the Annotation panel and select Single Line from the menu. The command prompt reads

   ```
   Current text style:  "Standard"
   Text height:  1'-0"  Annotative:  No
   Specify start point of text or [Justify/Style]:
   ```

   Type **J** (for justify) and press Enter.

6. The command prompt now reads as follows:

   ```
   Enter an option [Align/Fit/Center/Middle/
   Right/TL/TC/TR/ML/MC/MR/BL/BC/BR]:
   ```

   Type **F** (for fit) and press Enter. Click points A and B in Figure 10.5.

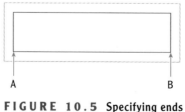

**FIGURE 10.5 Specifying ends
of fit baseline**

7. Type **OFFICE** and press Enter twice. The TEXT command ends and the single line of text appears on the drawing canvas (see Figure 10.6).

FIGURE 10.6 Making single-line
text fit within a predefined space

 8. Select the inner rectangle and press the Delete key.

9. Toggle on Ortho mode on the status bar.

 10. Click the Move tool on the Modify panel, type **L** (for last), and press
Enter twice. Click an arbitrary point on the drawing canvas, move
the cursor upward from that point, type **2"** (or **5** cm), and press
Enter. The text moves up so that the word OFFICE is centered within
the rectangle (see Figure 10.7).

FIGURE 10.7 Centering the text
within the rectangle by moving it upward

11. Save your work as Ch10-C.dwg or Ch10-C-metric.dwg.

Justifying Text

AutoCAD has numerous options that let you justify text to suit almost any
conceivable geometric situation. In the following steps, you will align text so
that it appears centered within a *callout symbol* indicating the drawing and
sheet number:

1. If the file is not already open from performing the previous step, go to
the book's web page, browse to Chapter 10, get the file Ch10-C.dwg or
Ch10-C-metric.dwg, and open it.

2. Click the Pan tool in the Navigation bar and drag to the right to
reveal the circle with a line running through it.

3. Type **text** and press Enter. The command prompt reads

```
Specify start point of text or [Justify/Style]:
```

Type **J** (for justify) and press Enter.

4. The command prompt now reads

```
Enter an option [Align/Fit/Center/Middle/Right/
TL/TC/TR/ML/MC/MR/BL/BC/BR]:
```

Type **mc** (for middle center) and press Enter. Type **cen** (for center) and click the circle to make the center of the circle the middle point of the text. Press Enter to accept zero as the default rotation angle. Type **3** and press Enter twice.

5. Click the Move tool on the Modify panel, type **L** (for last), and press Enter twice. Click an arbitrary point on the drawing canvas, move the cursor upward from that point, type **18**" (or **40** cm), and press Enter. The text is centered within the upper semicircle (see Figure 10.8).

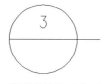

FIGURE 10.8 Moving the number upward to center it within the upper semicircle

6. Save your work as Ch10-D.dwg or Ch10-D-metric.dwg.

Transforming and Creating Text

Text objects can be transformed with the same commands you might use on other types of objects, commands such as MOVE, COPY, ROTATE, SCALE, and MIRROR. In the following steps, you will mirror and copy existing text to create new text objects whose content you will alter later in the "Editing Text" section. In addition, you will create new text in a different style.

1. If the file is not already open, go to the book's web page, browse to Chapter 10, get the file Ch10-D.dwg or Ch10-D-metric.dwg, and open it.

2. Click the Mirror tool on the Modify panel, select the text object (3), and press Enter. Click the Endpoint at point A and the Center point at B, as shown in Figure 10.9, to define the mirror. The command line reads

```
Erase source objects? [Yes/No] <N>:
```

3. Press Enter to accept the default, No, and the MIRROR command is done.

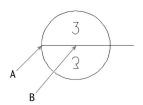

FIGURE 10.9 Mirroring text to create a duplicate text object

MIRRORING TEXT

Set the MIRRTEXT system variable to 1 to mirror text as well as objects with the MIRROR command. Text mirrored with MIRRTEXT set to 1 appears backward or upside down.

4. Click the Copy tool on the Modify panel, type **L** (for last), and press Enter twice. Click an arbitrary point on the drawing canvas, move the cursor to the right from this point, type **4'** (or **140** cm), and press Enter twice. A new text object is created to the right of the text you mirrored in the previous step.

> ◄
> **Transforming and editing existing text is an alternative to creating new text objects from scratch.**

5. Click the Single line text tool on the Annotation panel. The command prompt reads

```
Specify start point of text or [Justify/Style]:
```

6. Type **S** (for style) and press Enter. Type **Title** (the name of one of the styles you created in the "Creating Text Styles" section) and press Enter. Title is now the current style.

7. Click point A in Figure 10.10 as the start point of text. The command prompt now reads

```
Specify height <6">:
```

8. Type **1'6˝** (or **45** cm) to specify the text height and press Enter. Press Enter again to accept a default rotation of zero degrees (horizontal). Type **Drawing Title** and press Enter twice to end the TEXT command.

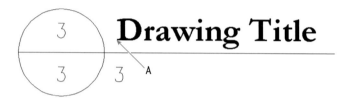
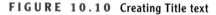

FIGURE 10.10 Creating Title text

9. Save your work as Ch10-E.dwg or Ch10-E-metric.dwg.

Writing and Formatting Paragraphs of Text Using MTEXT

The MTEXT command is a word processing program within AutoCAD that treats all the lines and paragraphs you write as a single object. The powerful MTEXT command gives you word wrap, per-letter style overrides, tabs, inline spell checking, control over line spacing, bulleted and numbered lists, column formatting, and many other features.

MTEXT is ideally suited to writing general notes on drawings and other lengthy blocks of text. In the following steps, you will create and format some unusual general notes. Instead of typing multiple paragraphs, you'll import one of the most famous monologues in the English language and turn it into a series of hypothetical steps.

1. If the file is not already open, go to the book's web page, browse to Chapter 10, get the file Ch10-E.dwg or Ch10-E-metric.dwg, and open it. In addition, get the file Hamlet.txt and double-click the file to open it in Notepad on the PC or TextEdit on the Mac (see Figure 10.11). Select Format ➢ Word Wrap in Notepad to see the text wrap onto multiple lines if necessary.

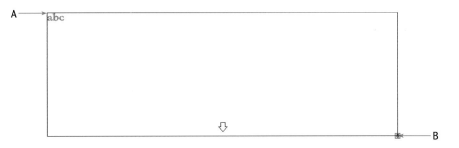

FIGURE 10.11 Hamlet's famous soliloquy

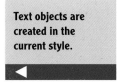

Text objects are
created in the
current style.

2. Press Alt+Tab to switch back to AutoCAD. Pan over to the large rectangle in Ch10E-dwg or Ch10-E-metric.dwg.

3. Type **ST** (for style) and press Enter. Double-click Standard in the Styles list on the left side of the Text Style dialog box. Standard is now the current style. Click the Close button.

Certification
Objective

4. Open the menu under the Text tool on the Annotation panel and select Multiline Text from the menu. Click points A and B, as shown in Figure 10.12.

A —— abc

                                    ⇩

                                                      B

FIGURE 10.12 Specifying the opposite corners of a block of multiline text

5. The Text Editor context tab appears on the ribbon. Expand its Tools panel and click the Import Text button, as shown in Figure 10.13.

FIGURE 10.13 The Text Editor context tab appears when you're creating or editing MTEXT objects.

CONTEXT TAB OR IN-PLACE EDITOR

If you are in a workspace that doesn't support the ribbon (such as AutoCAD Classic), then the Text Editor context tab cannot appear. Instead, you will see the In-Place Editor, which has most of the same functionality.

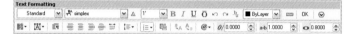

The built-in spell checker identifies misspelled words by underlining them in red. Perhaps this is not surprising for English written 400 years ago, but in your own projects right-click any underlined word that seems incorrect (which wouldn't include company or product names, or technical jargon most likely) for correctly spelled suggestions.

6. Click Hamlet.txt in the Select File dialog box that appears. Click Open and text appears within the large rectangle (see Figure 10.14).

To be, or not to be – that is the question: whether 'tis nobler in the mind to suffer the slings and arrows of outrageous fortune or to take arms against a sea of troubles, and by opposing end them. To die to sleep no more; and by a sleep to say we end the heartache, and the thousand natural shocks that flesh is heir to. 'Tis a consummation devoutly to be wish'd. To die to sleep. To sleep perchance to dream: ay, there's the rub! For in that sleep of death what dreams may come when we have shuffled off this mortal coil, must give us pause. There's the respect that makes calamity of so long life. For who would bear the whips and scorns of time, th' oppressor's wrong, the proud man's contumely, the pangs of despis'd love, the law's delay, the insolence of office, and the spurns that patient merit of th' unworthy takes, when he himself might his quietus make with a bare bodkin? Who would these fardels bear, to grunt and sweat under a weary life, but that the dread of something after death the undiscover'd country, from whose bourn no traveller returns puzzles the will, and makes us rather bear those ills we have than fly to others that we know not of? Thus conscience does make cowards of us all, and thus the native hue of resolution is sicklied o'er with the pale cast of thought, and enterprises of great pith and moment with this regard their currents turn awry and lose the name of action. Soft you now! The fair Ophelia! Nymph, in thy orisons be all my sins rememb'red.

FIGURE 10.14 Importing text with the MTEXT command

Click within a block of text you are creating or editing to place the cursor at that location. Double-click to select an entire word. Triple-click to select an entire paragraph.

7. Drag the cursor from the end to the beginning of the block of text and highlight all the text. Open the Bullets And Numbering menu and choose Numbered from the list. The number 1 appears at the start of the text. Click strategic points in the text and press Enter to separate the paragraph into the numbered notes shown in Figure 10.15. Don't worry if the text extends below the lower edge of the rectangle (it should).

8. Click within the block of text to deselect all text. Drag out a selection that includes the phrase "To be or not to be – that is the question." Open the Text Editor Color Gallery drop-down in the Formatting panel and select Red. Click the Make Uppercase button in the same panel (see Figure 10.16).

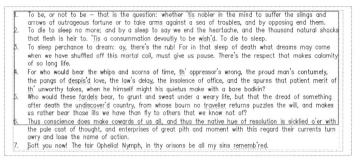

FIGURE 10.15 Turning a block of text into a series of numbered notes

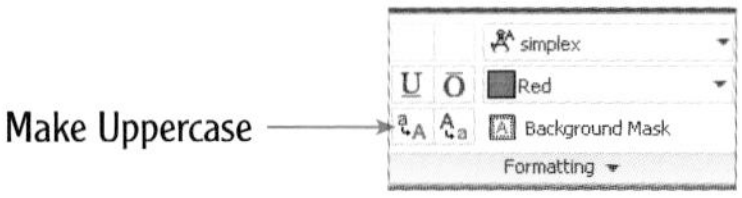

Make Uppercase

FIGURE 10.16 Formatting selected text

9. Click anywhere outside the block of text on the drawing canvas to end the MTEXT command.

10. Save your work as Ch10-F.dwg or Ch10-F-metric.dwg.

You can format selected letters or words independently with the MTEXT command.

Editing Text

Editing text can mean many different things, from changing content (the words) and text object properties, to creating multiple columns of text. You would be very frustrated indeed if you couldn't correct typographical errors because everyone seems to make them. Fortunately, editing text is as simple as double-clicking, highlighting the text in question, and retyping. It is also easy to create multiple columns in AutoCAD by dragging a grip. Creating columns of text can help you fit the required words into the space available on your drawings.

Editing Content and Properties

Editing text content is as simple as double-clicking existing text and typing something new. Editing text properties requires you to use the Quick Properties palette or the Properties panel. In the following steps, you will edit both content and properties:

1. If the file is not already open, go to the book's web page, browse to Chapter 10, get the file Ch10-F.dwg or Ch10-F-metric.dwg, and open it.

2. Double-click the text in the lower semicircle of the drawing title symbol to invoke the DDEDIT command. The number 3 is highlighted. Type **A-4**, click outside the editing window on the drawing canvas, and press Esc to stop editing. The bubble now references the hypothetical drawing 3 on sheet A-4 (see Figure 10.17).

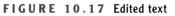

FIGURE 10.17 Edited text

3. Toggle on Quick Properties on the status bar and select the 3 under the text Drawing Title. In the Quick Properties window that appears, change Justify to Middle Left and type **Scale: 1/8" = 1'-0"** (or **Scale: 1:20**) in the Contents text box (Figure 10.18).

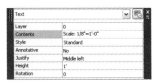

FIGURE 10.18 Editing text content and justification using Quick Properties

> Use the Properties palette to access more property values than Quick Properties shows.

4. Press Enter to update the selected object. Press Esc to deselect. Toggle off Quick Properties. Figure 10.19 shows the result.

5. Save your work as Ch10-G.dwg or Ch10-G-metric.dwg.

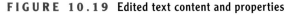

FIGURE 10.19 Edited text content and properties

Working with Columns

You can create multiple columns easily with any multiline text object. This feature is perfect if the text you have written doesn't fit into the space between the drawing and its title block on a typical drawing. Creating multiple columns gives you more layout options, allowing you to find the best fit for paragraphs of text within the space available. In the following steps, you will move object grips to create and size two columns:

1. If the file is not already open, go to the book's web page, browse to Chapter 10, get the file Ch10-G.dwg or Ch10-G-metric.dwg, and open it.

2. Click once on the numbered Hamlet text to select it and reveal its grips. Click the Column Height (bottom) grip and move it upward, automatically creating two columns as shown in Figure 10.20.

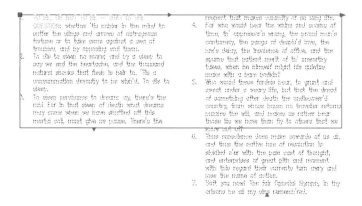

FIGURE 10.20 Moving the bottom grip up to create two columns

3. Click the Column Width (middle) grip and move it to the left to reduce the size of both columns simultaneously. Move the right grip until it reaches the right edge of the rectangle and then click to set its new position (see Figure 10.21).

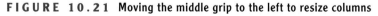

FIGURE 10.21 Moving the middle grip to the left to resize columns

4. The first column is too short compared to the right column. Move the Column Height (bottom) grip down until the text in both columns is roughly equalized. Press Esc to deselect the text. Select the rectangle and press the Delete key. Figure 10.22 shows the result.

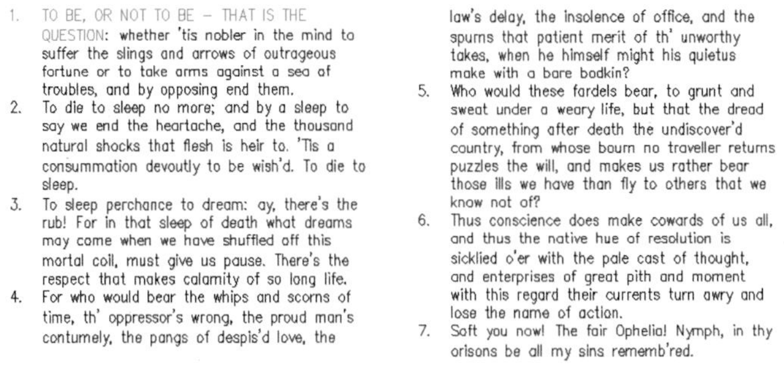
1. TO BE, OR NOT TO BE – THAT IS THE QUESTION: whether 'tis nobler in the mind to suffer the slings and arrows of outrageous fortune or to take arms against a sea of troubles, and by opposing end them.
2. To die to sleep no more; and by a sleep to say we end the heartache, and the thousand natural shocks that flesh is heir to. 'Tis a consummation devoutly to be wish'd. To die to sleep.
3. To sleep perchance to dream: ay, there's the rub! For in that sleep of death what dreams may come when we have shuffled off this mortal coil, must give us pause. There's the respect that makes calamity of so long life.
4. For who would bear the whips and scorns of time, th' oppressor's wrong, the proud man's contumely, the pangs of despis'd love, the law's delay, the insolence of office, and the spurns that patient merit of th' unworthy takes, when he himself might his quietus make with a bare bodkin?
5. Who would these fardels bear, to grunt and sweat under a weary life, but that the dread of something after death the undiscover'd country, from whose bourn no traveller returns puzzles the will, and makes us rather bear those ills we have than fly to others that we know not of?
6. Thus conscience does make cowards of us all, and thus the native hue of resolution is sicklied o'er with the pale cast of thought, and enterprises of great pith and moment with this regard their currents turn awry and lose the name of action.
7. Soft you now! The fair Ophelia! Nymph, in thy orisons be all my sins rememb'red.

FIGURE 10.22 **The result after resizing the column length and deleting the rectangle**

5. Save your work as `Ch10-H.dwg` or `Ch10-H-metric.dwg`.

The Essentials and Beyond

In this chapter you learned how to work with text. You created text styles, wrote and justified single lines of text, and imported multiple paragraphs of text. In addition, you edited and styled multiline text and learned to control its appearance. You should now be able to express yourself in written form within AutoCAD, and thus convey your design intent both graphically and literally.

Additional Exercise

Explore the `FIND` command on your own. Use it not only to find but also to replace specific words within any of the text in the drawing, its blocks, attributes, dimensions, tables, and/or Xrefs. You can confine a find and replace operation specifically using search options such as Match Case, Search Xrefs, search within Dimension Or Leader Text, and many others. There is an arrow in the lower-left corner of the Find And Replace dialog box that you click to expand the dialog box and thus access all the search options and searchable text types.

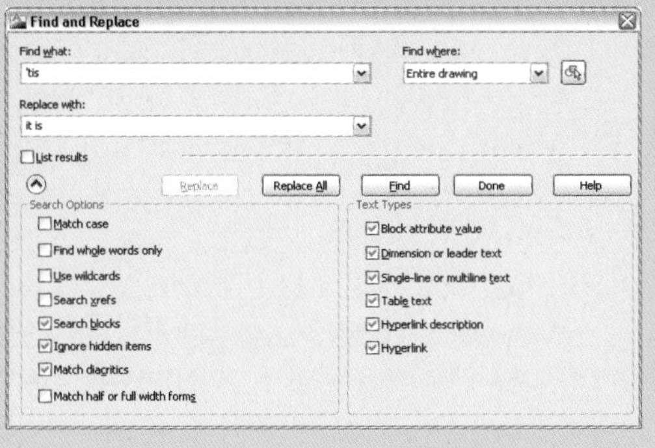
Find and Replace
Find what:
'tis
Find where:
Entire drawing
Replace with:
it is
List results
Replace
Replace All
Find
Done
Help
Search Options
Match case
Find whole words only
Use wildcards
Search xrefs
Search blocks
Ignore hidden items
Match diacritics
Match half or full width forms
Text Types
Block attribute value
Dimension or leader text
Single-line or multiline text
Table text
Hyperlink description
Hyperlink

CHAPTER 11

Dimensioning

Dimensioning is the art of annotating drawings with precise numerical measurements. The process is generally straightforward in AutoCAD because everything is typically drawn in real-world scale. Dimensions will automatically display the correct measurements as long as the geometric objects they refer to are drawn to actual size. In this chapter, you'll learn the mechanics of dimensioning in model space. Dimensioning in paper space and in viewports is covered in Chapter 13, "Working with Layouts."

▶ **Styling dimensions**

▶ **Adding dimensions**

▶ **Editing dimensions**

Styling Dimensions

The appearance of dimensions (the size of text and arrows, the length of extension lines, and so on) is controlled by dimension styles. Every drawing comes with a Standard dimension style, which of course is the current style as there is only one by default. When you have more than one dimension style, you must choose which one is current. New dimension objects are assigned the current dimension style, in much the same way that objects and layers or text and text styles work.

You can customize dimension styles and even create substyles to control the way different types of dimensions appear according to your personal preferences or to adhere to a corporate or industry standard established for dimensions. For example, if you want to use architectural tick marks rather than arrowheads for linear and aligned dimensions but want to use arrowheads for radius, diameter, and angular dimensions, these preferences can be encoded in a dimension style and a series of substyles.

In the following steps, you will modify the Standard dimension style and create a few substyles for specific types of dimensions in preparation for adding dimension objects in the next section.

Modifying dimension styles in a particular drawing in no way affects the dimensions or styles in other drawings. If you want to use the same dimension styles in future drawings, customize the dimension styles in your drawing template.

▶

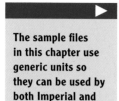
1. Go to the book's web page at **www.sybex.com/go/ autocad2012essentials**, browse to Chapter 11, get the file Ch11-A.dwg, and open it (see Figure 11.1).

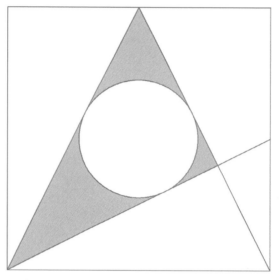

FIGURE 11.1 The geometric drawing you will dimension

Certification Objective

2. Select the Home tab on the ribbon if it is not already selected. Expand the Annotation panel and click the Dimension Style tool (see Figure 11.2).

FIGURE 11.2 Accessing the Dimension Style Manager on the ribbon

3. As you can see in the Dimension Style Manager, every drawing has Standard and Annotative dimension styles by default (see Figure 11.3). The Standard style is selected by default. Click the Modify button to alter the Standard style.

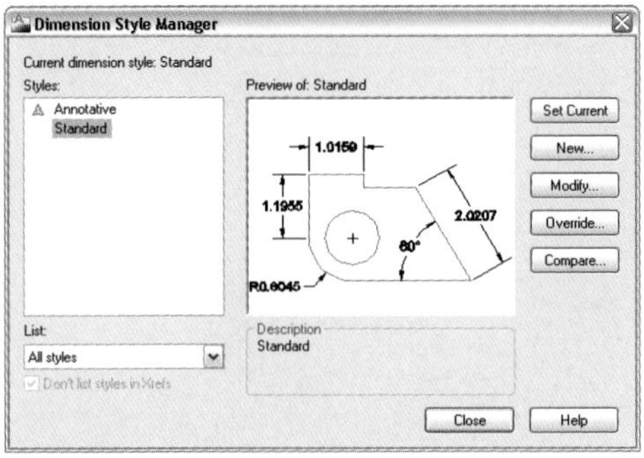

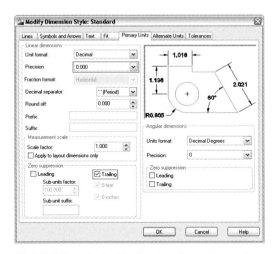

FIGURE 11.3 Dimension Style Manager

4. Select the Primary Units tab in the Modify Dimension Style: Standard dialog box. Set Precision to 0.000 and select Trailing in the Zero Suppression section (see Figure 11.4). If you are in a country that uses a comma instead of a period as a decimal separator, select "," (Comma) in the Decimal Separator drop-down menu.

◄

You will learn about Annotative styles in Chapter 13.

FIGURE 11.4 Configuring dimension style primary units

5. Select the Symbols And Arrows tab. In the Arrowheads section, choose Open 30 from the First drop-down (see Figure 11.5). The Second drop-down automatically matches the first by default as it now says Open 30.

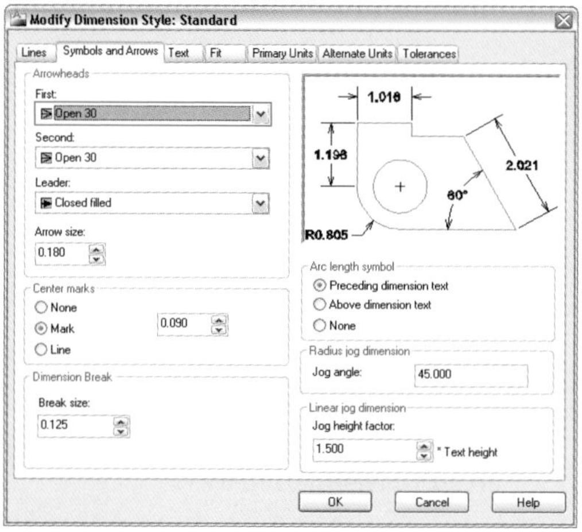

FIGURE 11.5 Changing arrowheads in the Standard dimension style

6. Select the Lines tab. Double-click the Offset From Origin value to select it, type **0.125**, and press Tab (see Figure 11.6). Observe in the preview image how the distance between the object and its extension lines increases. Click OK and Close to save the modifications you've made to the Standard style.

UNDERSTANDING DIMENSION STYLES

Changing a dimension style automatically updates all existing dimension objects in the current drawing that have that style assigned.

7. Type **D** (for dimension style) and press Enter. The Dimension Style Manager reappears. Click the New button to open the Create New Dimension Style dialog box. Verify that Start With is set to Standard. Choose Angular Dimensions from the Use For drop-down (see Figure 11.7). Click Continue.

8. The New Dimension Style: Standard: Angular dialog box appears. Select the Symbols And Arrows tab. Change the First arrowhead drop-down to Closed Filled. The Second arrowhead automatically changes to Closed Filled as well (see Figure 11.8). The preview image reveals how the angular dimension will appear. Click OK.

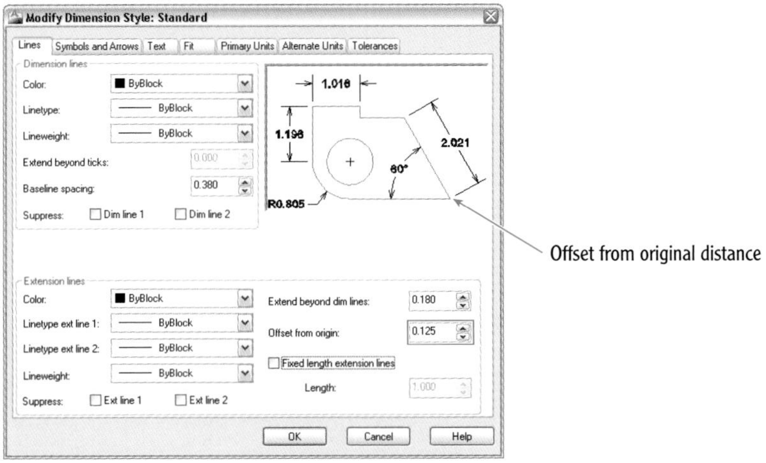

FIGURE 11.6 Increasing the offset from origin distance

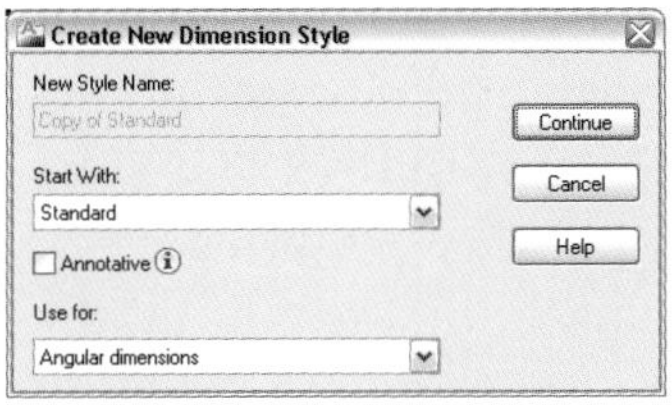

FIGURE 11.7 Creating a dimension substyle for angular dimensions

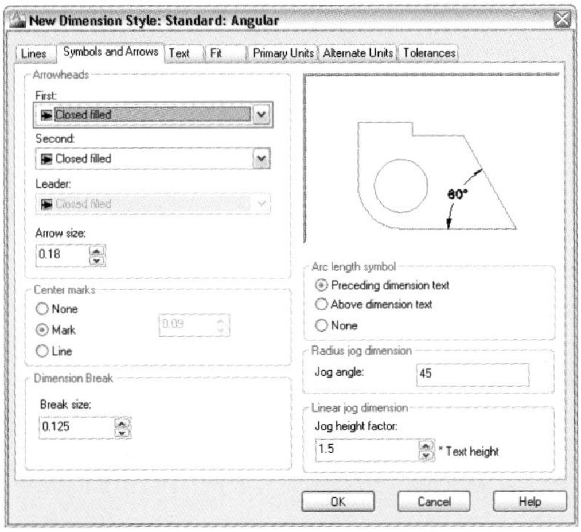

FIGURE 11.8 Customizing the arrowheads in the Angular substyle

9. Click the New button again in the Dimension Style Manager. Select Radius Dimensions in the Use For drop-down and click Continue. Select Closed Filled in the Second arrowhead on the Symbols And Arrows tab. The preview image again reveals what a radial dimension will look like governed by this substyle; click OK.

▶ Linear dimensions can either be horizontal or vertical. Aligned dimensions measure linear distances at angles other than horizontal or vertical.

10. Select Standard in the styles list in the left pane of the Dimension Style Manager. The preview image now shows the cumulative effect of the style and its substyles: open arrowheads for linear and aligned dimensions and closed filled arrowheads for angular and radial dimensions. Figure 11.9 lists these types. Click Close.

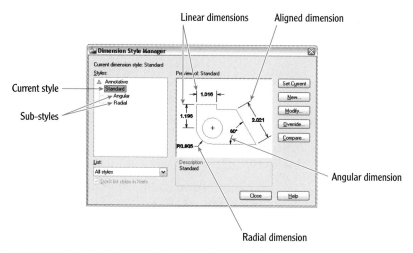

FIGURE 11.9 The preview image shows how different types of dimensions will appear when they are added to the drawing.

11. Save your work as Ch11-B.dwg. Dimension styles are saved within the drawing.

Adding Dimensions

In technical drawings, dimensions are typically measurements for which the designer may be legally responsible. So while it is essential to know how to add specific dimensions to a drawing, it is also useful for your own information to use *inquiry commands* that measure linear objects (MEASUREGEOM or DIST) or find areas (AREA) without making specific annotations in the drawing (thus avoiding potential liability). We will discuss how to do this in the following section. In addition, we will add a variety of dimension objects that show specific measurements on the drawing. We will then end the section with a discussion on how to add a *multileader*, which is text pointing to a specific feature with an arrow, to a drawing.

Using Inquiry Commands

Use inquiry commands when you want to find out (but not document) how long, what angle, what name, or what area a specific feature has without annotating the drawing with this information. In the following steps, you'll explore inquiry commands to get these specific types of information from a drawing:

1. If the file is not already open, go to the book's web page, browse to Chapter 11, get the file Ch11-B.dwg, and open it.

2. Toggle on Object Snap mode on the status bar if it is not already on. Right-click the Object Snap button and turn on Endpoint and Intersection running object snap modes.

3. Click the Distance tool in the Utilities panel of the Home tab on the ribbon. Click points A and B, as shown in Figure 11.10. The command prompt reads

Certification Objective

```
Distance = 5.000,  Angle in XY Plane = 26.565,
Angle from XY Plane = 0.000 Delta X = 4.472,
Delta Y = 2.236,   Delta Z = 0.000
```

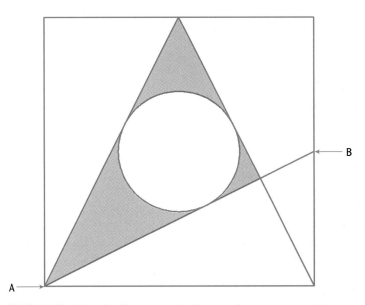

FIGURE 11.10 Measuring the distance between two points

The number of decimal places shown in the inquiry commands is controlled by the Precision drop-downs in the Drawing Units dialog box (accessed with the UNITS command).

4. Open the Measure menu in the Utilities panel, select the Radius tool, and select the circle. The command prompt reads

```
Radius = 1.000
Diameter = 2.000
```

5. Type **A** (for Angle) and press Enter. Select lines A and B, as shown in Figure 11.11. The command prompt now gives the value:

```
Angle = 36.87°
```

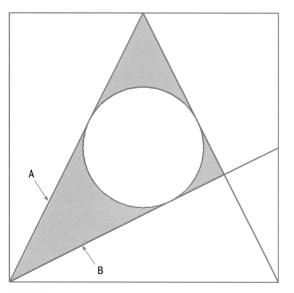

FIGURE 11.11 Measuring the angle between two lines

6. Type **AR** (for area) and press Enter. The command prompt reads

```
Specify first corner point or
[Object/Add area/Subtract area/eXit]
<Object>:
```

7. Press Enter to accept the default Object option and select the circle. The command prompt gives the values:

```
Area = 3.142, Circumference = 6.283
```

8. The area within the circle turns green to give you a visual indication of which area and circumference are measured. Figure 11.12 shows the circle's area of π and circumference of 2π. Press Esc and the MEASUREGEOM command ends.

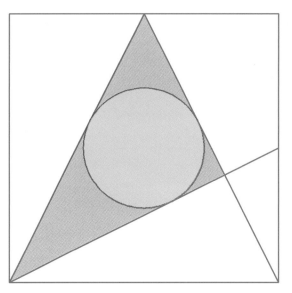

FIGURE 11.12 Measured area shown in green

Adding Dimension Objects

In the following steps you'll add dimension objects one at a time using a variety of specialized tools to produce dimensions that are linear, aligned, angular, radial, and so on.

1. If the file is not already open from performing the previous step, go to the book's web page, browse to Chapter 11, get the file Ch11-B.dwg, and open it.

2. Toggle on Object Snap mode on the status bar if it is not already on. Right-click this button and turn on Endpoint and Intersection running object snap modes if necessary.

3. Click the Linear dimension tool on the Annotation panel. Click points A and B to specify the first and second extension line origin points, as shown in Figure 11.13. Click point C to specify the dimension line location.

Dimension objects are typically associated with the geometry to which they refer so that when you modify the geometry, the dimensions automatically update with new measurements.

Certification
Objective

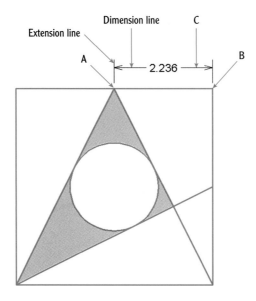

FIGURE 11.13 Creating a linear
dimension by clicking three points

4. Press the spacebar to repeat the last command. The command
   prompt reads

   ```
   Specify first extension line origin or <select object>:
   ```

   Press Enter to accept the default option (Select Object). Click the
   top red line and then click point A, as shown in Figure 11.14.

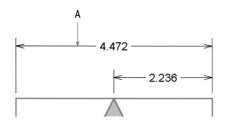

FIGURE 11.14 Creating a linear dimension by
selecting an object and its dimension line location

**Certification
Objective**

5. Type **DIMCENTER** (for dimension center mark) and press Enter. Select the
   circle and a small crosshair symbol appears at the center of the circle.

6. Type **DIMLIN** (the alias for the DIMLINEAR command) and press Enter. Click points A, B, and C, as shown in Figure 11.15.

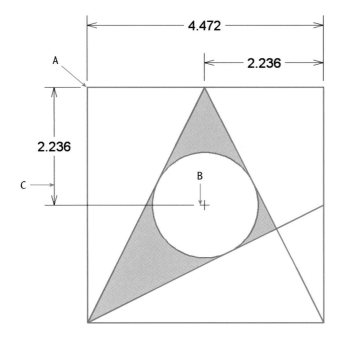

FIGURE 11.15 Creating another linear dimension

7. Type **DIMCONTINUE** (for dimension continue) and press Enter. Click point A as shown in Figure 11.10 to add another linear dimension below the previous one. Press Esc to end the command.

8. Open the dimension menu in the Annotation panel and select the Aligned tool. Click points A, B, and C, as shown in Figure 11.16.

9. Add the four additional aligned dimensions shown in Figure 11.17 measuring 1, 2, 3, and 4 units.

10. Open the dimension menu in the Annotation panel and select the Angular tool. Select lines 1 and 2, as shown in Figure 11.19, and then click point A. Press the spacebar to repeat the DIMANGULAR command, select lines 2 and 3, and then click point B.

Using DIMCONTINUE to add adjacent linear dimensions is more efficient than using DIMLINEAR.

◄

Certification Objective

Certification Objective

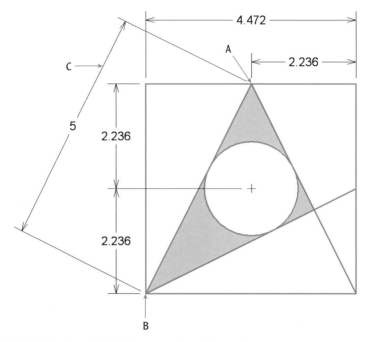

FIGURE 11.16 Adding an aligned dimension

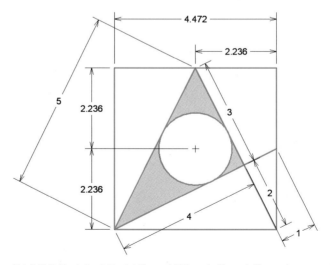

FIGURE 11.17 Adding additional aligned dimensions

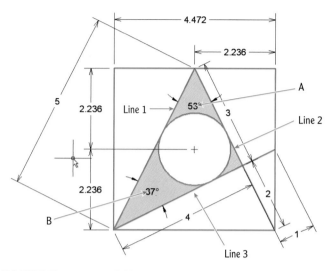

FIGURE 11.18 Adding angular dimensions

Certification
Objective

11. Open the dimension menu in the Annotation panel and select the Radius tool. Select the circle and then click a point inside the circle to locate the radius value (see Figure 11.19).

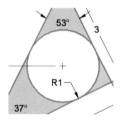

FIGURE 11.19 Adding a radius dimension

12. Save your work as Ch11-C.dwg.

Adding and Styling Multileaders

A multileader is text with a line tipped by an arrowhead that leads the eye to specific geometric features. Multileader styles control the appearance of leader objects in much the same way that dimension styles control the appearance of dimensions. In the following steps, you will add a leader object and then configure the multileader style.

1. If the file is not already open, browse to Chapter 11, get the file Ch11-C.dwg, and open it.

2. Select the Leader tool in the Annotation panel. Click points A and B and type **Area of circle = 3.142** (as shown in Figure 11.20) and then press Ctrl+Enter.

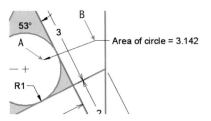

FIGURE 11.20 Adding a leader object

3. Expand the Annotation panel and select the Multileader Style button. Click the Modify button in the Multileader Style Manager dialog box that appears.

4. Choose Dot from the Symbol drop-down in the Arrowhead section on the Leader Format tab of the Modify Multileader Style: Standard dialog box (see Figure 11.21). Click OK and Close, and the leader object automatically has a dot on its end.

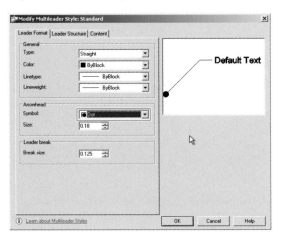

FIGURE 11.21 Editing a multileader style

5. Save your work as Ch11-D.dwg.

Editing Dimensions

Dimensions have grips that allow you to reposition extension lines, the dimension line, and dimension text independently of one another. In the following steps, you will edit the length and location of extension and dimension lines directly with grips, adjust a dimension style to affect the appearance of dimension objects, and use a few specialized dimension-editing commands:

1. If the file is not already open, browse to Chapter 11, get the file Ch11-D.dwg, and open it.

2. Toggle on Object Snap mode on the status bar if it is not already on. Right-click the Object Snap button and turn on Endpoint and Intersection running object snap modes.

3. Click the horizontal linear dimension with a value of 2.236 to select it. Click the lower-left grip to adjust the length of this extension line. Snap the grip to point A, as shown in Figure 11.22. Press Esc to deselect.

Certification Objective

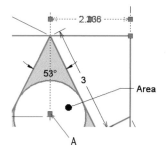

FIGURE 11.22 Grip-editing a dimension object

4. Type **D** (alias for the DIMSTYLE command) and press Enter. Select the Angular substyle in the Dimension Style Manager that appears and click the Modify button.

5. Select the Fit tab in the Modify Dimension Style: Standard: Angular dialog box. Select the Text radio button in the Fit Options section (see Figure 11.23). Click OK and Close to close all open dialog boxes. The angular values appear outside the lines being measured.

6. Type **DIMEDIT** (for dimension edit) and press Enter. The command prompt reads

Certification Objective

```
Enter type of dimension editing
[Home/New/Rotate/Oblique] <Home>:
```

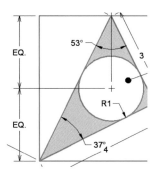

FIGURE 11.23 Changing a fit option in the dimension style

7. Type **N** (for new) and press Enter. A text-editing window appears below the last text you entered. Press the right arrow key to move the cursor to the right of the text field and then press the Backspace key to delete the zero.

8. Type **EQ.** (abbreviation for equal) and then press Ctrl+Enter to end text entry mode. Select both vertical linear dimensions having values of 2.236 and press Enter. Figure 11.24 shows the result.

FIGURE 11.24 Editing dimension text content with DIMEDIT

Certification
Objective

9. Type **DIMTEDIT** (for dimension text edit) and press Enter. Select the aligned dimension with a value of 2 and press Enter. The command prompt reads

```
Specify new location for dimension text or
[Left/Right/Center/Home/Angle]:
```

10. Type **L** (for left) and press Enter. The dimension text is now left-justified in relation to the dimension line, so the 2 is more easily read within the whitespace left within the red lines (see Figure 11.25).

FIGURE 11.25 Changing dimension text justification with DIMTEDIT

11. Select the ribbon's Annotate tab and click the Break tool on the Dimensions panel. The command prompt reads

```
Select dimension to add/remove break or [Multiple]:
```

12. Type **M** (for multiple) and press Enter. Select the dimensions with values of 2.236, 3, and 5 and press Enter. The command prompt reads

```
Select object to break dimensions or [Auto/Remove] <Auto>:
```

13. Press Enter to accept the default Auto option and the DIMBREAK command ends. Breaks are made in the selected dimensions where they cross other objects (see Figure 11.26).

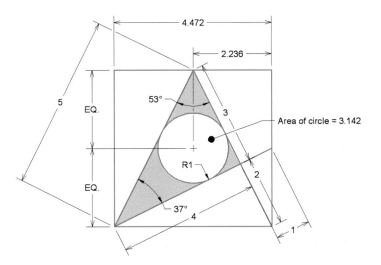

FIGURE 11.26 Using DIMBREAK to clean up overlapping dimension objects

14. Your drawing should now resemble Ch11-E.dwg, which is available at this book's web page.

THE ESSENTIALS AND BEYOND

In this chapter you took your first steps in the art of dimensioning. You learned how to adjust dimension styles and create new substyles; how to add linear, aligned, angular, and radial dimension objects; and how to edit dimensions using a variety of techniques.

ADDITIONAL EXERCISE

Explore the DIMBASELINE command on your own. Baseline dimensions all reference the same base point to eliminate cumulative errors that can crop up due to rounding errors between consecutive adjacent dimensions. Try creating two sets of baseline dimensions that reference the left and bottom edges of the diagram shown here:

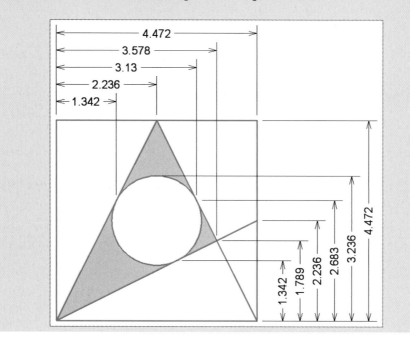

CHAPTER 12

Keeping In Control with Constraints

Constraints are specific restrictions applied to objects that allow for design exploration while maintaining object shape and/or size within predefined limits. In this chapter, you will create three types of constraints: geometric, dimensional, and user-created. Once the design has been sufficiently constrained, you will make a host of geometric and dimensional changes by simply changing a single parameter.

▶ **Working with geometric constraints**

▶ **Applying dimensional constraints and creating user parameters**

▶ **Constraining objects simultaneously with geometry and dimensions**

▶ **Making parametric changes to constrained objects**

Working with Geometric Constraints

▶

AutoCAD LT cannot create constraints. However, LT users can view and edit constraints that were created in AutoCAD 2012. The sample files in this chapter use generic units so they can be used by both Imperial and metric users.

Geometric constraints allow you to force specific 2D objects to be coincident, collinear, concentric, parallel, perpendicular, horizontal, vertical, tangent, smooth, and symmetric; to have equal lengths; or to be fixed in world space. In the following steps, you will assign sufficient geometric constraints to ensure that a rectangle will always remain square even when it is stretched:

1. Go to the book's web page at **www.sybex.com/go/ autocad2012essentials**, browse to Chapter 12, get the file Ch12-A.dwg, and open it.

2. Select the Rectangle tool on the Draw panel. Click two points on the drawing canvas to create an arbitrarily sized rectangle.

3. Toggle Infer Constraints mode on in the status bar.

4. Press the spacebar to repeat the RECTANG (for Rectangle) command, and then click two more points to draw another arbitrarily

sized rectangle adjacent and to the right of the first one (see
Figure 12.1). AutoCAD automatically infers perpendicular and parallel constraints from the geometry of the second rectangle.

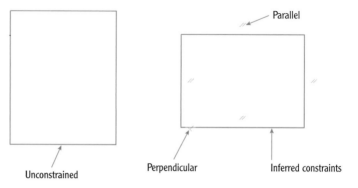

FIGURE 12.1 Drawing two rectangles, one unconstrained

5. Toggle off Infer Constraints mode by pressing Ctrl+Shift+I.

6. Select both rectangles with a crossing selection window. Hover the
   cursor over the upper-right grip of the left rectangle, select Stretch
   Vertex from the grip menu that appears, and stretch it up and to the
   right so the rectangle deforms. Hover the cursor over the upper-right
   grip of the right rectangle, select Stretch Vertex from the grip menu,
   and stretch it up and to the right. The rectangle remains a rectangle
   because of the constraints (see Figure 12.2). Press Esc to deselect.

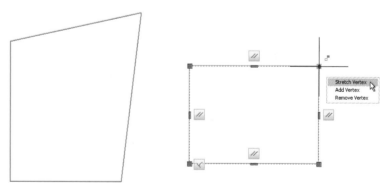

FIGURE 12.2 Stretching constrained geometry limits the types of
transformation that can occur.

7. Select the Parametric tab on the ribbon and select the Auto Constrain tool in the Geometric panel. Select the unconstrained rectangle on the left and press Enter. Two constraints are applied: perpendicular and horizontal (see Figure 12.3).

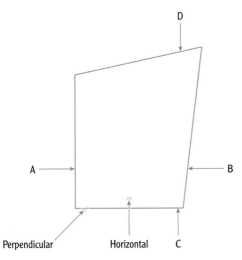

FIGURE 12.3 Applying constraints with the Auto Constrain tool

Objects are never repositioned when inferring constraints or when using the Auto Constrain tool. Objects can be repositioned when applying constraints manually.

8. Select the Parallel constraint tool in the Geometric panel. Click lines A and B, as shown in Figure 12.3. Line B is automatically repositioned to conform to the parallel constraint applied to line A.

9. Press the spacebar to repeat the GCPARALLEL (for geometric constraint parallel) command. Click lines C and D, as shown in Figure 12.3.

10. The left rectangle not only has parallel and perpendicular constraints like the right rectangle, but it also has a horizontal constraint that was applied by the Auto Constrain tool. Select the right rectangle and press the Delete key.

The order in which you select objects can be significant when you apply constraints. The second object will be repositioned in some cases, depending on the constraint that is applied and the shape and position of the objects.

11. Select the Equal constraint tool in the Geometric panel. Click lines A and C, as shown in Figure 12.3. The rectangle becomes a square (see Figure 12.4).

12. Multiple constraints are grouped together in what is called a *constraint bar*. Position the cursor over the constraint bar and you'll see a tiny close box. Click it to hide the constraint bar.

Hiding constraints does not remove them; it merely reduces visual clutter.

Show All **13.** Click the Show All button in the Geometric panel. The hidden constraint bar reappears.

14. Right-click the horizontal constraint and choose Delete from the context menu. The rectangle is no longer constrained horizontally (so you could rotate it if desired).

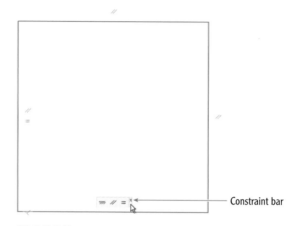

Constraint bar

FIGURE 12.4 Applying Equal constraints to adjacent sides turns the rectangle into a square.

Hide All   15. Click the Hide All button in the Geometric panel. The constraints are hidden but still active.

16. Save your work as Ch12-B.dwg.

Applying Dimensional Constraints and Creating User Parameters

Dimensional constraints allow you to control object sizes with specific numerical values, and to set up dynamic dimensional relationships with mathematical equations and formulas. User constraints are not tied to specific geometry but hold values calculated from dimensional constraints. In the following steps, you will create dimensional and user constraints:

1. If the file is not already open from performing the previous step, go to the book's web page, browse to Chapter 12, get the file Ch12-B.dwg, and open it.

2. Select the ribbon's Home tab, open the Layer drop-down in the Layers panel, and select Layer 2 to make it the current layer.

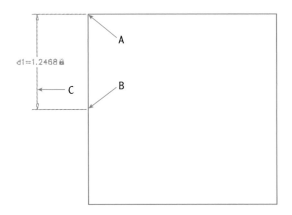

3. Select the Parametric tab on the ribbon. Select the Linear constraint tool in the Dimensional panel and click *constraint points* A and B, as shown in Figure 12.5. Constraint points highlight in red on screen when you are choosing them. Click point C to locate the dimension line. Press Enter to accept the default dimension text. This dimensional constraint is automatically given the variable name d1.

FIGURE 12.5 Creating a vertical linear dimensional constraint

Constraint points behave similarly to object snaps but are limited to endpoints, midpoints, center points, and insertion points.

4. Type **C** (for circle) and press Enter. Draw an arbitrarily sized circle anywhere within the square.

5. Click the Linear constraint tool in the Dimensional panel and click the first constraint point in the upper-left corner of the rectangle. Click the circle to accept its center as the second constraint point. Move the cursor upward (see Figure 12.6) and click to place the horizontal dimension line above the rectangle.

6. Type **d2=d1** and press Enter. The circle moves over so that it is horizontally centered within the rectangle and the constraint reads fx: d2=d1. The fx means the dimensional constraint is calculated by a function.

7. Press the spacebar to repeat the DCLINEAR (for dimensional constraint linear) command. Click the first constraint point in the upper-right corner of the rectangle. Click the circle to accept its center as the second constraint point. Move the cursor to the right and click to place the vertical dimension line to the right of the rectangle. Type **d3=d1** and press Enter. The circle is now centered within the square.

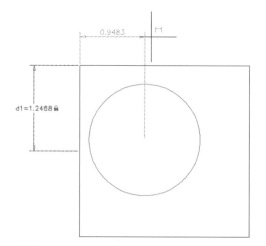

FIGURE 12.6 Creating a horizontal linear dimensional constraint

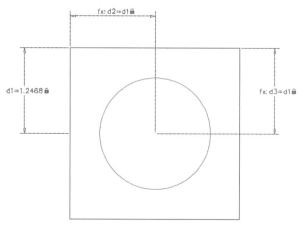

FIGURE 12.7 Adding another linear constraint that is calculated by a function

You can convert an existing dimension into a dimensional constraint with the DIMCONSTRAINT command.

fx
Parameters
Manager

8. Click the Parameters Manager button in the Manage panel to open the Parameters Manager palette. All the dimensional constraints that you have created are listed here (d1, d2, and d3). Click the Fx button to create a new user parameter.

9. Type **P** (for perimeter) as the user parameter name and press Enter. Double-click the Expression value and type **d1*8** (d1 times 8) and press Enter (see Figure 12.8). The perimeter of the square is equal to eight times the length of half of one of its sides. Close the Parameters Manager.

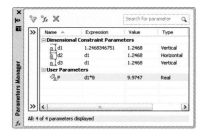

FIGURE 12.8 Adding a user parameter in the Parameters Manager

10. Select the Hide All button in the Dimensional panel.

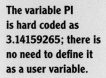
|⊡| Hide All

11. Select the Diameter constraint tool in the Dimensional panel, select the circle, click a point inside the circle to locate the dimension line, type **dia=P/PI**, and press Enter. The circumference of the circle is now equal to the perimeter of the square, traditionally called *squaring the circle* (see Figure 12.9).

◀

You can give constraints any name you like. We identified the diameter constraint with the letters dia to represent the green circle's diameter. If you wanted to later constrain the diameter of another circle you might call it dia2, for example.

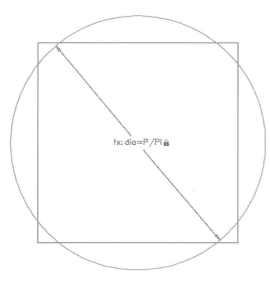

fx: dia=P/PI

FIGURE 12.9 Squaring the circle with constraints defined by formulas

◀

The variable PI is hard coded as 3.14159265; there is no need to define it as a user variable.

12. Save your work as Ch12-C.dwg.

Constraining Objects Simultaneously with Geometry and Dimensions

You can use geometric and dimensional constraints together to force objects to conform to your design intent. In the following steps you will draw two more circles and constrain their positions and sizes using a combination of geometric and dimensional constraints.

1. If the file is not already open, go to the book's web page, browse to Chapter 12, get the file Ch12-C.dwg, and open it.

2. Select the ribbon's Home tab and open the Layer drop-down in the Layers panel and select Layer 3 to make it the current layer.

3. Type **C** (for circle) and press Enter. Draw an arbitrarily sized circle anywhere within the square.

4. Select the ribbon's Parametric tab and then click the Concentric constraint tool in the Geometric panel. Select the green circle and then the blue circle. The blue circle immediately moves to conform to the geometric constraint so that it is concentric within the larger circle.

5. Select the Radius constraint tool in the Dimensional panel, select the blue circle, and click a point inside the circle to locate the dimension line. Type **rad=d1** and press Enter. The blue circle changes size so it fits perfectly within the square (see Figure 12.10).

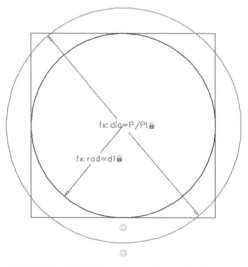

FIGURE 12.10 Constraining the blue circle geometrically and dimensionally

6. Select the Hide All button in the Dimensional panel. ⌐ᵍ⌐ Hide All

7. Select the ribbon's Home tab and open the Layer drop-down in the Layers panel and select Layer 4 to make it the current layer.

8. Type **C** (for circle) and press Enter. Draw an arbitrarily sized circle anywhere above the square.

9. Select the ribbon's Parametric tab and click the Tangent constraint tool in the Geometric panel. Select the top line of the square as the first object and the magenta circle as the second object. The circle moves down to conform to the tangent constraint (see Figure 12.11).

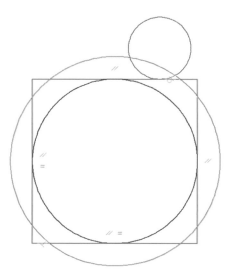

FIGURE 12.11 Applying a tangent geometric constraint

10. Press the spacebar to repeat the GCTANGENT (for geometric constraint tangent) command. Select the blue circle first and then select the magenta circle. The magenta circle moves on top of the blue circle to conform to the new tangent constraint.

11. Click the Linear constraint tool in the Dimensional panel. Click the magenta circle, the blue circle, and then a point off to the right to place the dimension line. Type **d4=dia/2** and press Enter (see Figure 12.12). The center of the magenta circle is anchored effectively at the top quadrant (or top cardinal point if you will) of the green circle.

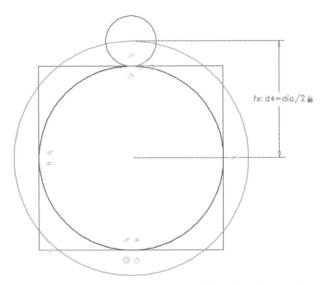

FIGURE 12.12 Adding the last dimensional constraint

 Hide All

Hide All

12. Click the Hide All button in the Dimensional panel and click the Hide All button in the Geometric panel. All constraints are hidden but still active.

13. Save your work as Ch12-D.dwg.

Making Parametric Changes to Constrained Objects

Once you have intelligently applied geometric and/or dimensional constraints, it is easy to make parametric changes that affect the shape and/or size of multiple interconnected objects. In the following steps, you will change a single parameter (d1) and see how it affects the objects you have constrained. In addition, you will add dimensions to two circles and uncover an amazing coincidence.

1. If the file is not already open, go to the book's web page, browse to Chapter 12, get the file Ch12-D.dwg, and open it.

fx

Parameters Manager

2. Select the ribbon's Parametric tab and click the Parameters Manager button in the Manage panel.

3. Double click the d1 parameter's expression. Type **3** and press Enter. All parameter values are recalculated because they are all based on the first parameter you created earlier in this chapter (see Figure 12.13).

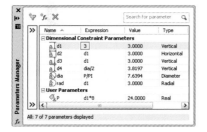

FIGURE 12.13 Changing a single parameter has a cascading effect.

4. Click the Zoom Extents tool in the Navigation bar. The form of the diagram remains unchanged; only the scale has changed.

5. The Earth's polar radius is 3949.9 miles (or 6356.8 km). I suggest you verify this measurement at http://en.wikipedia.org/wiki/Earth. Double-click the d1 parameter's expression. Type **6356.8** and press Enter.

6. Click the Zoom Extents tool in the Navigation bar.

7. Select the ribbon's Home tab and open the Layer drop down in the Layers panel and select 0 to make it the current layer.

8. Select the ribbon's Annotate tab, open the Dimension menu in the Dimensions panel, and click the Radius tool. Select the blue circle and then click a point inside the circle to locate the dimension object.

9. Press the spacebar to repeat the DIMRADIUS (dimension radius) command. Select the magenta circle and click a point outside the circle to locate the dimension object. Figure 12.14 shows the result.

10. The Moon's polar radius is 1078.7 miles (or 1735.97 km). I suggest you verify this measurement at **http://en.wikipedia.org/wiki/ Moon**. The diagram amazingly encodes the sizes of Earth and Moon with accuracy exceeding 99.9%.

11. Your drawing should now resemble Ch12-E.dwg, which is available at the book's web page.

◀

John Michell was the first to discover this geometric relationship in his 1973 book *City of Revelation*.

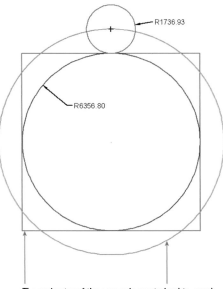

R1736.93

R6356.80

The perimeter of the square is constrained to equal
the circumference of this circle

FIGURE 12.14 Dimensioning two radii in
the squaring the circle diagram

THE ESSENTIALS AND BEYOND

In this chapter you learned how to apply constraints to cause objects to conform to specific
geometric, dimensional, and formulaic requirements. You saw how changing constraint
expressions make objects automatically change their shapes and sizes to conform to the
sum total of all applied constraints.

(Continues)

THE ESSENTIALS AND BEYOND *(Continued)*

ADDITIONAL EXERCISE

Explore annotational constraints on your own. For example, show all dimensional constraints, then select the d1 constraint and open the Properties palette. Change the Constraint Form property to Annotational. Annotational constraints cannot be hidden but instead annotate the drawing, somewhat like dimension objects. However, the padlock symbol identifies them as dimensional constraints.

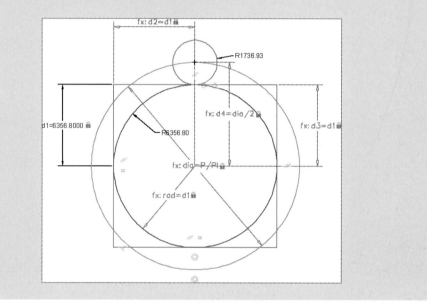

CHAPTER 13

Working with Layouts and Annotative Objects

There are two distinct spaces in which you can create drawings: *model-space* and *paperspace*. Typically, 2D drawings and 3D models are created in modelspace. *Layouts* in paperspace bring together annotations and drawings to be ultimately plotted on paper or published electronically. *Viewports* display drawings at specific scales on layouts, which is where you'll draw title blocks that frame the drawings. We will discuss all of these in this chapter and explain how to use each.

▶ **Creating annotative styles and objects**

▶ **Creating layouts**

▶ **Adjusting floating viewports**

▶ **Overriding layer properties in layout viewports**

▶ **Drawing on layouts**

Creating Annotative Styles and Objects

All the geometry you draw in AutoCAD is created at its actual size. However, the heights of text, dimensions, and attributes present a potential problem. As drawings are scaled down from their real-world size to be represented on paper using viewport scale (which you'll be learning more about in the "Adjusting Floating Viewports" section), text, dimensions, and attributes are likewise scaled down to fit on paper.

To compensate, users of versions before AutoCAD 2008 had to intentionally scale text, dimensions, and attributes much larger in modelspace than their intended size on paper so that when being reduced in a viewport, they appeared at the correct size on paper. Complicating this issue is the fact if you wanted to display the same drawing at different scales on the same sheet of paper (a common occurrence), you would have to duplicate all the annotation, assign copies to different layers, and scale the annotation according to each viewport's scale.

Fortunately, annotative objects overhaul and greatly simplify this process by automatically displaying text, dimensions, and/or attributes at different heights on the same drawing according to the viewport scale in which they are displayed.

The purpose of annotative styles is to control the appearance of annotative objects such as text, dimensions, and/or attributes. We will discuss both text and dimensions in upcoming sections but will hold off on attributes until Chapter 15, "Storing, Presenting, and Extracting Data." As you'll see, annotative objects change their sizes automatically to fit the drawing scale.

Working with Annotative Text

In the following steps you will configure an annotative text style to display text at ⅛″ (or 0.4 cm) high on paper. All the text objects assigned to this style will automatically adjust their heights to ⅛″ (or 0.4 cm), no matter what scale the drawing is shown in. In this way annotative objects automatically change their sizes relative to other geometry in the drawing.

1. Go to the book's web page at **www.sybex.com/go/ autocad2012essentials**, browse to Chapter 13, get the file Ch13-A.dwg (or Ch13-A-metric.dwg), and open it.

2. Type **ST** (for style) and press Enter. Click the New button in the Text Style dialog box that appears. Type **Annotative** as the style name in the New Text Style dialog box and click OK.

3. Select Arial as the font name, select Annotative in the Size area, type **1/8″** (or **0.4** cm) for Paper Text Height, and type **0.9** for the Width Factor (see Figure 13.1). Click Apply and then click Close.

4. Zoom into the room with the round table at the top of the floor plan.

 5. Click the Multiline text tool in the Annotation panel on the ribbon's Home tab. Select 1/16″ = 1′-0″ (or 1:200 for metric) from the drop-down menu in the Select Annotation Scale dialog box that appears (see Figure 13.2). Click OK.

6. Click the first corner at some arbitrary point inside the round table. Type **J** (for justify) and press Enter. The command prompt reads

       Enter justification [TL/TC/TR/ML/MC/MR/BL/BC/BR] <TL>:

If you don't see the Select Annotation Scale dialog box (it can be suppressed), you can still set the annotation scale on the status bar.

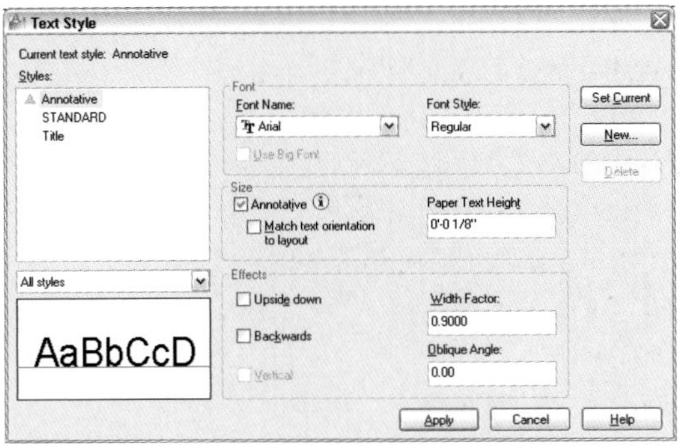

FIGURE 13.1 Creating an annotative text style

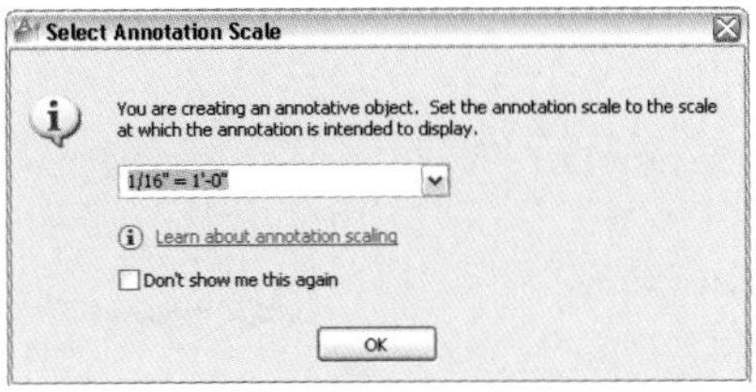

FIGURE 13.2 Selecting an annotation scale in modelspace

Type **MC** (for middle center) and press Enter. Click the second point a short distance down and to the right. Type **Council Room** and press Ctrl+Enter to end the MTEXT command. Pressing Enter moves you to the next line in multiline text so you must hold Ctrl while pressing Enter to end the command.

7. Click the Move tool on the Modify panel, type **L** (for last), and press Enter twice. Type **ins** (for insert) and click the text object. Type **cen** (for center) and press Enter. Click the circular table to center the text on the table (see Figure 13.3). This text appears ⅛˝ high in 1/16˝ = 1´-0˝ scale (or 0.4 cm high in 1:200 scale).

8. Select the two toggles adjacent to Annotation Scale on the status bar so that both have yellow icons indicating they are turned on (see Figure 13.4).

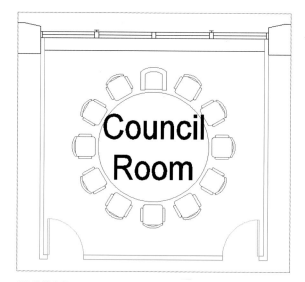

FIGURE 13.3 Centering multiline text on the circular table

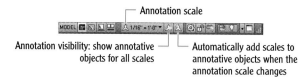

FIGURE 13.4 Annotative controls on the status bar

ANNOTATION SCALES

Annotative objects do not automatically hold representations at all conceivable scales. You can add or delete scales for individual annotative objects in the right-click context menu.

9. Change the Annotation Scale to 1/2″ = 1′-0″ (or 1:20 for metric) in the status bar. The text you created appears much smaller. This text will appear ⅛″ high in 1/2″ = 1′-0″ scale (or 0.4 cm in 1:20 scale).

Select the text object and observe both scales simultaneously (see Figure 13.5). Press Esc to deselect.

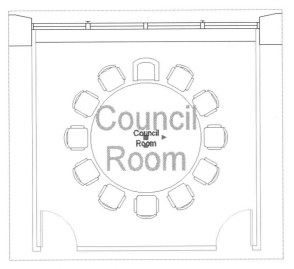

FIGURE 13.5 Annotative text shown in two scales

10. Save your work as Ch13-B.dwg or Ch13-B-metric.dwg.

Working with Annotative Dimensions

In much the same way as text, dimensions can be made annotative so that they change sizes when the annotative scale is changed. In the following steps, we will explore how to do this by creating an annotative dimension style and then adding an annotative linear dimension.

1. If the file is not already open from performing the previous step, go to the book's web page, browse to Chapter 13, get the file Ch13-B.dwg or Ch13-B-metric.dwg, and open it.

2. Type **D** (for dimension style) and press Enter. Click the New button in the Dimension Style Manager to bring up the Create New Dimension Style dialog box. Type **Annotative** in New Style Name and click the Annotative check box (see Figure 13.6). Imperial users click Continue, OK, and then Close. Metric users should click OK, select Decimal Units and Precision of 0 (whole centimeters) on the Primary Units tab of the Modify Dimension Style dialog box, click OK, and click Close.

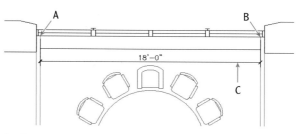

FIGURE 13.6 Creating an annotative dimension style

3. Toggle on Object Snap. Verify that endpoint running object snap mode is on by right-clicking the icon in the status bar.

4. Click the Linear dimension tool in the Annotation panel. Click points A, B, and C, as shown in Figure 13.7.

FIGURE 13.7 Drawing a linear dimension

1/16" = 1'-0" ▼

5. Select the 1/16″ = 1′-0″ (or 1:200 in metric) scale button in the Annotation Scale menu on the status bar. A much larger dimension object appears in the drawing canvas. Select the dimension object and, using one of the dimension line grips at either end of the dimension line, move it upward so that the dimension does not overlap the exterior wall. Press Esc to deselect. Figure 13.8 shows the result.

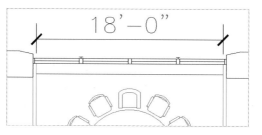

FIGURE 13.8 Moving the 1/16″ = 1′-0″ (or 1:200 in metric) scale dimension line upward for clarity

6. Save your work as Ch13-C.dwg or Ch13-C-metric.dwg.

Creating Layouts

Think of layouts as sheets of virtual paper because that's what they represent. You will create layouts whether you plan to ultimately publish the drawing on paper or in electronic form. Each drawing can have multiple layouts to publish in a variety of formats. In the following steps, you will create two layouts, one for an 8.5″ × 11″ sheet of paper (or ISO A4) and another for a 30″ × 42″ drawing (or ISO A0), standard business and drawing sizes.

1. If the file is not already open, go to the book's web page, browse to Chapter 13, get the file Ch13-C.dwg or Ch13-C-metric.dwg, and open it.

2. Click the Layer Properties tool in the Layers panel on the ribbon's Home tab.

3. Click the New Layer button in the Layer Properties Manager that appears. Type **Z-Viewport** and press Enter. With the Z-Viewport line still highlighted, press Alt+C to make the new layer current. Click the printer icon in the Z-Viewport layer's Plot column to make this layer nonplotting (see Figure 13.9). Close the Layer Properties Manager.

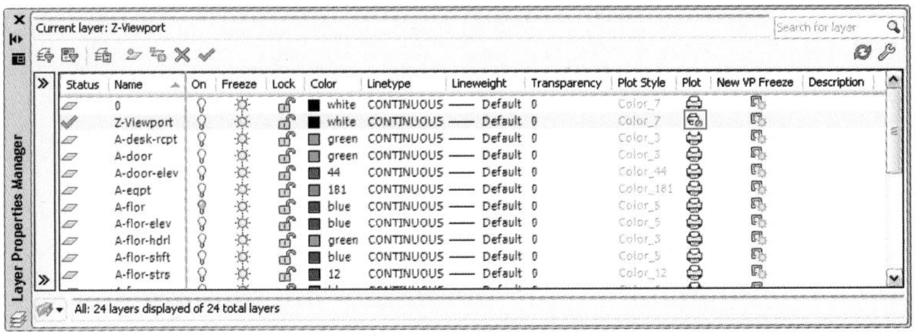

FIGURE 13.9 Creating a nonplotting viewport layer and setting it current

LAYOUT AND MODEL TABS

Layout and model tabs are a legacy interface that longtime AutoCAD users may prefer to keep using. If you see tabs at the bottom of the drawing canvas labeled Model and Layout1, then you are looking at the older interface. Right-click either of these tabs and choose Hide Layout And Model Tabs to use the more streamlined modern interface.

4. Click the Layout1 button on the status bar. The image in the drawing canvas changes as you enter paperspace: a white representation of paper appears having an automatically created viewport through which you see the drawing in modelspace. The viewport object is on the Z-Viewport layer. The viewport frame will not appear in the output because it is on a nonplotting layer. The contents of the viewport will be output, however. The dashed lines indicate the limits of the plotting device's printable area (see Figure 13.10).

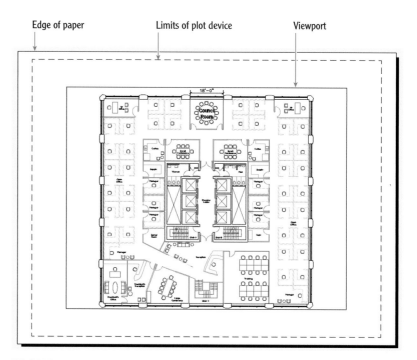

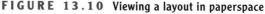

FIGURE 13.10 Viewing a layout in paperspace

Paperspace is a 2D space representing a sheet of virtual paper. Modelspace is a 3D space containing both 2D drawings and 3D models. ▶

5. Select the ribbon's Output tab. Click the Page Setup Manager tool in the Plot panel and click the Modify button in the Page Setup Manager dialog box that appears. When the Page Setup: Layout1 dialog box opens, select the DWG To PDF.pc3 plotter from the Name drop-down, choose monochrome.ctb from the Plot Style Table drop-down, check Display Plot Styles, and select ANSI Expand A (8.50 × 11.00 Inches)—or ISO Full Bleed A4 (297.00 × 210.00 MM) in metric—as the paper size (see Figure 13.11). Imperial users leave the plot scale at 1 inch = 1 unit, and metric users set the plot scale to 10 mm = 1 unit. Click OK and then click Close.

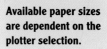

FIGURE 13.11 Configuring a page setup

Available paper sizes are dependent on the plotter selection.

6. Click Quick View Layouts in the status bar. Click the New Layout icon at the bottom of the Quick View Layouts interface that appears at the bottom of the drawing canvas. Click Layout2 to open it (see Figure 13.12). Click the Close Quick View Layouts icon.

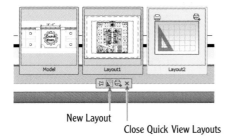

New Layout

Close Quick View Layouts

FIGURE 13.12 Creating a new layout through the Quick View Layouts interface

7. Click the Page Setup Manager in the Plot panel. Click the Modify button in the Page Setup Manager dialog box that appears. Select the DWG To PDF.pc3 plotter, select monochrome.ctb from the Plot Style Table drop-down, and check Display Plot Styles. Imperial users select ARCH E1 (30.00 × 42.00 Inches) as the paper size; metric users select ISO A0 (841.00 × 1189.00 MM) as the paper size. Imperial users leave the plot scale at 1 inch = 1 unit; metric users set the plot scale to

10 mm = 1 unit. Select the DWG To PDF.pc3 plotter to solve this problem. Click OK and then click Close.

8. A single tiny viewport was automatically created on the current layer in the corner of the layout. You will configure this viewport in the next section and create an additional viewport. Save your work as Ch13-D.dwg or Ch13-D-metric.dwg.

Adjusting Floating Viewports

Think of floating viewports as windows that exist in paperspace through which one sees into modelspace. Viewports are termed *floating* because you can position and size their frames however you like in relation to the paper represented in a layout. You will configure a single floating viewport on Layout1 and two separate viewports on Layout2 to gain experience with viewports.

Working on Layout1

In the following steps, you will set the scale of the building floor plan on Layout 1 and then adjust its viewport to fit the floor plan:

1. If the file is not already open, go to the book's web page, browse to Chapter 13, get the file Ch13-D.dwg or Ch13-D-metric.dwg, and open it.

2. Click the Quick View Layouts icon on the status bar. Select Layout1 and then press Esc to exit Quick View Layouts mode.

3. Click the PAPER icon on the status bar. This icon toggles between paperspace and modelspace, and the word shows you which space you are in (now modelspace). The viewport's frame highlights with a thicker representation when displaying modelspace (see Figure 13.13). Move the cursor inside the viewport and observe that the crosshair cursor is available only within the viewport.

4. Choose 1/16″ = 1′-0″ (or 1:200 in metric) from the Viewport Scale menu button on the status bar, as shown in Figure 13.14. The viewport zooms into the Elevator Lobby, which is in the center of the plan. At this exact zoom magnification, the plan appears in ¹⁄₁₆″ scale (or 1:200) in the layout.

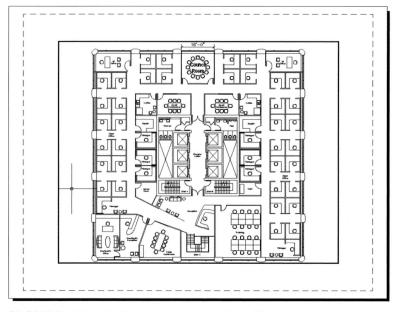

FIGURE 13.13 Modelspace active inside a floating viewport

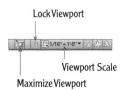

Lock Viewport

Viewport Scale

Maximize Viewport

FIGURE 13.14 The status bar's appearance when a floating viewport is active

MODEL 5. Click the MODEL icon on the status bar to switch back to paperspace. Move the crosshair cursor across the drawing canvas and observe that it appears across the entire paper.

6. Viewport frames exist in paperspace only. Click the single viewport frame to select it. Select the upper-right grip and move it upward and to the right until it is close to the upper-right corner of the paper but inside the plot device limits. Click the lower-left grip and move it to the lower-left corner inside the device limits (see Figure 13.15). Press Esc to deselect the viewport.

7. Save your work as Ch13-E.dwg or Ch13-E-metric.dwg.

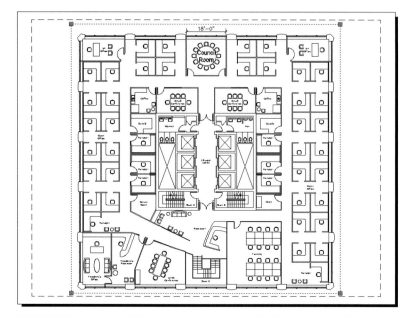

FIGURE 13.15 Adjusting the viewport to display the entire floor plan at ¹⁄₁₆˝ scale (or 1:200 in metric)

Working on Layout2

In the following steps you will adjust the viewport on Layout2, and in the process discover that certain combinations of building geometry, viewport scales, and paper sizes do not always mesh. You will fix the problem by selecting a different viewport scale and then adjust the viewport to fit the floor plan. In addition you'll create a viewport from scratch and adjust it.

1. If the file is not already open, go to the book's web page, browse to Chapter 13, get the file Ch13-E.dwg or Ch13-E-metric.dwg, and open it.

2. Click the Quick View Layouts icon on the status bar. Select Layout2 and then press Esc to exit Quick View Layouts mode.

3. As an alternative to clicking PAPER on in the status bar, double-click inside the viewport to activate it: the Paper/Model toggle now indicates you are in the modelspace of the viewport.

4. Choose 1/4˝ = 1´-0˝ (or 1:40 in metric) from the Viewport Scale menu on the status bar. Modelspace zooms in to the Elevator Lobby.

5. Double-click the layout outside of the viewport to switch back into paperspace. Move the cursor across the drawing canvas and observe that you can move it now that it is active across the entire paper.

6. Viewport frames exist in paperspace only. Click the viewport frame to select it. Select the upper-right grip and move it upward until it is close to the upper-right corner of the paper but inside the plot device limits. Click the lower-left grip and move it to the lower-left corner inside the device limits. Press Esc to deselect.

7. Double-click inside the viewport to switch back into modelspace. Drag the mouse wheel (but do not turn the wheel) to pan the drawing over within the viewport to center it on the paper. The ¼″ (or 1:40 in metric) scale drawing almost fits, but it's too tight to fit comfortably on ARCH E1 or ISO A0 paper (see Figure 13.16). We couldn't have known this without first creating the layout and trying to fit the drawing to the paper at this specific scale.

> Changing the viewport scale automatically triggers a corresponding change in the annotation scale.

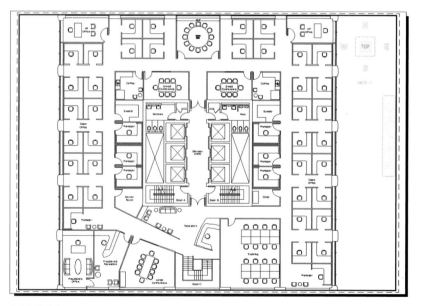

FIGURE 13.16 Discovering that the drawing at ¼″ scale (or 1:40 scale in metric) doesn't quite fit on the paper

8. Verify that the option Automatically Add Scales To Annotative Objects When The Annotation Scale Changes is toggled on in the status bar and then select 3/16″ = 1′-0″ scale (or 1:50 in metric) in the Viewport Scale menu. The floor plan now fits the layout.

9. Double-click the paper outside the viewport to switch back into paper-space. Select the viewport and grip-edit it so it closely surrounds the plan geometry. Move the plan to the left on the paper to make room for another drawing on this layout. Figure 13.17 shows the result.

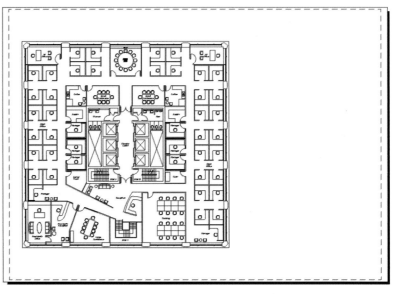

FIGURE 13.17 The drawing fits the paper at ³⁄₁₆″ scale (or 1:50 in metric)

Certification
Objective

10. Type **MV** (for make viewport) and press Enter. Click two arbitrary corner points to the right of the existing viewport to create a new viewport. The MVIEW command ends.

11. Double-click within the new viewport to enter its modelspace. Select 1/2″ = 1′-0″ (or 1:20 in metric) in the Viewport Scale menu on the status bar; the viewports zoom into the Elevator Lobby again. Pan downward until you center the view on the Council Room. Double-click outside the viewport to return to paperspace. Figure 13.18 shows the result.

> **I recommend that you lock viewports immediately after configuring them so that you don't inadvertently change the drawing scale by zooming.**
>
> ▶

12. Select both viewport objects and then click the Lock Viewport icon on the status bar. Press Esc to deselect. Double-click inside the new viewport and roll the mouse wheel forward to zoom in. Whereas before when you locked the viewport only the space within the viewport zoomed in, now the entire layout zooms in.

13. Save your work as Ch13-F.dwg or Ch13-F-metric.dwg.

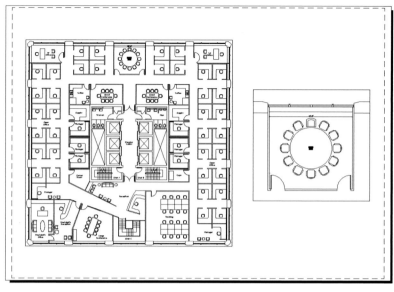

FIGURE 13.18 Creating and configuring a new viewport detailing the
Council Room

Overriding Layer Properties in Layout Viewports

Each viewport maintains its own set of layer properties that can override the drawing's basic layer properties. In the following steps, you will use this feature to turn off a selection of layers in a particular viewport, while continuing to display these same layers in another viewport.

1. If the file is not already open, go to the book's web page, browse to Chapter 13, get the file Ch13-F.dwg or Ch13-F-metric.dwg, and open it.

2. Double-click within the larger viewport on Layout2 that shows the entire floor plan to activate it and switch into floating modelspace.

3. Click the Layer Properties tool on the Layers panel on the ribbon's Home tab.

4. Expand the palette to the right by dragging its edge. Observe a set of properties in columns preceded with the letters VP (viewport). Freeze layers A-furn and A-furn-syst in the VP Freeze column (see Figure 13.19).

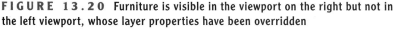

FIGURE 13.19 Freezing selected layers in the current viewport only

You can override the color, linetype, lineweight, transparency, and/or plot style layer properties independently in each viewport if so desired.

5. Double-click on the paper outside the viewport to switch back into paperspace. The furniture and furniture systems disappear from the current viewport but the Council Room round table is still visible in the viewport on the right of Layout2 (see Figure 13.20). Close the Layer Properties Manager.

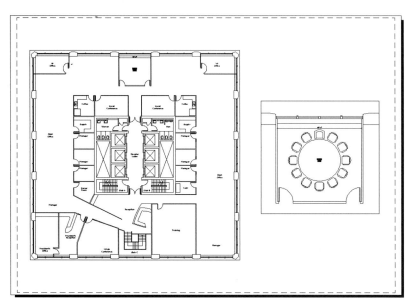

FIGURE 13.20 Furniture is visible in the viewport on the right but not in the left viewport, whose layer properties have been overridden

6. Click Maximize Viewport on the status bar. The layout disappears and is replaced by a maximized modelspace view shown with a red border (see Figure 13.21). This viewport's overridden layer properties are respected when you're working in maximized mode (the furniture remains frozen).

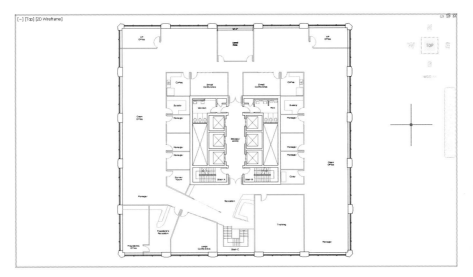

F I G U R E   1 3 . 2 1 Working in a maximized viewport

7. Zoom into the Council Room.

8. Click the Isolate tool in the Layers panel, type **S** (for settings) and press Enter. The command prompt reads

   ```
   Enter setting for layers not isolated
   [Off/Lock and fade] <Off>:
   ```

   Type **0** (for off) and press Enter. Create a crossing window around the Council Room, including its walls, doors, text, and dimension but excluding the exterior shell walls and glazing. Press Enter to isolate the selected layers.

9. Click the Stretch tool in the Modify panel; then click points A and B in Figure 13.22 and press Enter. Press the F8 key to toggle Ortho mode on. Click an arbitrary first point on the drawing canvas, move the cursor to the left, type **4″** (or **10** cm) and press Enter.

10. Press the spacebar to repeat the STRETCH command. Click points C and D in Figure 13.22 and press Enter. Click an arbitrary first point on the drawing canvas, move the cursor to the right, type **4″** (or **10** cm) and press Enter. The walls are stretched outward a distance equal to their thicknesses so that the dimension reads 18′-8″ or 569 cm (see Figure 13.23).

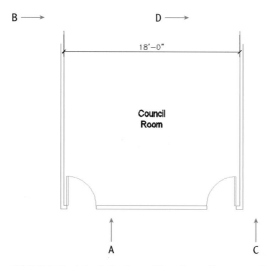

FIGURE 13.22 Stretching the walls outward

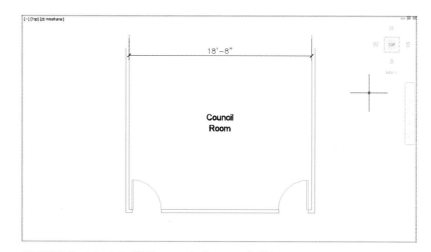

FIGURE 13.23 Walls stretched outward 4″ (or 10 cm) in each direction

 11. Click the Unisolate tool in the Layers panel.

12. Click the Extend tool in the Modify panel and press Enter to select all as potential boundary edges. Click points A and B on the sill line (shown in Figure 13.24) to extend it to the surrounding piers. Press Esc to end the EXTEND command.

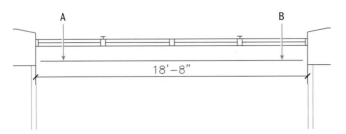

FIGURE 13.24 Extending the sill to meet the surrounding piers

13. Click Minimize Viewport in the status bar. The drawing canvas returns to Layout2. Zoom in and verify the 18´-8˝ (or 569 cm in metric) dimension is visible in both viewports.

14. Save your work as Ch13-G.dwg or Ch13-G-metric.dwg.

Drawing on Layouts

You can draw on layouts just as you can draw in modelspace. However, the types of content drawn on layouts will necessarily be of a different character, such as a title block, viewports, and optionally dimensions. Layouts have the measurements of physical sheets of paper and are not meant to hold real-world geometry directly (that is what modelspace is used for).

One way to draw directly on layouts is to use *title blocks*, which are borders surrounding the drawing that also have rectangles wherein text identifying the sheet is placed. You can also draw dimensions directly on layouts. Dimensions added in paperspace are associated with geometry in modelspace, so if the real-world geometry changes, the dimensions will automatically update.

In the following steps, you will draw a title block and add a dimension to the paperspace of the layout:

1. If the file is not already open, go to the book's web page, browse to Chapter 13, get the file Ch13-G.dwg or Ch13-G-metric.dwg, and open it.

2. Type **LA** (for Layer Properties Manager) and press Enter. Click the New Layer icon, type **Z-Title**, and press Enter. Double-click the new layer to make it current. Select a Lineweight value of 0.039˝ (or 1.00 mm) for a thick border. Toggle the Plot icon on. Close the Layer Properties Manager.

3. Click the Rectangle tool in the Draw panel. Click the corner points as close as possible (you cannot snap to the paper) to the edges of the paper in Layout2. The rectangle won't be visible initially because it overlaps the paper borders.

4. Click the Offset tool in the Modify panel. The command prompt reads

```
Specify offset distance or [Through/Erase/Layer] <0'-0">:
```

Type **E** (for erase) and press Enter. Type **Y** (for yes) and press Enter. Type **1˝** (or **2.5** cm) and press Enter. Select the rectangle you drew in the previous step and then click inside the rectangle to offset it inwardly.

TITLE BLOCKS

Drawings are legal documents and as such typically indicate the drawing scale, sheet name, and sheet number. This information is traditionally shown with text or attributes in a title block, which is drawn directly on the layout.

FLOOR PLAN

Scale 1:40

AutoCAD 2012 and
AutoCAD LT 2012
Essentials

A1

Dimensions added in paperspace are necessarily specific to each drawing and cannot be shown simultaneously in multiple viewports as annotative; modelspace dimensions can.

5. Set layer A-note current by selecting it in the Layer drop-down in the Layers panel.

6. Verify that the PAPER/MODEL toggle on the status bar reads PAPER. Zoom into the viewport on the right of Layout2.

7. Click the Linear tool in the Annotation panel, click points A, B, and C as shown in Figure 13.25. A dimension measuring 16´-10 1/2˝ (or 514 cm) appears on the layout in paperspace that looks similar to the dimension you drew earlier in this chapter in modelspace.

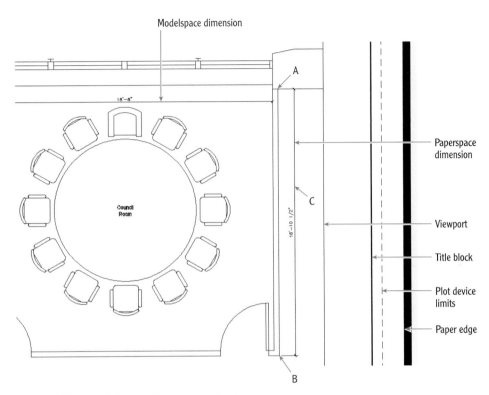

FIGURE 13.25 Drawing a dimension in paperspace

8. Click Maximize Viewport on the status bar. You are actually working in the larger viewport on Layout2, but this suits our purposes because the furniture layers are frozen, making it easier to stretch the walls. Pan over to the Council Room by dragging the mouse wheel.

WORKING IN MULTIPLE MAXIMIZED VIEWPORTS

When you work in a maximized viewport on a layout that has more than one viewport, the Next and Previous arrows appear surrounding the status bar toggle. Click these arrow icons to cycle through each and every viewport on a layout while staying in maximized mode.

9. Click the Stretch tool on the Modify panel. Create a crossing window around both doors and the lower portion of the walls in the Council

Room and press Enter. Click an arbitrary point on the canvas, move the cursor downward in the drawing canvas, type **1.5˝** (or **6** cm), and press Enter.

10. Click Minimize Viewport in the status bar. The drawing canvas returns to Layout2. The dimension in paperspace is automatically updated with the value of 17´-0˝ (or 520 cm in metric).

11. Select the Output tab on the ribbon and click the Preview tool in the Plot panel. What you now see is what you would get if you published this drawing (see Figure 13.26). Press Esc to exit the preview.

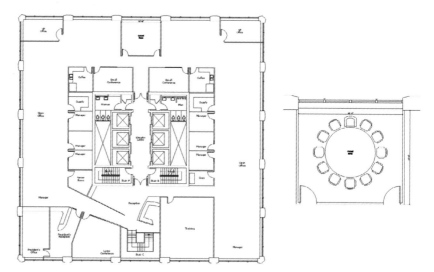

FIGURE 13.26 Plot preview of Layout2

12. Save your work as Ch13-H.dwg or Ch13-H-metric.dwg. Your drawing should now resemble the files available on the book's web page.

THE ESSENTIALS AND BEYOND

In this chapter you learned the differences between modelspace and paperspace. You created layouts and viewports, and set viewport scales and adjusted viewports to fit the real-world geometry. In addition you overrode layer properties in viewports, worked in maximized viewports, drew a title block, and dimensioned in paperspace. In short you are fully prepared to create physical and electronic output in the next chapter.

(Continues)

ADDITIONAL EXERCISE

TILEMODE is the system variable that switches between modelspace where tiled viewports are possible (TILEMODE=1) and a paperspace where floating viewports are possible (TILEMODE=0). Create tiled modelspace viewports with the VPORTS command on your own. You can alternatively create tiled viewports using the leftmost menu in the upper-left corner of the drawing canvas.

Tiled viewports are most useful when working on 3D models to get multiple simultaneous views of complex geometry, but can also be used to get a simultaneous overview and detailed view of a 2D drawing. Try working at a few different magnifications in Ch13-H.dwg or Ch13-H-metric.dwg with three viewports so you can see the overall plan and two detailed views simultaneously.

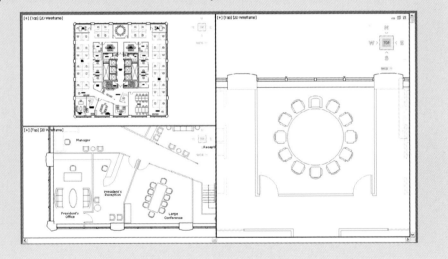

CHAPTER 14

Printing and Plotting

Plotting is the term for producing physical prints using a large-format printer, which is either networked or directly connected to an AutoCAD workstation. There is much more to plotting a drawing or publishing an entire sheet set than hitting the Print icon, however. Before you can successfully print, you must first learn to configure a plotter and a plot style table; you'll then learn how to create professional output from model- and/or paperspace. As you'll see in this chapter, you'll also have the option to keep everything digital and export DWF or PDF files that can be shared on the Internet with your partners and clients.

▶ **Configuring output devices**

▶ **Creating plot style tables**

▶ **Using plot style tables**

▶ **Plotting in modelspace**

▶ **Plotting layouts in paperspace**

▶ **Exporting to an electronic format**

Configuring Output Devices

In the most general sense everything you do on a computer is a form of *input*. Creating physical or even electronic drawings, on the other hand, are forms of *output*. Output devices are more commonly known as printers.

Large-format (24″ wide or larger) printers are marketed as "plotters" because of the history of technology. When I started my career more than 20 years ago, plotters had technical pens in them that you had to individually refill with ink. The paper (actually Mylar film) was rolled back and forth and the pens literally *plotted* one line at a time. Thankfully modern inkjet technology is much faster so you no longer wind up with clogged pens and ink on your hands.

In the following sections you will configure an output device by setting up a system printer and also an AutoCAD plotter. Once these steps are completed, you won't have to perform them again on the same computer.

Setting Up a System Printer

The first thing you'll need to do is set up a system printer, which contains *drivers* that your operating system uses to control the output device. System printers are not specific to AutoCAD; device manufacturers supply drivers, which you then install to become printers on your system.

If you are reading this book at work you undoubtedly already have a system printer or your CAD manager has installed one for you. For the purposes of this book however, you will install a driver for the HP DesignJet 800 plotter (an industry workhorse), whether you own this device or not. I will be using the HP DesignJet 800 system printer in this chapter. The following steps guide you in installing this typical system printer:

1. Open your browser and type **HP DesignJet 800 42 driver** as a Google search. Select the first search result or go to **www.hp.com** and search for Download Drivers and Software.

2. Select your operating system from the list and download the appropriate driver.

3. Install the driver following the manufacturer's instructions.

Setting Up an AutoCAD Plotter

AutoCAD for Mac doesn't use AutoCAD plotters but instead outputs directly to the system printers listed under System Preferences.

Most programs send output directly to system printers, but AutoCAD is an exception. AutoCAD has another layer of software between the program and the operating system known as an AutoCAD plotter. In this section you will set up an AutoCAD plotter that sends its output to the system printer, which in turn hands off the print job to the output device itself.

1. In AutoCAD type **PLOTTERMANAGER** and press Enter. The Windows Explorer dialog box appears displaying the Add-A-Plotter Wizard and various AutoCAD plotters that have the .pc3 file extension (see Figure 14.1).

2. Double click Add-A-Plotter Wizard. Read the Introduction page and click Next.

3. Select the System Printer radio button (see Figure 14.2) and click Next.

FIGURE 14.1 Explorer window showing two folders, the Add-A-Plotter Wizard and various AutoCAD plotters

PLOTTING RASTER IMAGES TO SCALE

For more information on setting up and plotting to a raster plotter driver in AutoCAD, see my book *Enhancing Architectural Drawings and Models with Photoshop* (Sybex, 2010). Raster images of drawing layers can be output to scale from AutoCAD and enhanced in Photoshop for presentation.

FIGURE 14.2 Selecting the System Printer option in the Add Plotter wizard

4. Select the HP DesignJet 800 system printer from the list in the Add Plotter dialog box (see Figure 14.3). The listed printers will differ on your computer depending on which drivers you (or your CAD manager) have already installed on your system. Click Next.

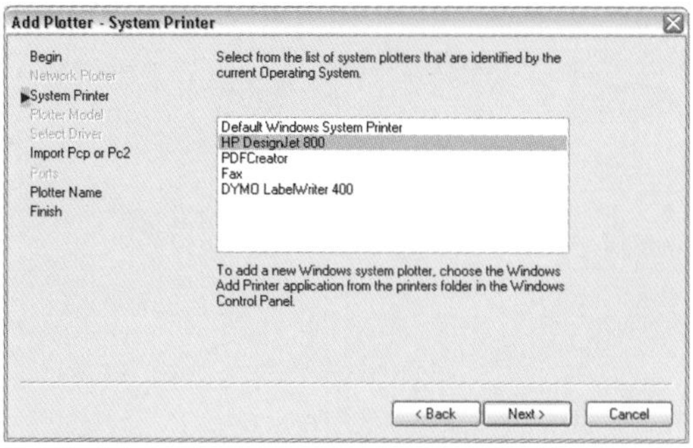

FIGURE 14.3 Selecting a system printer for the plotter to send data to

5. The next page allows you to import a legacy PCP or PC2 file from older versions of AutoCAD. Since we are creating a PC3 file from scratch, click Next to open the Plotter Name page.

6. AutoCAD now suggests a name for the plotter that is identical to the name of the system printer. Type the name **HP DesignJet 800 Plotter** to differentiate the new printer name from the system printer (see Figure 14.4). Click Next.

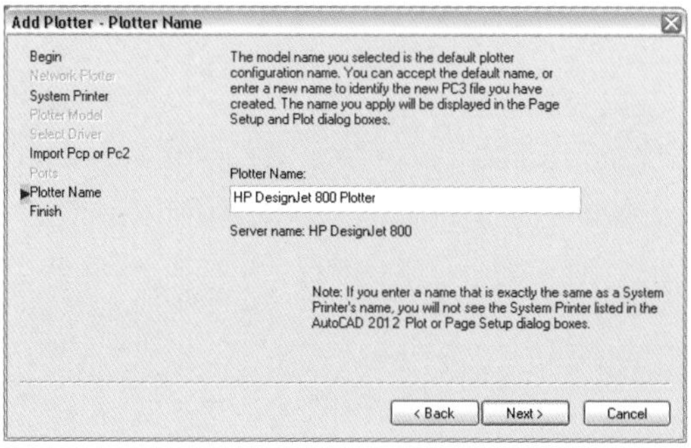

FIGURE 14.4 Giving the plotter a unique name

7. The final page of the Add Plotter wizard allows you to edit the newly created plotter driver itself. Click the Edit Plotter Configuration button to do this.

8. Select the Device And Document Settings tab and then select the Filter Paper Sizes node in the Plotter Configuration Editor dialog box that appears. Click the Uncheck All button. You should filter the list

of paper sizes to display only the sizes you use. Scroll down the list and select the following paper sizes: Arch C (landscape) and Arch D (landscape). Figure 14.5 shows the result.

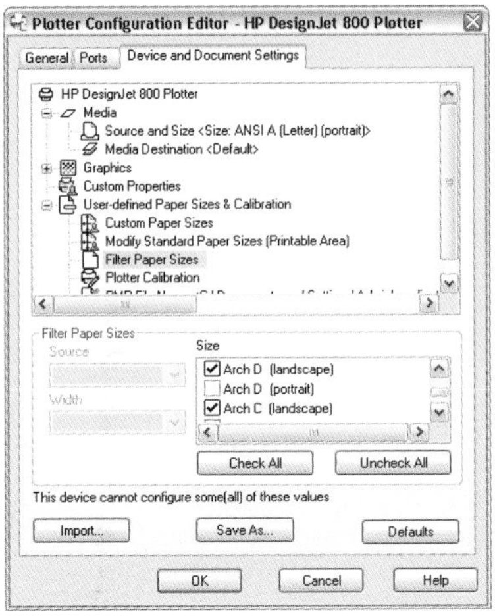

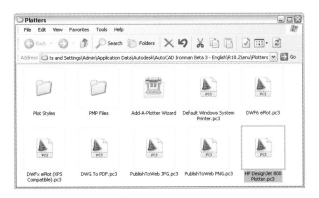

FIGURE 14.5 Filtering out all unused paper sizes

Edit the Custom Properties in the Plotter Configuration Editor to access settings specific to the system printer driver.

9. Click OK to close the Plotter Configuration Editor. Click Finish to close the Add-A-Plotter Wizard.
10. The new AutoCAD plotter driver you just created, `HP DesignJet 800 Plotter.pc3`, appears in the Windows Explorer window that was opened in step 1 (see Figure 14.6). Close Windows Explorer.

FIGURE 14.6 The new AutoCAD plotter driver appears in Windows Explorer

Creating Plot Style Tables

Plot style tables determine the final appearance of objects in terms of their color, linetype, lineweight, end cap, line fill, and screening percentage. Plot style tables trump layer properties when the drawing is printed, meaning the plot style tables take precedence.

In addition to creating a system printer and AutoCAD plotter, you will need to create a plot style table or use an existing one. AutoCAD has two types of plot style tables: color-dependent and named.

Color-Dependent Plot Style Tables (CTB Files) These have been used since the days of pen plotters when you assigned a number of colors in AutoCAD to a specific physical pen. For example, red objects might plot using the 0.5 mm pen and green and yellow objects might use the 0.7 mm pen. You can still use color-dependent plot style tables today, and many firms still do.

Named Plot Styles (STB Files) These were a new feature in AutoCAD 2000. Named plot style tables offer greater flexibility as compared with color-dependent plot styles because plot criteria can be assigned by layer or by object rather than by color only. In the following exercise you will create a named plot style. Named plot styles use the .stb file extension.

> **You cannot create or modify plot styles on the Mac version of AutoCAD—you can use only the default plot styles.**

1. Type **STYLESMANAGER** and press Enter. The Windows Explorer appears displaying a number of preset plot style table files (see Figure 14.7).

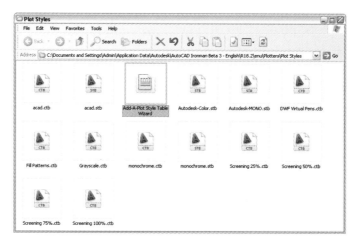

FIGURE 14.7 Windows Explorer showing the plot styles folder

2. Double-click the Add-A-Plot Style Table Wizard. Click Next after reading the introductory page.

3. Select Start From Scratch on the next page (see Figure 14.8). Click Next.

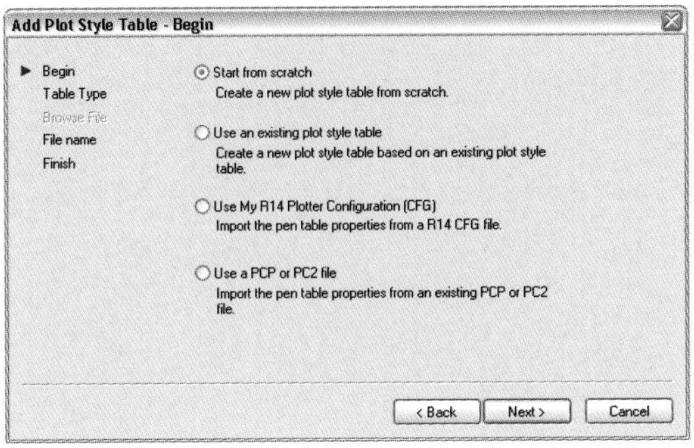

FIGURE 14.8 Starting a plot style table from scratch

4. Select the Named Plot Style radio button on the next page. This will create a named plot style having one default style called Normal. Click Next.

5. For lack of a more descriptive name, type **My plot style** on the File Name page (see Figure 14.9). Click Next.

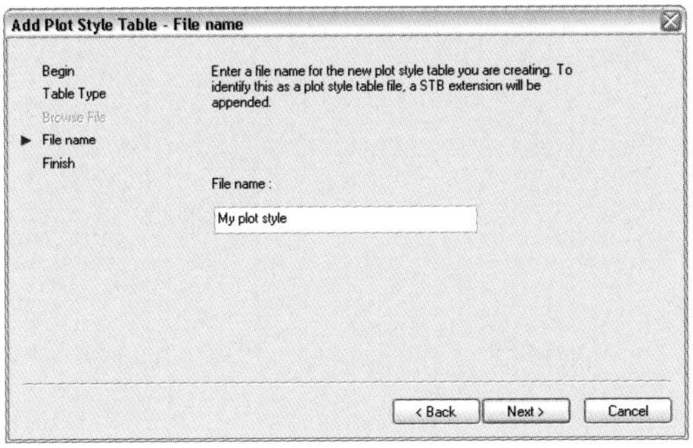

FIGURE 14.9 Typing a name for the plot style

6. The final page of the wizard allows you to edit the newly created STB file itself. Click the Plot Style Table Editor button.

7. Select the Form View tab in the Plot Style Table Editor that appears. Click the Add Style button. Type **Black** and press Enter.

8. Open the Color drop-down and select Black (see Figure 14.10).

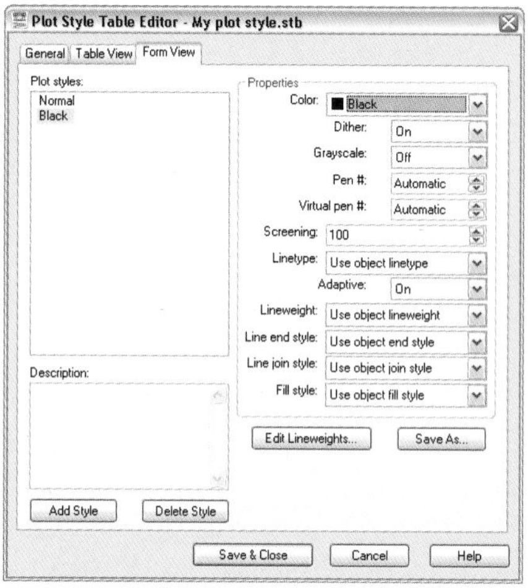

FIGURE 14.10 Creating a Black plot style

Screening refers to the intensity of ink sprayed on the paper while plotting. Selecting 100 sprays at full intensity whereas 0 sprays no ink. Intermediate values produce varying levels of grayscale.

9. Click the Add Style button again, type **20% Screen**, and press Enter. Highlight the value next to the word Screening, type **20**, and press Tab. Click Save & Close to close the Plot Style Table Editor.

10. Click Finish to close the Add Plot Style Table wizard. The named plot style table you just created, `My plot style.stb`, appears in the Windows Explorer that was opened in step 1 (see Figure 14.11). Click the close box in the Windows Explorer.

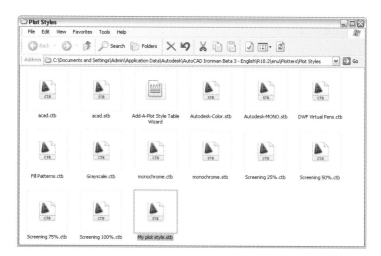

FIGURE 14.11 The new named plot style table appears in the Windows Explorer.

Using Plot Style Tables

New drawings are created using either color-dependent or named plot style tables. A setting in the Options dialog box controls this behavior. Existing drawings must go through a conversion process to switch from utilizing one plot style table type to the other.

After you or your CAD Manager decides which type of plot style table to use consistently, you will want to save a template that records this preference so that you don't have to revisit this issue every time you create a new drawing.

In the following exercise, you will configure new drawings to utilize named plot style tables and learn how to use plot styles by layer or by object.

Configuring New Drawings for Named Plot Style Tables

In the following steps, you will configure new drawings to use named plot styles and will save a template having a named plot style table assigned:

1. Type **OP** (for options) and press Enter. Select the Plot and Publish tab in the Options dialog box that appears.

2. Click the Plot Style Table Settings button in the lower right of the Options dialog box. Select the Use Named Plot Styles radio button in the Plot Style Table Settings dialog box that appears. Select My plot style.stb from the Default Plot Style Table drop-down menu. Select Black from the Default Plot Style For Layer 0 drop-down menu. Select ByLayer as the Default Plot Style for Layer 0 if it is not already selected (see Figure 14.12). Click OK and OK again to close both open dialog boxes.

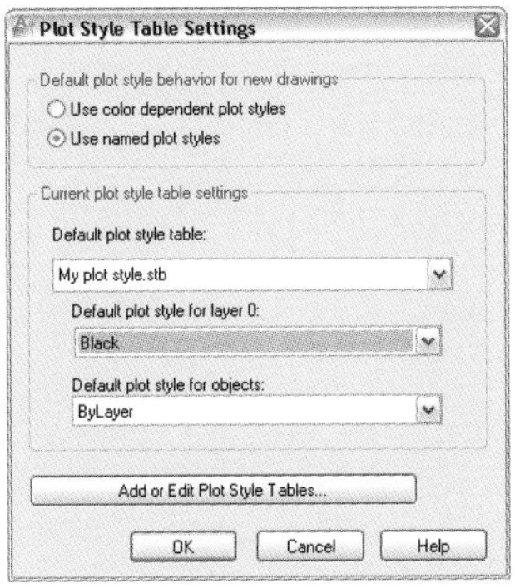

FIGURE 14.12 Configuring the default plot style behavior and settings for new drawings

3. Click the New button in the Quick Access toolbar. Click the arrow button adjacent to the Open button in the Select Template dialog box that appears. Choose Open With No Template – Imperial from the drop-down menu (see Figure 14.13).

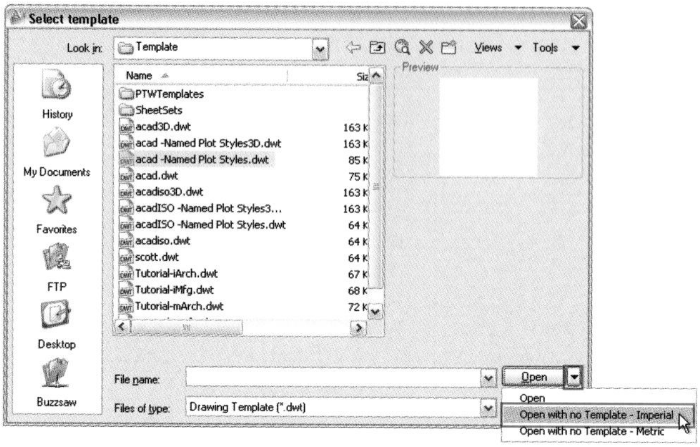

FIGURE 14.13 Creating a new drawing without using a template

4. Type **UN** (for units) and press Enter. Choose Architectural units (or Decimal units in metric) with a precision of ¼″ (metric users choose a precision of 0.0). Set Insertion Scale to Inches (or Centimeters in metric) (see Figure 14.14). Click OK.

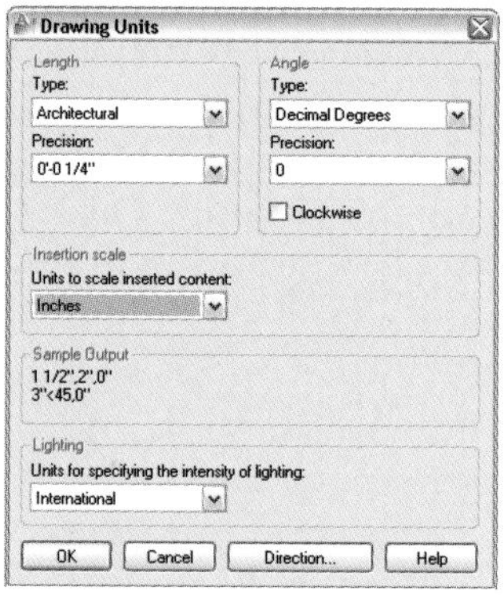

FIGURE 14.14 Setting architectural drawing units

5. Click the Save As button in the Quick Access toolbar. Change the Files Of Type drop down in the Save Drawing As dialog box that appears to AutoCAD Drawing Template (*.dwt). Type **My template** in the File Name text box (see Figure 14.15). Click Save.

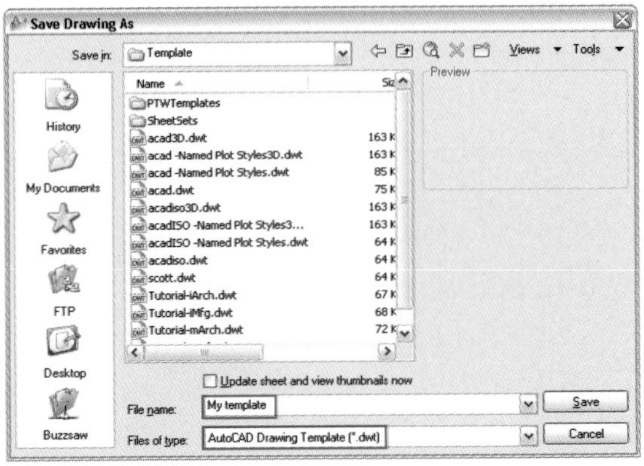

FIGURE 14.15 Saving a new drawing template

6. Type **Named plot styles and architectural units** in the Template Options dialog box that appears (see Figure 14.16). Click OK.

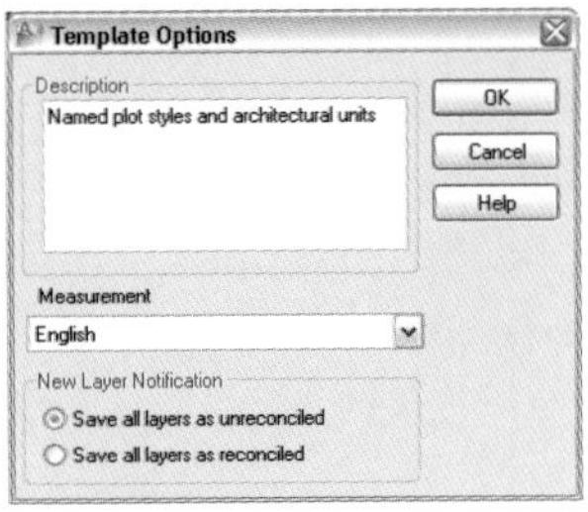

FIGURE 14.16 Describing the template

7. Type **close** and press Enter.

You can now create new drawings having named plot styles (and architectural or decimal units) simply by selecting "My template"—no other configuration is required.

SWITCHING PLOT STYLE TABLE TYPES IN EXISTING DRAWINGS

If you are switching from named plot styles to color-dependent plot styles in an existing drawing, use the CONVERTPSTYLES command to make the conversion. If you are going the other direction and converting an existing drawing from color-dependent plot styles to named plot styles, you must first use the CONVERTCTB command and then use CONVERTPSTYLES.

Assigning Plot Styles by Layer or by Object

If you are working in a drawing that uses a color-dependent plot style table, then the plot styles are automatically configured by color. When working on a drawing that uses a named plot style table, you will need to assign named plot styles by layer and/or by object, as shown in the following exercise:

1. Go to the book's web page at **www.sybex.com/go/ autocad2012essentials**, browse to Chapter 14, click on the file Ch14-A.dwg, and open it.

2. Type **LA** (for layer) and press Enter. Right-click any one of the layer names in the Layer Properties Manager that appears and choose Select All from the context menu. Click the word Normal in the Plot Style column. The plot style table you created earlier (My plot style.stb) is selected. Choose Black in the Select Plot Style dialog box (see Figure 14.17). Click OK. Now all the layers will plot in black.

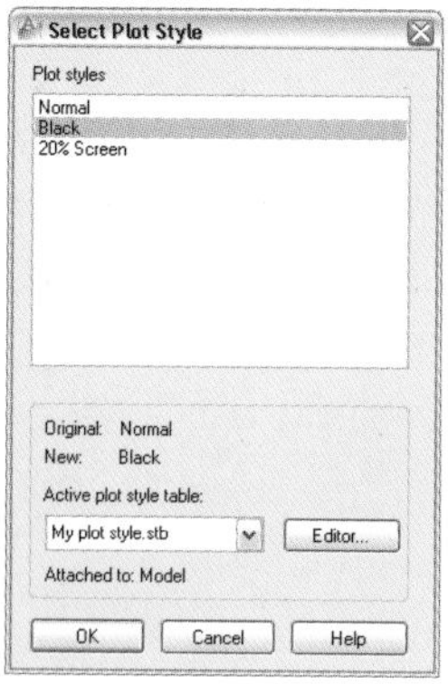

FIGURE 14.17 Selecting a plot style to assign to a layer

3. Click the Title layer in the Layer Properties Manager to select it; all the other layers automatically deselect. Click the plot style on the Title layer and change it to Normal in the Select Plot Style dialog box that appears (see Figure 14.18). The title text will now appear in red.

◀

The Normal plot style in My plot style.stb **outputs objects in color.**

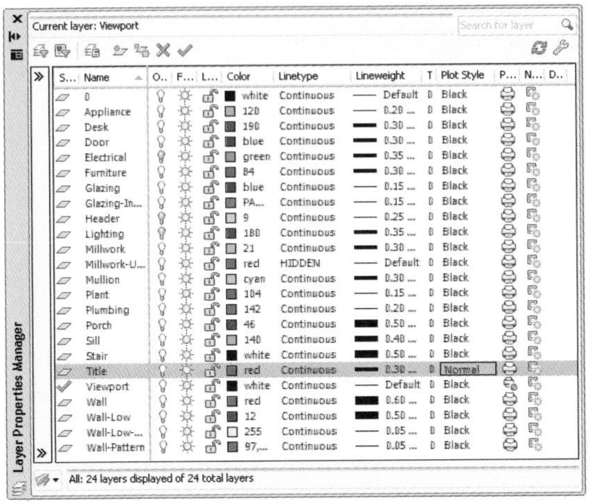

FIGURE 14.18 Configuring named plot styles by layer

4. Close the Layer Properties Manager.

5. Select the ribbon's View tab. Click the Properties button in the Palettes panel.

6. Click the solid hatch of the flooring in Marketing to select it (see Figure 14.19).

7. Open the Plot Style drop-down in the Properties palette and select Other from the menu. Select 20% Screen in the Select Plot Style dialog box that appears. Click OK and 20% Screen is listed as the plot style for the Hatch object in the Properties palette (see Figure 14.20). This object will plot with reduced intensity, so the hatch appears lighter.

8. Press Esc to deselect. Close the Properties palette.

9. Save your work as Ch14-B.dwg.

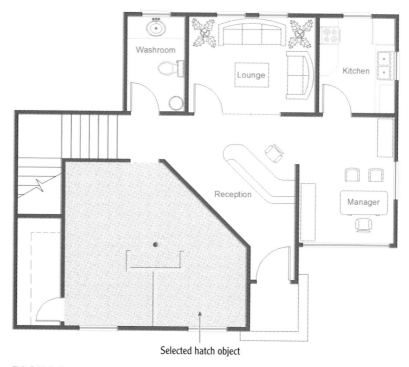

FIGURE 14.19 Selecting a hatch object

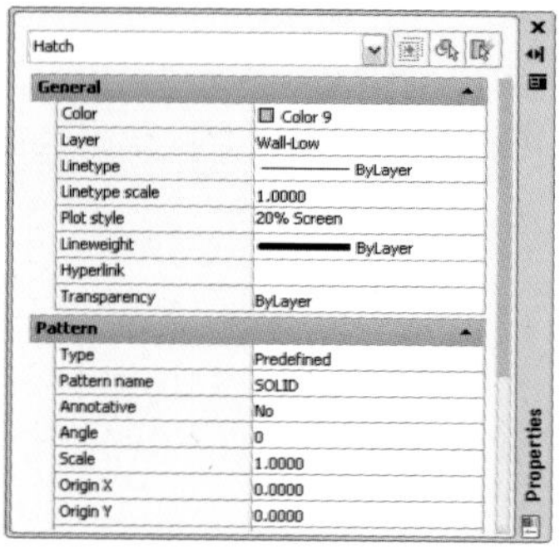

FIGURE 14.20 Changing the plot style assigned to a specific object

Plotting in Modelspace

You can plot what you are working on in modelspace at any time. This is usually done to create a *test plot*, so you (or your colleagues) can check and possibly mark up the evolving design on paper. In the following steps, you will create a test plot in modelspace.

1. Open the Ch14-B.dwg file. If this file is not open, find it on the book's web page.

2. Click the Plot tool in the Quick Access toolbar. Open the Name drop-down menu in the Plot – Model dialog box (see Figure 14.21). Observe that both a system printer and an AutoCAD plotter appear for the HP DesignJet 800 device. Click Cancel.

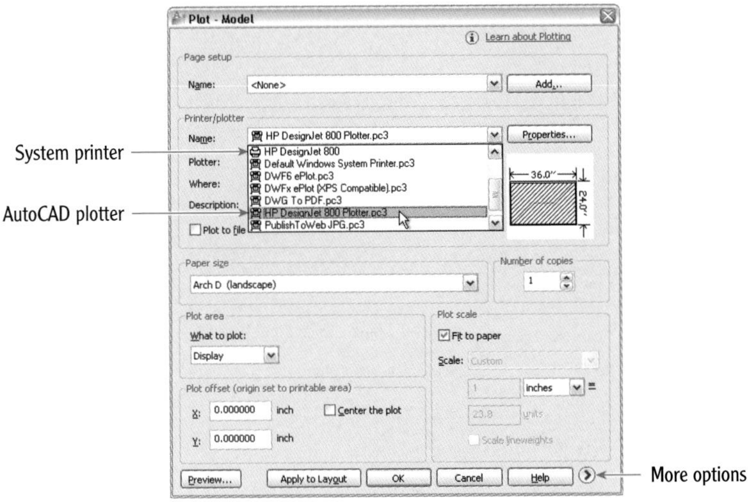

FIGURE 14.21 Selecting a plotter driver in the Plot dialog box

3. It can be confusing seeing the system printers and AutoCAD plotters in the same drop-down menu in the Plot dialog box. You should hide the system printers to remove this doubling of potential output drivers. Type **OP** (for options) and press Enter.

4. Select the Plot And Publish tab. Select Hide System Printers in the General Plot Options area (see Figure 14.22). Click OK.

5. Type **PLOT** and press Enter. Select the HP DesignJet 800 Plotter.pc3 from the Name drop-down menu (no system printers appear). Select Arch C (landscape) in the Paper Size area and Extents in the What To Plot drop-down menu. Select Center The Plot in the Plot Offset area, deselect Fit To Paper in the Plot Scale area, and 3/8″ = 1′-0″ from the Scale drop-down menu. Click the More Options button to

Choose the Fit To Paper option if you don't care about plotting to scale. Pay attention to the plot thumbnail when selecting specific scales to see if the drawing will fit on the chosen paper size.

◄

Certification
Objective

expand the dialog box as previously shown in Figure 14.20. Select My plot style.stb in the Plot Style Table area. Select Plot Stamp On (see Figure 14.23).

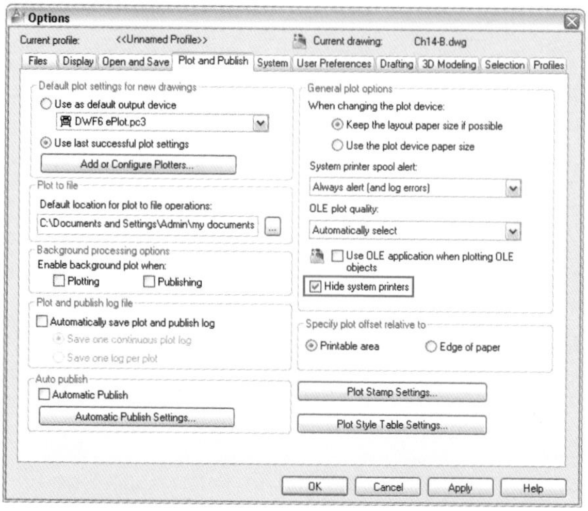

FIGURE 14.22 Hiding the system printer drivers in the Options dialog box

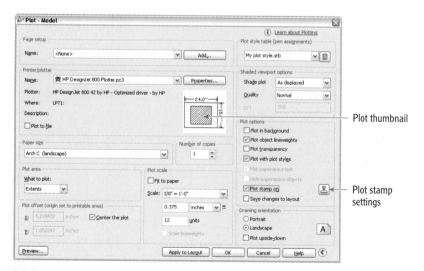

FIGURE 14.23 Configuring the Plot dialog box for output

6. Click the Plot Stamp Settings button as shown in Figure 14.23. Select Drawing Name, Device Name, and Plot Scale in the Plot Stamp dialog box that appears (see Figure 14.24). Click OK.

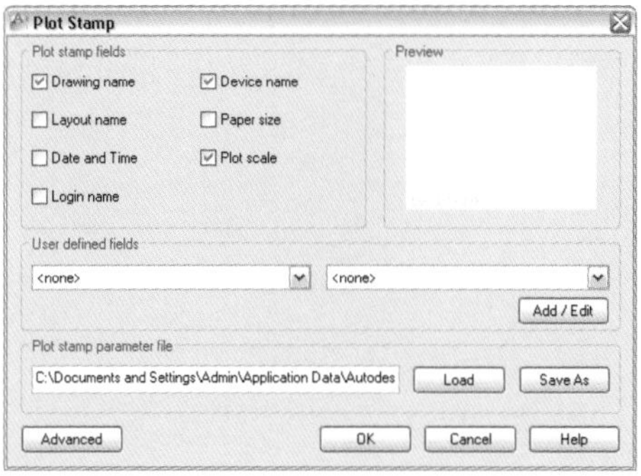

FIGURE 14.24 Configuring the Plot Stamp feature

7. Click the Preview button in the Plot dialog box. Click Continue in the Plot – Plot Scale Confirm dialog box that appears. A preview window temporarily replaces the user interface (see Figure 14.25).

FIGURE 14.25 What you see is what you get in the plot preview window.

8. Click the Plot icon as shown in Figure 14.25. The plot is immediately sent to the hypothetical HP DesignJet 800 output device. If this

device were really attached to your computer, it would start plotting within a few seconds. Once the plot has been sent, a notification window appears in the lower-right corner of AutoCAD's user interface (see Figure 14.26). The plot is complete; click the close box in the notification window.

FIGURE 14.26 Plot notification window

9. Save your work as Ch14-C.dwg.

Plotting Layouts in Paperspace

Layouts are the preferred plotting environment where one can display multiple scaled drawings within viewports, surrounded by title blocks containing text, and/or having dimensions in paperspace. In the following steps, you will create and plot two layouts from paperspace:

> **Layouts are always plotted at 1:1 scale in Imperial units. Metric layouts are also plotted at 1:1 scale if one millimeter equals one drawing unit, or at 10:1 scale if you decide one centimeter equals one drawing unit.**

1. Open the Ch14-C.dwg file. If this file is not open, find it on the book's web page.

2. Click the Layout1 icon on the status bar. A single viewport is automatically generated on the layout.

3. Click the ribbon's Output tab and click the Page Setup Manager icon in the Plot panel. Click the New button in the Page Setup Manager dialog box that appears. Click OK in the New Page Setup dialog box to accept the default name of Setup1. Click OK.

4. In the Page Setup dialog box that appears, open the Name drop-down menu and select HP DesignJet 800 Plotter.pc3, select Arch C (landscape) in the Paper Size drop-down menu, and select My plot style.stb in the Plot Style Table drop-down menu (see Figure 14.27). Click OK.

5. The Page Setup Manager dialog box now lists Setup1 as a saved page setup. Select Display When Creating A New Layout (see Figure 14.28). Click the Set Current button and then click Close.

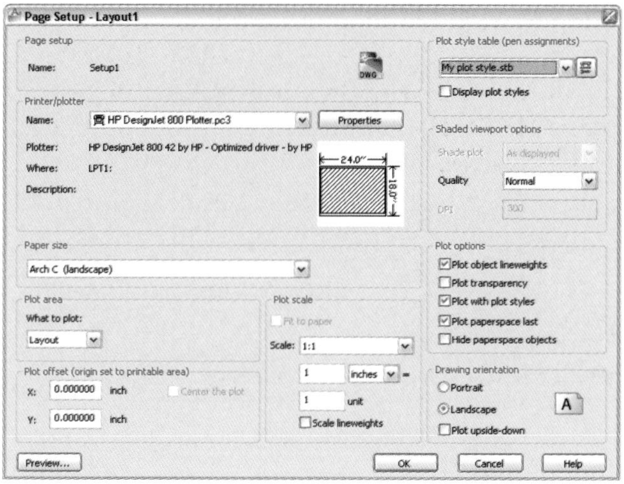

FIGURE 14.27 Configuring a new layout in the Page Setup dialog box

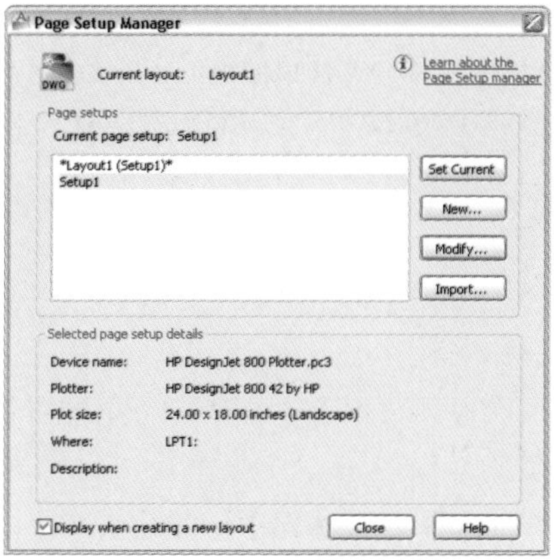

FIGURE 14.28 Saving a page setup for use in the next layout

6. Double-click within the viewport to activate floating modelspace. Select 3/8″ = 1′-0″ from the Viewport Scale menu on the status bar. Double-click outside the viewport on the drawing canvas to return to paperspace.

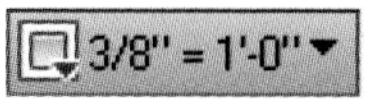

7. Select the viewport and stretch its grips to reveal and center the entire building as shown in Figure 14.29. You might need to move the viewport to center the building on the page, depending on how you stretch the grips.

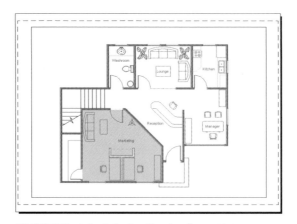

FIGURE 14.29 Configuring Layout1 to display the drawing in ⅜″ scale

8. Press Ctrl+P to execute the PLOT command. Deselect Plot Stamp On in the Plot dialog box that appears. Click OK and the plot is processed. Close the plot notification window when it appears.

9. Click the Quick View Layouts icon in the status bar. Click New Layout in the toolbar that appears and then click the Layout2 icon to initialize it.

10. Select Setup1 in the Page Setup Manager that appears and click the Set Current and Close buttons. Layout2 is configured the same way as Layout1.

11. Double click inside the viewport to activate floating modelspace. Select 3/8″ = 1′-0″ from the Viewport Scale menu on the status bar.

12. Type **LAYERSTATE** and press Enter. Select the Reflected Ceiling Plan layer state and then click the Restore button (see Figure 14.30).

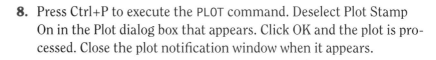

FIGURE 14.30 Restoring a layer state in floating modelspace

13. Double-click outside the viewport on the drawing canvas to return to paperspace. Open the Application menu and choose the Print category and then click Plot. Click the Preview button to open a preview window (see Figure 14.31).

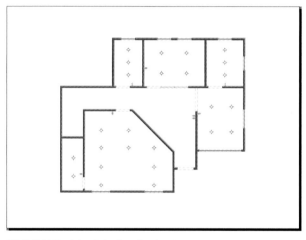

FIGURE 14.31 Previewing Layout2

You may remove the HP DesignJet 800 plotter from your system or use it for practicing plotting.

14. Click the Plot icon in the upper-left corner of the preview window and the plot is processed. Close the plot notification window.

15. Your drawing should now resemble Ch14-D.dwg, which is available among the book's download files.

Exporting to an Electronic Format

If you'd like to reduce the amount of paper you use and eliminate reprographics and drawing shipment costs, Windows users can consider exporting their drawings to electronic formats such as DWF (Design Web Format) and/or PDF (Portable Document Format). Mac for AutoCAD users can't export to DWF (but they can however save as PDF in the Plot dialog box). You can email, FTP, or use an online service to transfer electronic files to your subcontractors and clients for collaboration or approval purposes. In the following steps, you will export a DWF file:

DWFx files are written in XML (Extensible Markup Language) as opposed to Autodesk's proprietary DWF format. DWFx files can be viewed in the Internet Explorer browser without installing a plug-in.

1. Open the Ch14-D.dwg file on the book's web page.

2. Click the ribbon's Output tab and in the Export To DWF/PDF panel click on the drop-down arrow under the Export icon. Select DWFx from the menu that appears.

3. Click the Save button in the Save As DWFx dialog box (see Figure 14.32).

4. Right-click the Ch14-D.dwfx file on your hard drive; select Open With and select Microsoft Internet Explorer. After a few moments the vector drawing appears in the browser. Click the Fit To Width button at the bottom of the interface (see Figure 14.32).

► Use Autodesk Design Review if you want to view and markup DWF or DWFx files.

Fit to width

FIGURE 14.32 DWFx drawing displayed in Internet Explorer

THE ESSENTIALS AND BEYOND

In this chapter you learned how to configure a typical output device by creating both a system printer and an AutoCAD plotter. You configured a plot style table and created a template that uses it. In addition you plotted from both modelspace and layouts in paperspace, saved a page setup, and learned the entire plotting process. Finally you learned how to keep everything digital and export a DWFx file that can be shared over the Internet.

(Continues)

THE ESSENTIALS AND BEYOND *(Continued)*

ADDITIONAL EXERCISE

Explore the PUBLISH command on your own. Experiment with publishing multiple layouts from one drawing or any combination of modelspace views and layouts from multiple sheets all at once. The Publish feature is a great time-saver when you are ready to plot a stack of sheets. You can even try saving a sheet list for printing an identical set of the same drawings at another time.

Storing, Presenting, and Extracting Data

AutoCAD 2012 has several features that allow you to manipulate non-graphical data within your drawings. (Please note that AutoCAD LT doesn't support these features.) In this chapter you will begin by defining *attributes* within a block definition to store data. You will proceed to enter values in several block references, and then you will create a *table* to organize and display this data on a drawing layout. The data shown in the table will be a mixture of static text and dynamically linked *fields* that display textual information in modelspace. After creating this complex data management system, you will change one of the attribute's values and watch as the fields displaying data in the table automatically update.

▶ **Defining attributes and blocks**

▶ **Inserting attributed blocks**

▶ **Editing table styles and creating tables**

▶ **Using fields in table cells**

▶ **Editing table data**

Defining Attributes and Blocks

Blocks can be defined with *attributes* that contain any manner of textual information relevant to the object in question. Let's explore this topic in an exercise. First you will alter the Annotative text style that will be used by the attributes you create. Then you will create attribute definitions to store employees' names and ID numbers. Finally, you will define a simple block composed of two rectangles containing the attribute definitions.

1. Go to the book's web page at **www.sybex.com/go/ autocad2012essentials**, browse to Chapter 15, get

the file Ch15-A.dwg (or Ch15-A-metric.dwg, and open it. The drawing is an elaboration on the diagram you dimensioned in Chapter 11, "Dimensioning" (see Figure 15.1).

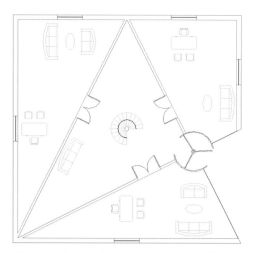

FIGURE 15.1 Diagram shown in Figure 11.1 converted into a floor plan for use in this chapter

2. Type **ST** (for style) and press Enter. Select the Annotative style in the Styles list on the left side of the Text Style dialog box. Select romans.shx in the Font Name drop-down menu. Type **1/8″** (or **0.30** cm) in the Paper Text Height box (see Figure 15.2). Click Apply, Set Current, and then Close.

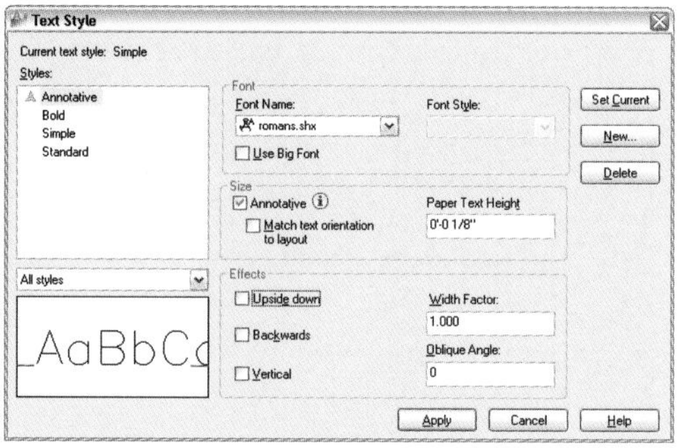

FIGURE 15.2 Setting the height of the Annotative text style

3. Click the Rectangle tool on the Draw panel of the ribbon's Home tab. Click a point at some arbitrary distance from the building as the start point, type **@3′,1′** (or **@90,25** in metric) and press Enter.

4. Click the Copy tool in the Modify panel, select the rectangle you just drew, and press Enter. Press F3 to toggle on Endpoint object snap if it is not already on, click the upper-left corner of the rectangle, and then click its lower-left corner to create two vertically stacked rectangles. Press Enter to end the COPY command.

5. Click the Line tool in the Draw panel, and click points A, B, and C in Figure 15.3. Press Enter to end the LINE command.

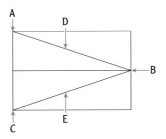

FIGURE 15.3 Drawing simple geometry to form the basis of an attributed block

6. Select 1/4″ = 1′-0″ scale (or 1:40 scale in metric) from the Annotation Scale menu on the status bar.

7. Right-click the Object Snap toggle on the status bar and turn on Midpoint running object snap mode if it is not already on.

8. Expand the Block panel and click the Define Attributes tool to open the Attribute Definition dialog box. Type **NAME** as the Tag, **Employee Name?** as the Prompt, and **Smith** as the Default. Set Justification to Middle Center and Text Style to Annotative (see Figure 15.4).

FIGURE 15.4 Specifying the properties of an attribute definition

UNDERSTANDING THE PARTS OF AN ATTRIBUTE

A Tag, Prompt, and Value plus a number of additional settings and optional modes define every attribute. The Tag is the programming name (typically capitalized without any spaces in the tag). The Prompt is the question you will be asking the person who inserts the attributed block, prompting them to enter the attribute value. The value is entered only when the attributed block is inserted and not when the attribute is defined (see the next section). The optional Default displays a default value when the attributed block is eventually inserted into a drawing.

9. Click OK to close the Attribute Definition dialog box. Click the midpoint at point D in Figure 15.3. Figure 15.5 shows the result.

FIGURE 15.5 Placing an attribute definition in relation to the block definition geometry

10. Press the spacebar to repeat the ATTDEF command. Type **IDNO** as the Tag, **Identification Number?** as the Prompt, and **1234** as the Default (see Figure 15.6). Set Justification to Middle Center and click OK. Click the midpoint of the lower diagonal line at point E in Figure 15.3.

Attribute	
Tag:	IDNO
Prompt:	Identification number?
Default:	1234

FIGURE 15.6 Creating another attribute definition

11. Click the Erase tool on the Modify panel, select the two diagonal lines, and press Enter.

12. Click the Create tool on the Block panel and type **Employee Data** in the Name text box.

13. Click the Pick Insertion Base Point icon and then click point C in Figure 15.3.

14. Click the Select Objects icon, click the NAME attribute definition, and then click IDNO. Select both rectangles and press Enter. Click the Delete radio button in the Objects area of the Block Definition dialog box and select Inches (or Centimeters) in the Block Unit drop-down menu (see Figure 15.7). Click OK and the attribute definitions and geometry disappear as expected.

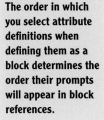

The order in which you select attribute definitions when defining them as a block determines the order their prompts will appear in block references.

FIGURE 15.7 Defining a block with attribute definitions

15. Save your work as Ch15-B.dwg or Ch15-B-metric.dwg.

Inserting Attributed Blocks

After you (or your CAD manager) has gone to the trouble of defining blocks with attributes, inserting them and entering values is easy. In the following steps, you will insert three Employee Name blocks and enter appropriate values in each block reference:

1. If the file is not already open, go to the book's web page, browse to Chapter 15, get the file Ch15-B.dwg or Ch15-B-metric.dwg, and open it.

2. Set the Symbol layer as current in the Layer drop-down menu in the Layers panel.

3. Click the Insert tool in the Block panel. Open the Name drop-down menu and select Employee Data. Verify that Specify On-Screen is selected in the Insertion Point area (see Figure 15.8).

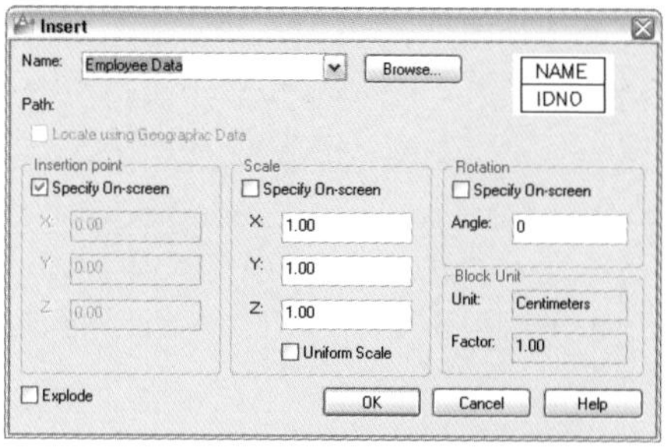

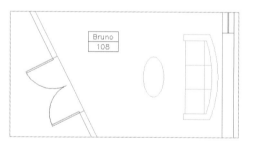

FIGURE 15.8 Inserting the Employee Data block you defined in the previous section

4. Click OK in the Insert dialog box and then click a point in the center of the room on the right. The command prompt reads

    Employee name? <Smith>:

    Type **Bruno** and press Enter. The prompt now reads

    Identification number? <1234>:

    Type **108** and press Enter. The block reference appears in the room with the values you typed in (see Figure 15.9).

FIGURE 15.9 Inserting a block and entering its attribute values at the command prompt

> ATTDIA **is a system variable that controls whether attribute values are input at the command prompt or entered in a dialog box.**
>
> ▶

5. Type **ATTDIA** and press Enter. Type **1** and press Enter.

6. Type **I** (for insert) and press Enter twice. Click a point in the center of the room on the left. Type **Andreae** as the employee name, press Tab, and type **864** as the identification number in the Edit Attributes dialog box (see Figure 15.10). Click OK.

7. Press the spacebar to repeat the INSERT command and press Enter. Click a point in the center of the room on the bottom. Type **Dee** as the

employee name, press Tab, and type **273** as the identification number in the Edit Attributes dialog box. Click OK. Figure 15.11 shows the result.

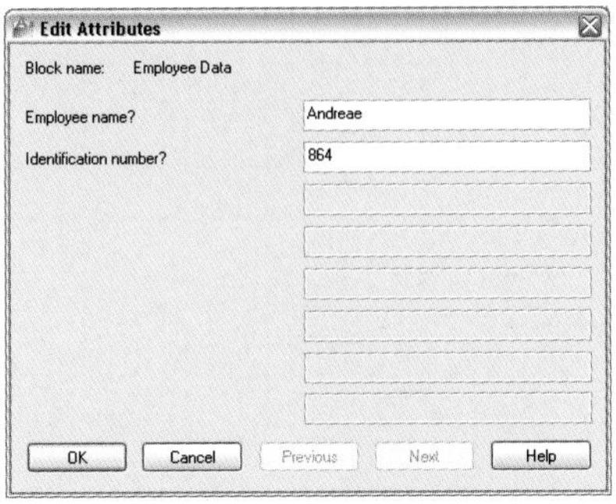

FIGURE 15.10 Entering values in the Edit Attributes dialog box

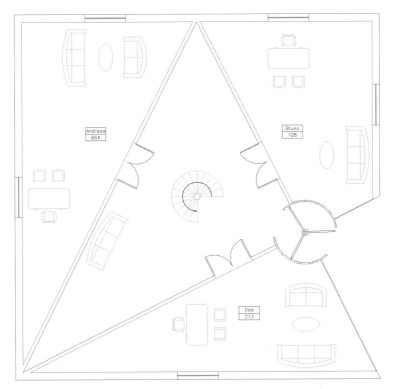

FIGURE 15.11 Three Employee Data blocks inserted and their attribute values entered

8. Save your work as Ch15-C.dwg or Ch15-C-metric.dwg.

Editing Table Styles and Creating Tables

Tables are like having Microsoft Excel or another spreadsheet program within AutoCAD. The overall appearance of tables is controlled by table styles. Cell spacing, borders, and background coloring is controlled by individual table cells. In the following steps, you will adjust a table style, create a new table, and begin adding content to its cells.

1. If the file is not already open, go to the book's web page, browse to Chapter 15, get the file Ch15-C.dwg or Ch15-C-metric.dwg, and open it.

2. Expand the Annotation panel and click the Table Style icon. Click the Modify button in the Table Style dialog box that appears.

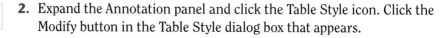

3. In the Modify Table Style: Standard dialog box that appears, open the Cell Styles drop-down menu and select Title. Select the General tab if it is not already selected. Double-click in the Horizontal text box in the Margins area. Type **1/16″** (or **0.20** cm), press Tab, and type **1/16″** (or **0.20** cm) to specify an equal vertical margin (see Figure 15.12).

> **Tables cell styles have three types: title, header, and data.**

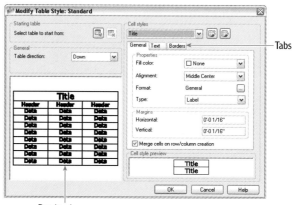

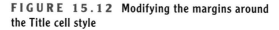

Preview image

FIGURE 15.12 Modifying the margins around the Title cell style

4. Select the Text tab within the Modify Table Style: Standard dialog box. Open the Text Style drop-down menu and select Bold. Double-click the Text Height text box and type **3/8″** (or **0.80** cm). See Figure 15.13.

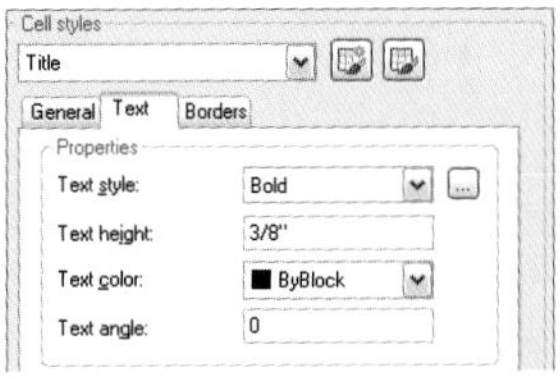

FIGURE 15.13 Editing the
Title cell style text properties

5. Open the Cell Styles drop-down menu and select Header. Open the Text Style drop-down menu and select Bold. Double-click the Text Height text box, type **1/4″** (or **0.50** cm), press Tab, and observe the preview image update.

6. Open the Cell Styles drop-down menu and select Data. Open the Text Style drop-down menu and select Simple. Double-click the Text Height text box and type **1/4″** (or **0.50** cm). Press Tab to update. The updates to the table style are complete. Click OK and then Close to end the TABLESTYLE command.

7. Click the Quick View Layouts tool on the status bar. Select Layout1 and press Esc to exit Quick View Layouts mode.

8. Open the Layer drop-down menu in the Layers panel and set the Table layer as current.

9. Click the Table tool in the Annotation panel. Set the number of Columns to 4 and Data Rows to 3 in the Insert Table dialog box. Set Column Width to 1″ (or 2.5 cm) (see Figure 15.14). The Title, Header, and Data cell styles you customized within the Standard table style will be used by default. Click OK.

LINKING TO TABLES IN EXTERNAL SPREADSHEETS

Select the From A Data Link radio button in the Insert Table dialog box and click the Launch The Data Link Manager icon to dynamically link to a spreadsheet in Microsoft Excel, for example.

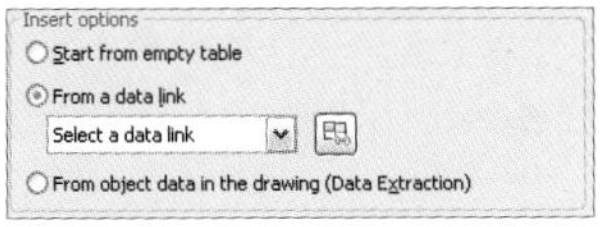

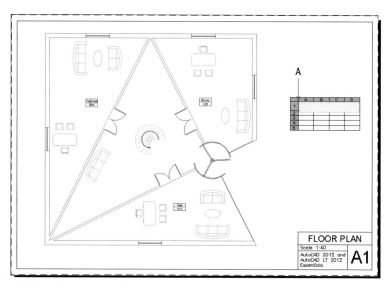

FIGURE 15.14 Specifying the number of columns and rows in the Insert Table dialog box

10. Click approximately at point A in Figure 15.15 to place the empty table on the layout.

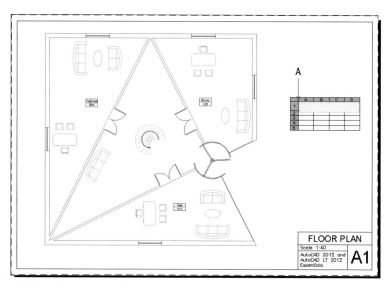

FIGURE 15.15 Placing a new table on the layout

11. The cursor is highlighted within the table's top cell. Zoom into the table by turning the mouse wheel. Type **Room Schedule** and press the Tab key. Type **Employee**, press Tab, and type **ID No**. The Tab key advances to the next cell from left to right, and then from top to bottom at the end of each row.

12. Type **Area (ft** in Imperial units or **Area (m** in metric units.

13. Right-click to open the context menu. Select Symbol ➤ Squared as shown in Figure 15.16. Type **)** and press Tab. Now the column header indicates an area in square feet (or square meters). Click outside the table on the layout to deactivate it.

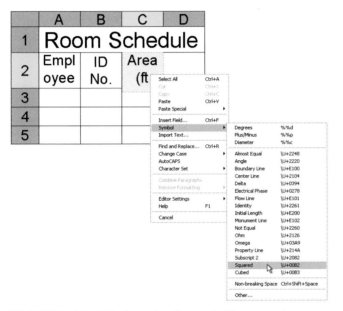

FIGURE 15.16 Accessing the symbol for squared

14. Click in the table to highlight it and then select cell D2 to highlight it for editing. Click the Delete Column tool in the Columns panel within the ribbon's contextual Table Cell tab.

15. Use the arrow keys to move between cells in the table. Press the left arrow key twice to move to cell A2. Each cell has four grips. Click cell A2's right grip and move it to the right to stretch column A wider. Click a point a short distance to the right to set the column width approximately as shown in Figure 15.17.

16. Press the right arrow key twice to move to cell B2. Click B2's right grip and stretch it to the right so that its entire header fits on one line. Repeat for cell C2. Press Esc to deselect (see Figure 15.18).

17. Save your work as Ch15-D.dwg or Ch15-D-metric.dwg.

You can insert or delete any number of rows and columns using tools on the Table Cell tab's Rows and Columns panels.

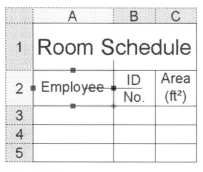

FIGURE 15.17 Resizing a column with cell grips

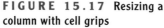

FIGURE 15.18 Formatted table

Using Fields in Table Cells

Fields are variables that are inserted into blocks of text that can change what they display over time. For example, you can insert a date field onto a title block that will update to show the current date every time the drawing is plotted. You can also link fields to objects in the drawing so that the field will display any one of the object properties. In the following steps, you will insert fields into cells within the table you designed in the previous section:

When selecting objects in the Field dialog box, you can select objects in floating viewports even when you are in paperspace.

1. If the file is not already open, go to the book's web page, browse to Chapter 15, get the file Ch15-D.dwg or Ch15-D-metric.dwg, and open it.

2. Select cell A3, which is the first data cell in the Employee column. Double-click within this cell to activate the Text Editor contextual tab on the ribbon. Click the Field tool on the Insert panel.

3. In the Field dialog box that appears, open the Field Category drop-down menu and select Objects. Select Object in the Field Names list.

Click the Select Objects button and select the attribute Bruno in the room on the right.

4. Select Value in the Property list that appeared after selecting the attribute in the previous step (see Figure 15.19). Click OK. The word Bruno appears in table cell A3.

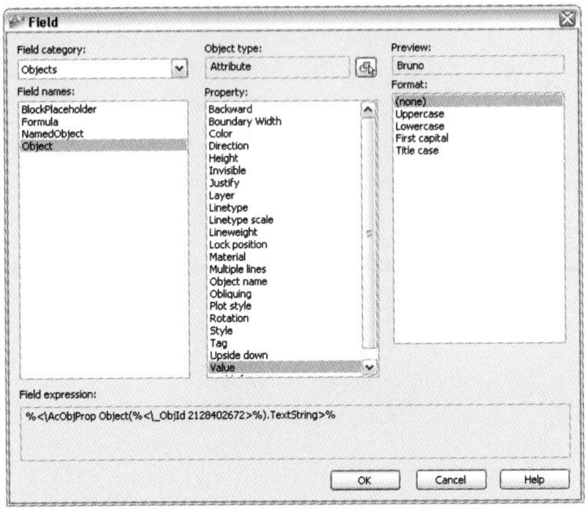

FIGURE 15.19 Accessing the attribute value in the Field dialog box

5. Press the down arrow and move to cell A4. Right-click and choose Insert Field from the context menu. Click the Select Objects button and select the attribute Andreae in the room on the left. Choose Value from the Property list and click OK.

6. Repeat the previous step, selecting the attribute Dee in the room at the bottom.

7. Continue adding fields in the ID No column, selecting each attribute value as shown in Figure 15.20.

	A	B	C
1	Room Schedule		
2	Employee	ID No.	Area (ft²)
3	Bruno	108	
4	Andreae	864	
5	Dee	273	

FIGURE 15.20 Inserting fields that link to attribute values in modelspace

Fields are displayed against a gray background to identify them as fields on screen. The gray field background does not appear in plotted output.

8. Double-click in cell C3 to activate the Text Editor. Press Ctrl+F to open the Field dialog box. Click the Select Objects button and select the magenta line in the doorway of Bruno's office. Choose Area from the Property list. The preview shows the area value as 347.014 SQ. FT. or 322388.23 (in units of square centimeters).

9. Click the Additional Format button. In Imperial units remove the SQ. FT. text from the suffix text box. In metric type **1/10000** in the Conversion Factor text box in order to manually convert square centimeters to square meters (see Figure 15.21). Click OK twice.

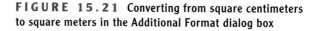

FIGURE 15.21 Converting from square centimeters to square meters in the Additional Format dialog box

> **AutoCAD automatically inserts a factor that converts from square inches to square feet in the Additional Format dialog box.**

10. Press the down arrow to move to cell C4. Repeat the previous two steps, selecting the magenta line in Andreae's office and displaying its area value in square meters.

11. Press the down arrow to move to cell C5. Repeat steps 8 and 9, selecting the magenta line in Dee's office and displaying its area value in square feet (or square meters). Click outside the table on the layout to deselect the table. Figure 15.22 shows the result.

12. Save your work as Ch15-E.dwg or Ch15-E-metric.dwg.

Room Schedule

Employee	ID No.	Area (ft²)
Bruno	108	347.014
Andreae	864	439.451
Dee	273	346.052

FIGURE 15.22 Adding all the relevant fields to the table

Editing Table Data

Beyond filling in a table with all the relevant information, you can also format it to display the data in an aesthetically pleasing fashion. You can change justification, alter border color and/or lineweight, and even change the background color of chosen cells to highlight them. In the following steps, you will format cells, add an additional row and a formula, and finally change an attribute and regenerate the drawing to see the table update:

1. If the file is not already open, go to the book's web page, browse to Chapter 15, get the file Ch15-E.dwg or Ch15-E-metric.dwg, and open it.

2. Click the word Dee (cell A5 in the table) to activate the ribbon's Table Cell contextual tab. Click the Insert Below button in the Row panel.

3. Press the down arrow and move to cell A6. Hold down Shift and click cell B6. Open the Merge Cells menu in the Merge panel and select Merge By Row. Cells A6 and B6 are merged. Type **Total** and click outside the table on the layout to deactivate Text Editing mode (see Figure 15.23).

Room Schedule

Employee	ID No.	Area (ft²)
Bruno	108	347.014
Andreae	864	439.451
Dee	273	346.052
Total		

FIGURE 15.23 Merging two cells and typing the word Total

fx

4. Click the cell to the right of the word Total to activate cell C6. Click the Formula button in the Insert panel and select Sum. Click points A and B, as shown in Figure 15.24. Press Enter to accept the formula =Sum(C3:C5).

	A	B	C
1	Room Schedule		
2	Employee	ID No.	Area (ft²)
3	Bruno	108	347.0
4	Andreae	864	439.4
5	Dee	273	346.0
6	Total		

A

B

FIGURE 15.24 Selecting a range of cells for a formula

5. Select the number 163082.582 (or 1052147.80 in metric) that appears in cell C6 (total area in square inches or square centimeters). Hold down Shift and select cell C3. Open the Data Format menu on the Cell Format panel and select Custom Table Cell Format from the context menu.

%..

6. Click the Additional Format button in the Table Cell Format dialog box that appears. Type **0.006944** (or **1/10000** in metric) in the Conversion Factor text box and click OK to close the Additional Format dialog box.

Formatting applied to a range of cells affects all selected cells.

7. Select Decimal in the Format list in the Table Cell Format dialog box. Open the Precision drop-down menu and select 0.0 (see Figure 15.25). Click OK.

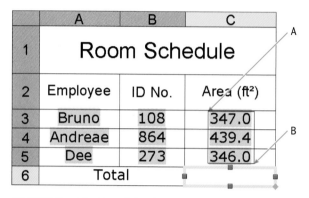

FIGURE 15.25 Formatting a range of cells

8. Open the text justification menu (currently set at Top Center) in the Cell Styles panel and select Top Right. Cells C3 through C6 are right-justified.

9. Select cell B3, hold down Shift, and select cell B5. Change the justification to Top Right in the Cell Styles panel. Select cell A3, hold down Shift, and select cell A5. Change its justification to Top Left. Select merged cell AB6. Change its justification to Top Right. Click outside the table to deselect. Figure 15.26 shows the result.

Room Schedule		
Employee	ID No.	Area (ft²)
Bruno	108	347.0
Andreae	864	439.4
Dee	273	346.0
	Total	1132.4

FIGURE 15.26 Table after adding a total row and justifying its data cells

10. Type **TABLESTYLE** and click the Modify button in the Table Style dialog box. In the Modify Table Style: Standard dialog box that appears, select Data from the Cell Styles drop-down menu if it is not already selected. Select the General tab if it is not already selected and double-click the Horizontal text box in the Margins area, type **1/8″** (or **0.15** cm), and press Tab. Type **1/8″** (or **0.15** cm) and click OK and then Close. There is a bit more space around the data cells.

11. Click the words Room Schedule to select merged cell ABC1. Open the Table Cell Background Color menu in the Cell Styles panel and choose Select Colors. Select the True Color tab in the Select Color dialog box that appears. Type **36,36,36** in the Color text box and press Tab (see Figure 15.27). Click OK.

12. Double-click in cell ABC1 to activate the Text Editor contextual tab on the ribbon. Drag a selection encompassing the entire phrase Room Schedule. Open the Text Editor Color Gallery in the Formatting panel and choose Select Colors. Select the True Color tab in the Select Color dialog box that appears. Type **255,255,255** in the Color text box, press Tab, and click OK. White text now appears on a black background. Click outside the table to exit Text Editor mode.

255,255,255

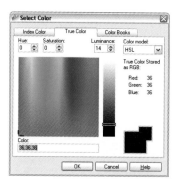

FIGURE 15.27 Selecting a very dark table cell background color

13. Toggle on Show/Hide Lineweight on the status bar if it is not already on.

14. Select cell ABC1, hold Shift, and select cell C6 to activate all the table's cells. Click the Edit Borders icon in the Cell Styles panel. Open the Lineweight drop-down menu and select 0.70 mm. Click the Outside Borders button to apply the properties and click OK (Figure 15.28). A thicker line appears around the outside borders of the table.

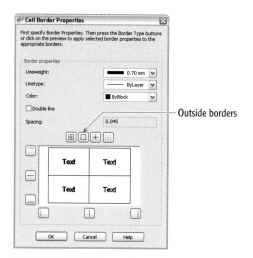

FIGURE 15.28 Changing cell border properties

15. Click the border of the table to select the table itself. Click the Uniformly Stretch Table Height grip on the lower left and move it upward until the table reaches its maximum compactness (see Figure 15.29). Press Esc to deselect the table.

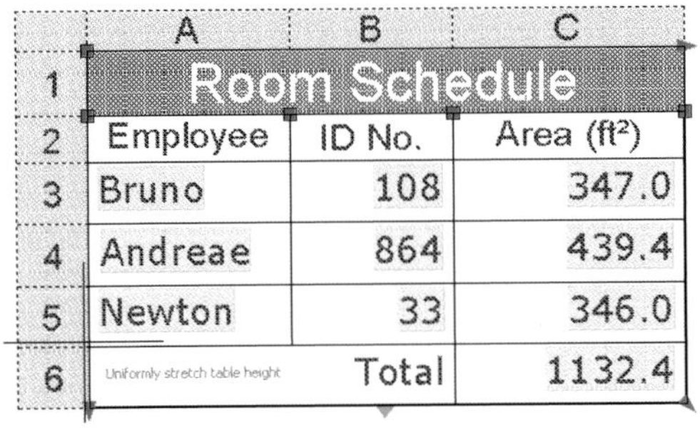

FIGURE 15.29 Stretching the table's height uniformly upward to compact its cells

16. Now you will change an attribute value and observe that this change appears automatically in the table through the fields linked to the attribute values. Click the Maximize Viewport icon in the status bar. Double-click the Employee Data block in Dee's office to open the Enhanced Attribute Editor. Type **Newton**, press Enter, type **33**, and press Enter again (see Figure 15.30). Click OK to end the EATTEDIT command.

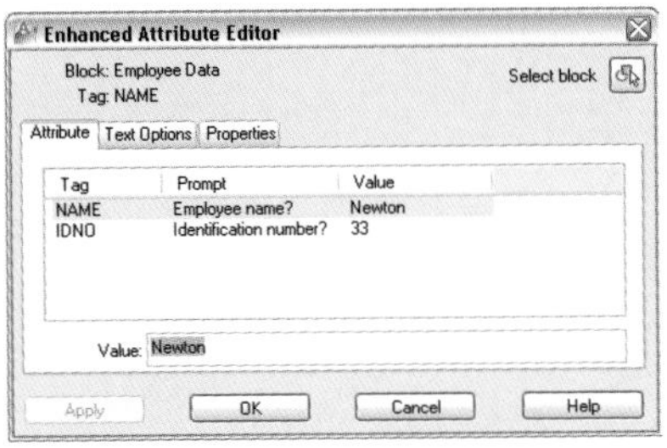

FIGURE 15.30 Editing attribute values in a maximized viewport

17. Click Minimize Viewport in the status bar. The table in Layout1 has automatically been updated and lists Newton and his newly entered identification number.

18. Select the Output tab and click the Preview icon on the Plot panel. The gray background in the fields disappears and you see the table exactly as it would plot (see Figure 15.31). Press Esc to exit preview mode.

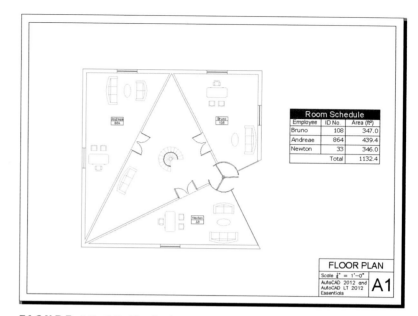

Room Schedule

Employee	ID No.	Area (ft²)
Bruno	108	347.0
Andreae	864	439.4
Newton	33	346.0
	Total	1132.4

FLOOR PLAN
Scale ¼" = 1'–0"
AutoCAD 2012 and
AutoCAD LT 2012
Essentials
A1

FIGURE 15.31 The final appearance of the drawing

19. Your drawing should now resemble Ch15-F.dwg (or
    Ch15-E-metric.dwg), which are available for download
    at the book's web page.

THE ESSENTIALS AND BEYOND

In this chapter you learned how to define attributes and embed them in block definitions.
You also inserted attributed blocks and adjusted their values in a drawing. In addition,
you created a table and adjusted its style to control the table's appearance, and you wrote
text and inserted fields within the table to link to nongraphical information associated
with attribute values and object data. In short, you now have the skills to manipulate
data within AutoCAD drawings.

ADDITIONAL EXERCISE

Use the ATTEXT command to extract attribute values from Ch15-F.dwg for analysis in an
external spreadsheet program such as Microsoft Excel. In order to extract attribute values
you must first create a template text file containing attribute tags and formatting codes.
The Template.txt file that has been supplied on the book's web page (found in the
Chapter 15 folder) is for this purpose. The letter C in the template indicates character

(Continues)

THE ESSENTIALS AND BEYOND *(Continued)*

format for words and N indicates numerical data. The numbers 016000 and 004000 control how many characters/digits are in the output (16 and 4, respectively).

Type **ATTEXT** and specify the location of both the template and output files. Click OK to create the CDF file. This standard file format can be imported into a spreadsheet program for analysis (or linking back into AutoCAD). In this simple example there are only six values; however, in real-world projects, programmatically extracting hundreds of attributes values can be quite a time-saver.

CHAPTER 16

Navigating 3D Models

The only tools you need to navigate 2D drawings are Pan and Zoom, which are simple to use. Getting around 3D models can be a bit more challenging. This chapter will delve into how to navigate 3D models in AutoCAD 2012. (Please note that AutoCAD LT doesn't support these features.) You'll learn various methods for visualizing and navigating 3D models, from selecting visual styles to using preset isometric views. You'll also learn how to orbit into custom views and interactively navigate in perspective.

▶ **Using visual styles**

▶ **Working with tiled viewports**

▶ **Navigating with the ViewCube**

▶ **Orbiting in 3D**

▶ **Using cameras**

▶ **Navigating with SteeringWheels**

▶ **Saving views**

Using Visual Styles

Visual styles control the way models appear in each viewport. The default visual style is 2D Wireframe, which is what you have been using in previous chapters. Consider for a moment how 3D models are displayed on a 2D screen—an illusion. Creating the illusion of where objects are situated in space requires some visual indication as to which objects are in front of other *occluded* objects. A wireframe representation does not give this indication. Rather, to show occlusion, objects need to be either hidden or covered by the shading of other objects according to the visual style that is selected.

Visual styles are never photorealistic like a rendering can be (see Chapter 18, "Presenting Your Design"), but many offer more realistic real-time views of your model compared to wireframe representations. In the following steps, you will sample the visual styles available in AutoCAD 2012.

The model in this chapter is a conceptual model of the O_2 Arena in London that you will build in Chapter 17, "Modeling in 3D." The O_2 Arena (designed by architect Richard Rogers) was originally known as the Millennium Dome because it opened on January 1, 2000. This distinctive, mast-supported, dome-shaped cable network structure will be one of the venues for the London 2012 Olympics (see Figure 16.1).

FIGURE 16.1 You will navigate a 3D conceptual model of the Millennium Dome in this chapter.

1. Go to the book's web page at **www.sybex.com/go/ autocad2012essentials**, browse to Chapter 16, get the file Ch16-A.dwg, and open it. The sample file is displayed in 2D Wireframe visual style by default.

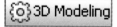

2. Select the 3D Modeling workspace from the Quick Access toolbar.

3. Select the ribbon's View tab and open the Visual Styles drop-down menu at the top of the Visual Styles panel (see Figure 16.2).

FIGURE 16.2 Selecting a visual style

4. Select the Wireframe icon. The UCS icon displays a colorful axis tripod in this visual style (see Figure 16.3).

You can change the uniform background color using the Colors button on the Display tab of the Options dialog box, invoked with the OPTIONS command.

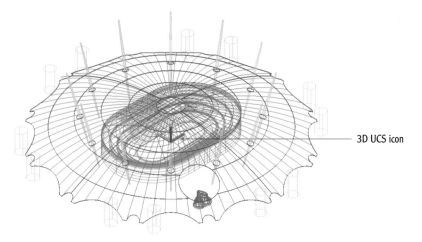

— 3D UCS icon

F I G U R E 1 6 . 3 Wireframe visual style

5. Select the Visual Styles Manager icon in the Palettes panel to alter visual style settings. Scroll down the list of Available Visual Styles In Drawing and select Shaded With Edges. Change Color to Tint in the Face Settings group (Figure 16.4).

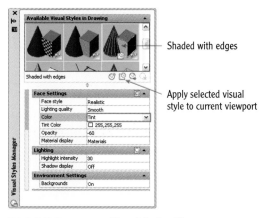

— Shaded with edges

— Apply selected visual style to current viewport

F I G U R E 1 6 . 4 Visual Styles Manager

6. Select the Apply Selected Visual Style To Current Viewport button, as shown in Figure 16.4. Close the Visual Styles Manager. Figure 16.5 shows the result in the drawing canvas.

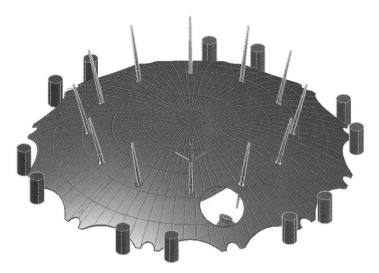

FIGURE 16.5 The altered Shaded With Edges visual style displays the model tinted with white.

7. Open the Visual Styles drop-down menu in the Visual Styles panel and select Save As A New Visual Style. The command prompt reads

```
Save current visual style as or [?]:
```

Type **Tinted with edges** and press Enter. These words appear on the Visual Styles drop-down menu showing this is now the current visual style.

8. You can also change visual styles using the in-canvas controls located in the upper-left corner of the viewport. Select the Visual Style Controls to open a menu (see Figure 16.6).

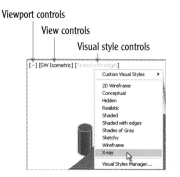

FIGURE 16.6 In-canvas controls

By saving a visual style, you can recall it later after switching to another visual style.

9. Choose X-ray from the in-canvas menu that appears. Figure 16.7 shows the result: a transparent, shaded view with edges.

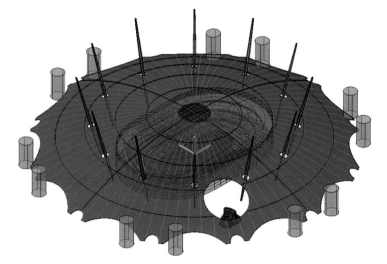

FIGURE 16.7 The X-ray visual style lets you see through solid objects.

10. Save your work as Ch16-B.dwg.

Working with Tiled Viewports

Tiled viewports allow you to visualize a 3D model from different simultaneous vantage points. By starting a command in one viewport and finishing it in another, you can more easily transform objects in 3D. To help you get a better grasp of how this works, the following steps show you how to divide the single default viewport into three tiled viewports.

1. If the file is not already open, go to the book's web page, browse to Chapter 16, get the file Ch16-B.dwg, and open it.

2. Type **VPORTS** and press Enter. In the Viewports dialog box that appears, select Three: Right in the Standard Viewports list. Open the Setup drop-down menu and select 3D (see Figure 16.8). Click OK.

3. Click anywhere inside the viewport showing the front view to activate it. Open the in-canvas Visual Style Controls menu in this viewport and select Shaded. Click anywhere inside the viewport showing the

◄

Tiled viewports can only exist in modelspace with the system variable TILEMODE **equal to 1. Floating viewports exist only on layouts.**

top view to activate it. Open the in-canvas Visual Style Controls menu in this viewport and select Wireframe. Figure 16.9 shows the result.

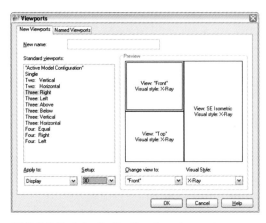

FIGURE 16.8 Configuring viewports

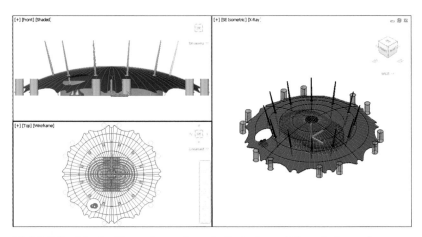

FIGURE 16.9 Three viewports each displaying a different view and visual style

You can maximize or minimize viewports as needed at any time to get a better view of a 3D object.

4. Select the plus (+) symbol in the upper-left viewport displaying the front view to open the in-canvas Viewport menu. Select Maximize Viewport. The front view fills the drawing canvas.

5. Observe that what was formerly a plus (+) symbol in the in-canvas Viewport menu is now a minus (−) symbol. Double-click the minus symbol to minimize this viewport, displaying the front view.

6. Click anywhere inside the right viewport showing the SE Isometric view to activate it. Double-click this viewport's plus symbol to maximize it. The SE Isometric view once again fills the drawing canvas.

7. Save your work as Ch16-C.dwg.

Navigating with the ViewCube

The ViewCube is a 3D navigation interface that lets you easily rotate through numerous preset orthogonal and isometric views. The ViewCube's instant visual feedback keeps you from getting lost in 3D space, even when you orbit into a custom view.

In AutoCAD 2012 the ViewCube helps you visualize the relationship between the current user coordinate system (UCS) and the world coordinate system (WCS).

In the following steps, you will experiment with the ViewCube and learn how to view a 3D model from almost any angle.

1. If the file is not already open, go to the book's web page, browse to Chapter 16, get the file Ch16-C.dwg, and open it.

2. Open the ViewCube menu (see Figure 16.10) and select Set Current View As Home.

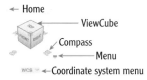

FIGURE 16.10 ViewCube navigation interface

3. Hover your cursor over the ViewCube and observe that different parts highlight in blue as you pass over them. Click the word Right. The view changes to an orthogonal view of the right side of the model (also known as an architectural elevation).

4. The ViewCube rotates with the view change. Hover the cursor over each of the elements on the right face and observe there are four corners, four edges, plus the right face itself that highlights in blue. In addition, there are four arrows facing the cube and two curved arrows in the upper right. Each of these interface elements rotates the view in a specific direction, as indicated in Figure 16.11.

Autodesk uses the ViewCube and SteeringWheel navigation controls in many 3D applications, including AutoCAD, Revit, Inventor, and 3ds Max.

You can select from a short list of preset views using the in-canvas View Controls menu as an alternative to the ViewCube.

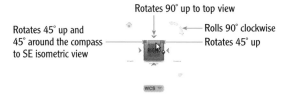

Rotates 90° up to top view

Rotates 45° up and
45° around the compass
to SE isometric view

Rolls 90° clockwise

Rotates 45° up

FIGURE 16.11 Additional ViewCube controls

5. Spend some time navigating with the ViewCube, rotating into multiple different views. Try Bottom, Left, Back, SE Isometric, and NW Isometric.

6. Click the Home icon in the ViewCube interface to return to the initial view.

7. Select the UCS icon at the center of the 3D model to activate it. Drag the tip of the blue z-axis. The command prompt reads

```
** Z AXIS DIRECTION **
Specify a point on Z axis:
```

Click an arbitrary point in the drawing canvas to rotate the UCS. Observe that the ViewCube rotates relative to the current UCS (see Figure 16.12). This feedback can help you visualize where the XY drawing plane is (parallel to the Top face of the ViewCube).

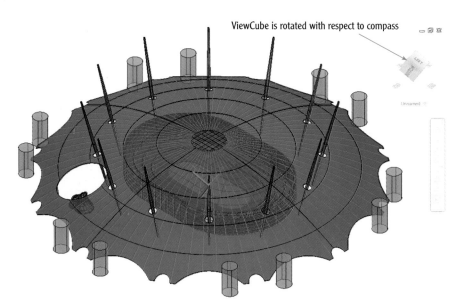

ViewCube is rotated with respect to compass

FIGURE 16.12 ViewCube aligned to the current UCS

8. Open the ViewCube's Coordinate System menu and select WCS to restore the original coordinate system.

9. Save your work as Ch16-D.dwg.

Orbiting in 3D

As you learned in the previous section, the ViewCube is limited to rotating the view in 45° increments. While the ViewCube might get you close to the angle you wish to view a 3D model, you will often need to *orbit* to fine-tune the view to the optimal angle to best see particular geometry. Orbiting refers to rotating the view at any arbitrary angle. In the following steps, you will learn a few methods of orbiting in 3D:

1. If the file is not already open, go to the book's web page, browse to Chapter 16, get the file Ch16-D.dwg, and open it.

2. Let's assume you want to get a close look at the ventilation towers that appear under a large elliptical hole in the dome membrane. Click the edge between the Top and Front faces and zoom into the ventilation towers, as shown in Figure 16.13.

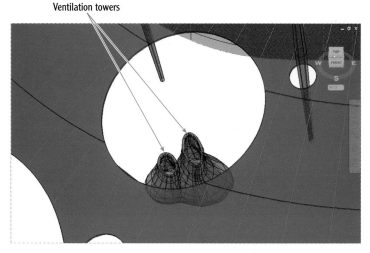

FIGURE 16.13 Using the ViewCube to view the ventilation towers

3. Position the cursor over the compass ring surrounding the ViewCube and drag it to the right to get a better view of the ventilation towers so the hole in the dome membrane appears more circular.

4. Click the Orbit tool in the Navigation bar. Drag down in the drawing canvas to orbit your point-of-view upward until you can see the ventilation towers unobstructed by the dome membrane (see Figure 16.14). Press Esc to end the 3DORBIT command.

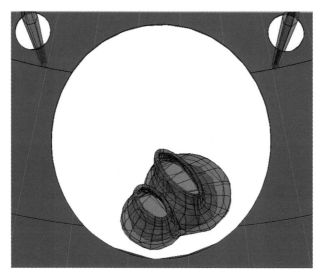

FIGURE 16.14 Orbiting for better view of subject

The Orbit tool is constrained so that it doesn't roll by default. Use 3DFORBIT to orbit with roll.

5. Hold down Shift and drag the mouse wheel to orbit (without roll) about the ventilation towers once more. You will find that it is not possible to gain an eye-level view of the towers without other objects obstructing the view. You will learn how to set up this type of view using a camera in the next section.

6. Save your work as Ch16-E.dwg.

Using Cameras

AutoCAD uses virtual cameras to set up views similar to those achieved in the real world with physical cameras. AutoCAD's CAMERA command creates a camera object that you can manipulate in an isometric view to position the viewpoint in relation to the camera target. In the following steps, you will create a virtual camera and position it in an isometric view:

1. If the file is not already open, go to the book's web page, browse to Chapter 16, get the file Ch16-E.dwg, and open it.

2. Open the in-canvas View Controls menu and select SW Isometric.

3. Zoom out by rolling the mouse wheel backward.

4. Toggle off Object Snap in the status bar.

5. Type **CAMERA** and press Enter. Click points A and B, as shown in Figure 16.15, and press Enter.

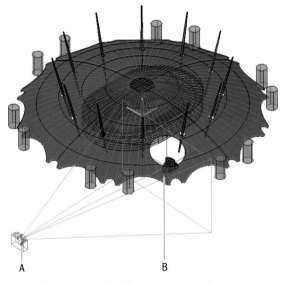

A   B

FIGURE 16.15 Placing a camera in an isometric view

6. Select the camera object. Select the Shaded visual style in the Camera Preview window that appears. Drag the Lens Length/FOV grip to the right and click approximately at point A to expand the field of view (see Figure 16.16).

7. Drag the Camera & Target Location grip forward until the camera is under the outer edge of the dome. Figure 16.17 shows the Camera Preview window. You will correct the fact that the camera is "on the ground" in the next step.

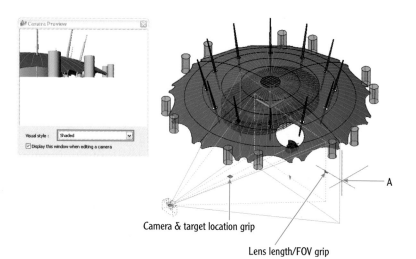

Camera & target location grip

Lens length/FOV grip

A

FIGURE 16.16 Placing a camera in an isometric view

FIGURE 16.17 Camera Preview window showing the new position of the camera "on the ground"

> Camera views are in perspective so that objects diminish in size according to their distances from the camera.

8. Right-click in the drawing window and choose Set Camera View. Drag the mouse wheel downward to move the camera and its target upward, as shown in Figure 16.18.

9. Save your work as Ch16-F.dwg.

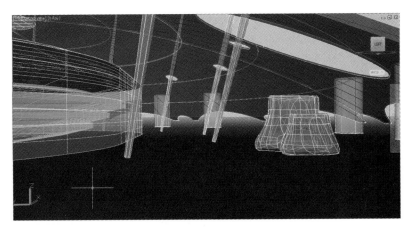

FIGURE 16.18 Looking through the camera

Navigating with SteeringWheels

The SteeringWheel is an interactive navigation control that Autodesk uses in many 3D applications, including AutoCAD. In the following steps, you will use the SteeringWheel's full navigation wheel feature (displaying all eight navigation tools) to compose a view under the dome.

1. If the file is not already open, go to the book's web page, browse to Chapter 16, get the file Ch16-F.dwg, and open it.

2. Select the SteeringWheel tool in the Navigation bar. The full navigation wheel appears in the drawing canvas in close proximity to the cursor (see Figure 16.19).

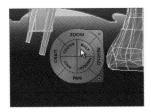

FIGURE 16.19 Full navigation SteeringWheel interface

3. Position the cursor over the Walk tool within the inner ring of the SteeringWheel. Click and hold the mouse button and observe a

walk circle appear in the lower portion of the drawing canvas. Drag the cursor relative to the walk circle to move in that direction (see Figure 16.20). The further from the walk circle you drag, the faster you walk in that direction. Release the mouse button.

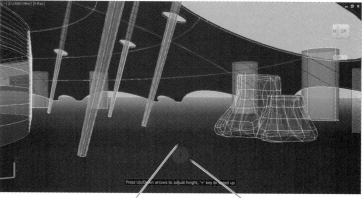

Cursor location for   Walk circle
walking forward

FIGURE 16.20 Walking under the dome

ADDITIONAL STEERINGWHEELS

There are eight commands appearing on variations of the SteeringWheels: Zoom, Pan, Orbit, Rewind, Center, Walk, Up/Down, and Look.

There are three basic SteeringWheels: Full Navigation, View Object, and Tour Building. The latter two wheels have four commands, each suitable to their purposes of navigating around an object or touring through a building.

Each one of the basic wheels has a corresponding mini-wheel with the same commands as the larger interface. I suggest starting with the basic wheels and then graduating to mini-wheels as you gain experience. Mini-wheels are more efficient because the mouse has less distance to travel to select navigation commands.

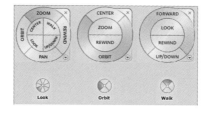

4. Position the cursor over the Look tool in the SteeringWheel's inner ring. Click and hold the mouse button and drag upward to rotate the camera to look up at the hole in the dome above the ventilation towers. Release the mouse button.

5. Position the cursor over the Rewind tool in the SteeringWheel's outer ring. Drag to the left to go backward in the history of movements made using the steering wheel. Drag back to the point before you looked up (see Figure 16.21). Press Esc to exit the SteeringWheel.

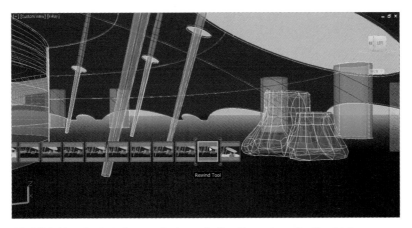

FIGURE 16.21 Interactively rewinding through navigation history

6. Save your work as Ch16-G.dwg.

Saving Views

Named views allow you to save where you are in space so you can recall these positions in the future. In the following steps you will save the current position in the viewport, change the view, switch out of perspective, and then return to the saved view.

1. If the file is not already open, go to the book's web page, browse to Chapter 16, get the file Ch16-G.dwg, and open it.

2. Type V (for view) and press Enter. Click the New button in the View Manager dialog box that appears.

3. In the New View / Shot Properties dialog box that appears, type **Camera2** as the view name (see Figure 16.22). Click OK twice to close both open dialog boxes.

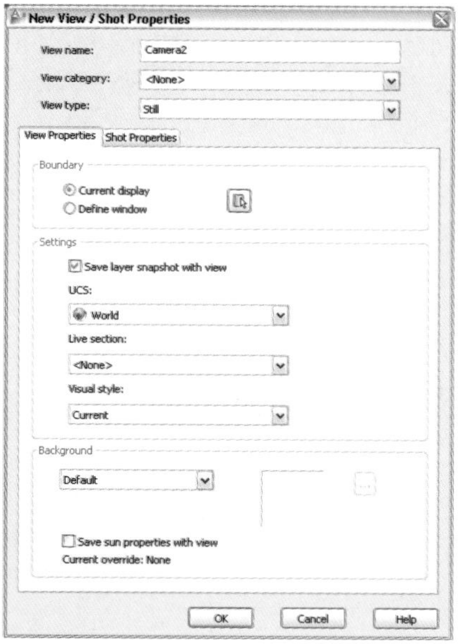

FIGURE 16.22 Saving a new view

▶

Many different properties can be saved with views, including Camera Position, Layer Snapshot, UCS, Live Section, Visual Style, and Background.

4. Click the upper-left corner of the left face of the ViewCube to switch to the NW Isometric view. The model is still in perspective even after switching out of the Camera2 view (see Figure 16.23).

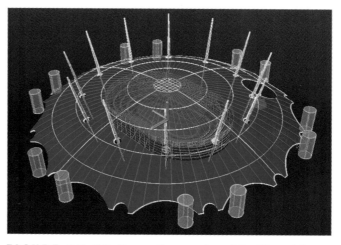

FIGURE 16.23 Perspective overview of the 3D model

5. You can toggle in and out of perspective view at any time. Open the in-canvas View Controls menu and select Parallel to switch out of perspective.

6. Type **V** (for view) and press Enter. Select Camera2 in the list of Model Views in the View Manager dialog box (see Figure 16.24). Click Set Current, Apply, and then OK. The initial perspective view is restored.

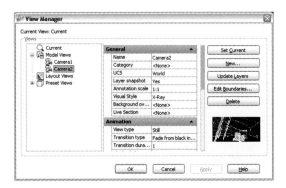

FIGURE 16.24 Restoring a view

7. Save your work as Ch16-H.dwg. Figure 16.25 shows the result.

FIGURE 16.25 The X-ray view from Camera 2

THE ESSENTIALS AND BEYOND

In this chapter you learned how to view a 3D model in a variety of ways, including changing its visual styles and working with tiled viewports. You also picked up important 3D navigation skills using the ViewCube, SteeringWheel, and 3DORBIT command. In addition, you placed a camera, adjusted its position and field of view in Isometric mode, looked through its virtual lens, and walked around an interior building space. Finally, you learned how to save and restore views so you can get back to the places AutoCAD's virtual camera has been.

ADDITIONAL EXERCISE

Did you know AutoCAD can create walkthrough and/or flyby animations? First draw a spline to act as a camera motion path. Edit the spline (see Chapter 5, "Shaping Curves," if necessary) so that the spline has a smooth 3D shape. Use the ANIPATH command to create a motion path animation, linking the camera's path to the spline you just drew. Export the animation to your hard drive and watch the video. You can share video files with people who don't have AutoCAD.

CHAPTER 17

Modeling in 3D

AutoCAD has three different 3D modeling toolsets comprising surfaces, solids, and meshes reflecting the historical evolution of computer graphics. Each toolset was initially developed to suit specific industries: surfaces for industrial design, solids for engineering, and meshes for games and movies. Each toolset has particular strengths and limitations that become evident the more you use them. Yet AutoCAD allows you to pick the best tool for the job no matter what type of work you do, so you can find the best solutions for your drawings. We will explore these tools throughout this chapter, where you will learn how to create and edit surfaces and solid models, and how to smooth out geometry with mesh tools.

▶ **Creating surface models**

▶ **Editing surface models**

▶ **Creating solid models**

▶ **Editing solid models**

▶ **Smoothing meshes**

Creating Surface Models

In this chapter you will create a conceptual model of the O_2 Arena in London, the same model used in Chapter 16, "Navigating 3D Models."

In AutoCAD, *surfaces* are defined as infinitely thin shells that do not contain any mass or volume. Two-dimensional profile shapes have been provided in the chapter's sample file that you will use to create 3D surfaces. You will begin the following exercise by creating a planar surface, and then revolving, sweeping, and extruding 2D profiles into 3D surfaces.

Making Planar Surfaces

Planar surfaces differ from flat bounded areas like circles and closed polylines in that they display surfaces rather than edges only, in shaded visual styles. In the following steps, you will create this simplest of all surfaces from a circle:

1. Go to the book's web page at **www.sybex.com/go/ autocad2012essentials**, browse to Chapter 17, get the file Ch17-A.dwg, and open it. The sample file is displayed in the Shaded With Edges visual style so surfaces will be visible when you create them.

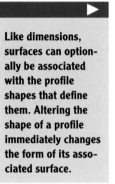

2. Select the 3D Modeling workspace from the Quick Access toolbar.

3. Select the ribbon's Home tab and click the Make Object's Layer Current tool in the Layers panel. Select the circle at the center of the drawing to set the Dome Membrane layer as current.

4. Select the ribbon's Surface tab and click the Surface Associativity toggle in the Create panel if it is not already highlighted in blue.

5. Select the Planar tool in the Create panel. The command prompt reads

   ```
   Specify first corner or [Object] <Object>:
   ```

   Press Enter to accept the default Object option. Select the blue circle at the center of the drawing and press Enter. A planar surface appears as the PLANESURF command ends.

6. Click the SW corner of the ViewCube to move to a SW isometric viewpoint. The blue planar surface you just created is visible at the top of the dome (see Figure 17.1).

Like dimensions, surfaces can optionally be associated with the profile shapes that define them. Altering the shape of a profile immediately changes the form of its associated surface.

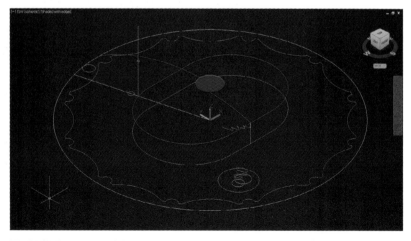

FIGURE 17.1 Creating a planar surface at the top of the dome

Revolving 2D Profile into a 3D Model

Much as you would turn wood on a lathe, you create 3D surfaces by revolving open profiles like lines, arcs, or polylines around an axis. In the following steps, you will revolve a single arc to generate the exterior surface of the dome:

1. Select the ribbon's Surface tab and toggle off the Surface Associativity icon in the Create panel.

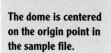

2. Select the Revolve tool on the Create panel of the ribbon's Surface tab. Select the blue arc running from the planar surface at the top of the dome down to the white circle at the periphery and press Enter.

3. The command prompt reads

   ```
   Specify axis start point or define axis by [Object/X/Y/Z]
   <Object>:
   ```

   Type **0,0** and press Enter.

4. The command prompt now says

   ```
   Specify axis endpoint:
   ```

   Type **0,0,1** and press Enter. Press Enter again to accept the default angle of revolution (360 degrees). The REVOLVE command ends and the dome surface appears (see Figure 17.2).

> ◀
>
> **The dome is centered on the origin point in the sample file.**

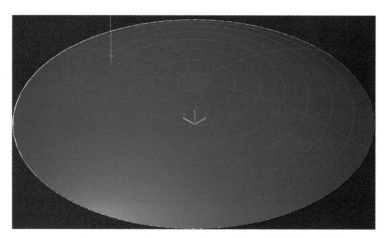

FIGURE 17.2 Revolving an arc to generate the dome surface

5. Type **E** (for erase) and press Enter. Type **P** (for previous) and press Enter. Press Enter again to erase the arc that generated the dome surface.

THREE-DIMENSIONAL CARTESIAN COORDINATES

The Z direction extending above and below the ground plane can be specified within Cartesian coordinates simply by adding a second comma followed by the Z value. For example, the coordinates of a point one unit above the origin point are 0,0,1.

6. Type **LA** (for layer) and press Enter to open the Layer Properties Manager. Double-click the icon representing the Arena layer to set it as current. Click the Dome Membrane layer's lightbulb icon to toggle it off. Click the Auto-hide toggle so the palette collapses when the cursor isn't over it (see Figure 17.3).

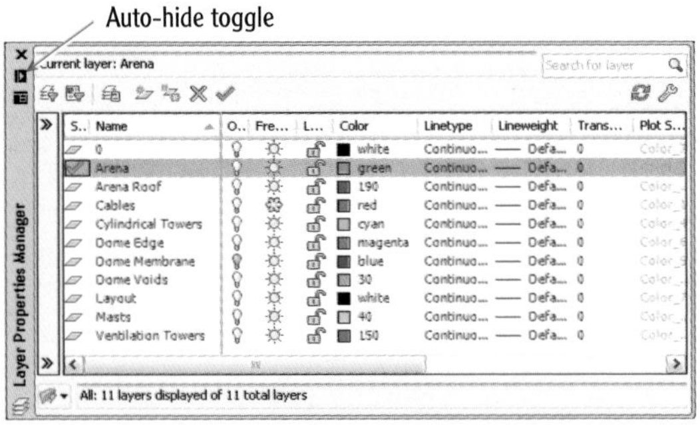

FIGURE 17.3 Changing layer properties

Sweeping Out 3D Geometry

The SWEEP command gives you the ability to create surfaces by pushing an open profile through space following a path. In these steps, you will model the arena within the Millennium Dome and its internal roof by sweeping open shapes along closed paths:

1. Select the Sweep tool on the Create panel of the ribbon's Surface tab. Select the green arena profile shown in Figure 17.4 and press Enter.

2. The command prompt reads

        Select sweep path or [Alignment/Base point/Scale/Twist]:

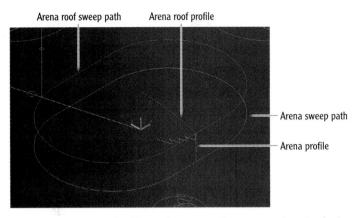

FIGURE 17.4 Profiles and sweep paths representing the O$_2$ Arena

Select the arena sweep path as shown in Figure 17.4 and press Enter. Figure 17.5 shows the resulting 3D arena.

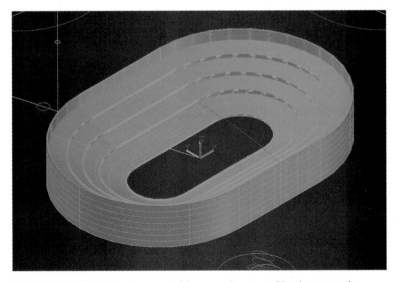

FIGURE 17.5 Arena created by sweeping a profile along a path

3. Hover the cursor over the Layer Properties Manager's title bar to reveal the palette. Double-click the Arena Roof layer's icon to set it as current.

4. Press the spacebar to repeat the SWEEP command. Select the arena roof profile and press Enter. Select the arena roof sweep path and press Enter again. Figure 17.6 shows the result.

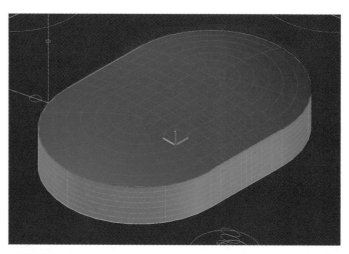

FIGURE 17.6 Sweeping the arena roof

5. Hover the cursor over the Layer Properties Manager's title bar to reveal the palette. Double-click the Dome Edge layer's icon to set it as current. Toggle off the Arena and Arena Roof layers.

Extruding 2D Geometry into 3D

Extruding means pushing forcibly through a die, like hot steel beams being extruded at a foundry. In the following steps, you will extrude the boundary representing the edge of the dome membrane as a curtain-like wall. In the next section, you will use this curtain to trim off the outer portion of the membrane.

 1. Select the Extrude tool on the Create panel of the ribbon's Surface tab. Select the magenta dome edge (see Figure 17.7) and press Enter.

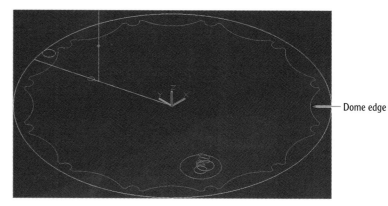

Dome edge

FIGURE 17.7 Selecting the dome edge

2. The command prompt reads

   ```
   Specify height of extrusion or [Direction/Path/Taper angle]
   ```

   Type **50** and press Enter. A 3D curtain-like wall rises up out of the 2D edge.

3. Hover the cursor over the Layer Properties Manager's title bar to reveal the palette. Toggle on the Dome Membrane layer. Double-click the Dome Membrane layer's icon to set it as current. Figure 17.8 shows the result.

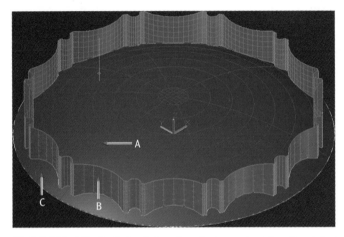

FIGURE 17.8 Extruded surface in magenta pokes through dome membrane in blue

4. Save your work as Ch17-B.dwg.

Editing Surface Models

Surface models have editing tools that modify existing surface boundaries. In the following sections you will modify surface boundaries using other surfaces or by projecting edges onto existing surfaces and using these projections to modify boundaries or cut holes in surfaces. In addition, you will project 2D objects onto 3D surfaces without altering the surfaces at all.

Trimming Surfaces with Other Surfaces

In the following steps, you will trim off the portion of the dome membrane that extends beyond the curtain wall extrusion you generated in the previous section.

1. If the file is not already open, go to the book's web page, browse to Chapter 17, get the file Ch17-B.dwg, and open it. Switch to the 3D Modeling workspace if it's not selected already in the Quick Access toolbar.

2. Select the Trim tool on the Edit panel of the ribbon's Surface tab. The command prompt reads

   ```
   Select surfaces or regions to trim or
   [Extend/PROjection direction]:
   ```

   Click point A in Figure 17.8 and press Enter.

3. The command prompt now says

   ```
   Select cutting curves, surfaces, or regions:
   ```

   Click point B in Figure 17.8 and press Enter.

4. The prompt says

   ```
   Select area to trim [Undo]:
   ```

   Click point C in Figure 17.8 and press Enter. The SURFTRIM command ends.

5. Hover the cursor over the Layer Properties Manager's title bar to reveal the palette. Click the Sun icon to freeze the Dome Edge layer. Figure 17.9 shows the resulting trimmed dome membrane.

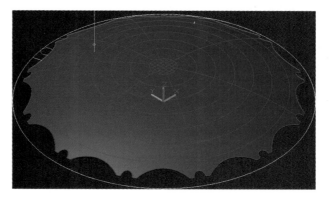

FIGURE 17.9 Trimmed dome membrane

Projecting Edges on Surfaces

In the following steps, you will project a series of 2D objects onto a 3D surface. More specifically, you will project the large hole for the ventilation towers, 12 smaller holes accommodating the structural masts, and numerous cables onto the surface of the dome membrane.

1. We want to see through the dome but cannot in the Shaded With Edges visual style. Using the in-canvas controls in the top-left corner of the viewport, click the Visual Style menu and select Wireframe.

2. Hover the cursor over the Layer Properties Manager's title bar to reveal the palette. Double-click the Dome Voids layer's icon to set it as current.

3. Zoom into the area where there is a large orange circle with a series of light blue circles and ellipses inside it.

4. Toggle on Auto Trim in the Project Geometry panel.

5. Select the Project to UCS tool in the Project Geometry panel on the ribbon's Surface tab. The command prompt reads

   ```
   Select curves, points to be projected or
   [PROjection direction]:
   ```

   Click the large orange circle and press Enter.

6. The command prompt now says

   ```
   Select a solid, surface, or region for
   the target of the projection:
   ```

   Select the blue dome membrane. A new orange spline appears on the surface of the trimmed dome (see Figure 17.10) and the PROJECTGEOMETRY command ends.

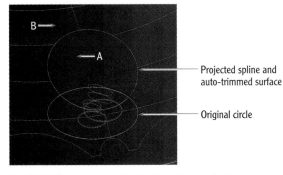

Projected spline and auto-trimmed surface

Original circle

FIGURE 17.10 Projecting the ventilation tower cutout upward onto the dome membrane's surface

7. Type **E** (for erase) and press Enter. Click points A and B in Figure 17.10 to create a crossing window that selects both the dome and the projected spline. Type **R** (for remove) and press Enter. Type **L** (for last) and press Enter twice to erase the projected spline but not the dome.

8. Pan over to the small orange circle with a white line running through it.

Auto
Trim

9. Toggle off Auto Trim in the Project Geometry panel.

You will array this
projected spline
around the dome in
the next section.

10. Select the Project to UCS tool in the Project Geometry panel, select the small orange circle, and press Enter. Select the blue dome and press Enter. A new projected spline appears on the dome surface (see Figure 17.11).

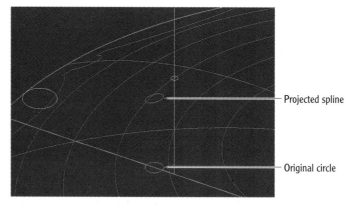

FIGURE 17.11 Projecting one mast void upward onto the dome membrane's surface

11. Type **E** (for erase) and press Enter. Select the original small orange circle on the ground and press Enter.

12. Select the ribbon's Home tab and click the Isolate tool in the Layers panel. Select the blue dome membrane and press Enter.

13. Hover the cursor over the Layer Properties Manager's title bar to reveal the palette. Click the Cables layer's snowflake and darkened lightbulb icons to both thaw and toggle the layer on. Double-click the Cables layer's icon to set it as current (see Figure 17.12).

14. Click the Top of the ViewCube. Click the Rotate Clockwise icon in the ViewCube interface if necessary so North is up.

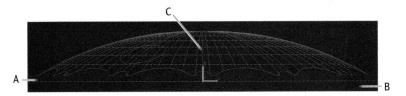

FIGURE 17.12 Changing layer states

15. Select the ribbon's Surface tab and click the Project To View tool in the Project Geometry panel. Select all the objects in the drawing canvas with a crossing selection and press Enter. The command prompt reads

```
Select a solid, surface, or region for
the target of the projection:
```

Select the blue dome and press Enter. Although the PROJECTGEOMETRY command ends, you can't see the projected objects in the top view.

16. Click the Front arrow below the ViewCube. Type **E** (for erase), click points A, B, and C in Figure 17.13 to select all the lines on the ground and one in the center. Press Enter to erase the selection.

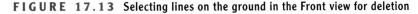

FIGURE 17.13 Selecting lines on the ground in the Front view for deletion

17. Click the upper-left corner of the ViewCube to switch into a SW Isometric viewpoint. Type **LAYUN** (for layer unisolate) and press Enter.

Trimming Surfaces with Edges

You already trimmed one surface when you projected the large orange circle onto the dome using Auto Trim mode in the previous section. You won't use Auto Trim in the next exercise because you need to retain the projected object. In the following steps, you will first array this projected spline around the dome and then manually trim all 12 voids that the structural masts will ultimately pass through.

1. Type **AR** (for array), press Enter, select the small orange spline that you projected on the dome in the previous section, and press Enter. Type **PO** (for polar) and press Enter. The command prompt reads

   ```
   Specify center point of array or
   [Base point/Axis of rotation]:
   ```

   Type **0,0** and press Enter.

2. The command prompt now says

   ```
   Enter number of items or
   [Angle between/Expression] <4>:
   ```

   Type **12** and press Enter. Press Enter again to accept the default angle of 360 degrees. Type **AS** (for associative) and press Enter. Type **N** (for no) and press Enter twice to end the ARRAY command. Twelve splines appear arrayed around the dome (see Figure 17.14).

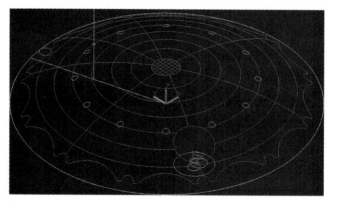

FIGURE 17.14 Arraying projected splines around the dome

> You cannot trim a surface with an array object. By making a nonassociative array, you end up with individual objects that can be used.

3. Open the in-canvas Visual Style Controls menu and select Shaded With Edges.

4. Select the Trim tool on the Edit panel of the ribbon's Surface tab. Select the dome, press Enter, select one of the orange splines, and press Enter. Click inside the spline and press Enter. A hole in the shape of the spline is cut in the dome.

5. Repeat the previous step 11 more times, one for each remaining orange spline.

6. Hover the cursor over the Layer Properties Manager's title bar to reveal the palette. Double-click the Cylindrical Towers layer's icon to set it as current. Toggle off the Dome Voids layer. Figure 17.15 shows the result.

7. Save your work as Ch17-C.dwg.

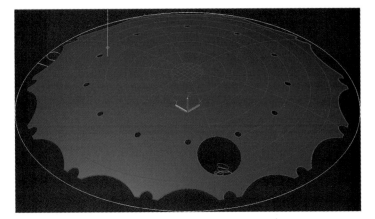

FIGURE 17.15 Trimming holes in the dome to accommodate the masts

Creating Solid Models

If surfaces cover a space, solid models enclose a volume. Only with solid objects can you use the MASSPROP command to calculate engineering properties such as volume, centroid, moments of inertia, and so on. Many of the solid modeling tools are the same as the surface modeling tools. If you start these commands with a closed path such as a circle, ellipse, or closed polyline, you will end up with a solid object while open paths generate surfaces. In the following sections you'll extrude and loft solid objects.

> The EXTRUDE, REVOLVE, LOFT, and SWEEP commands have Mode options that allow you to select either Solid or Surface.

Extruding Solid Objects

The difference between a surface extrusion and a solid extrusion is what's in the middle: nothing in the case of the surface model, and "mass" in the case of the solid. In the next section, you'll see how to affect the solid "mass" with Boolean tools. In the following steps, you'll extrude a circle into a solid and array it around the dome.

1. If the file is not already open, go to the book's web page, browse to Chapter 17, get the file Ch17-C.dwg, and open it. Switch to the

3D Modeling workspace if it's not selected already in the Quick Access toolbar.

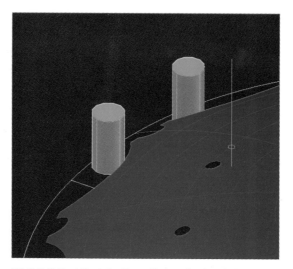

2. Select the ribbon's Solid tab and click the Extrude tool in the Solid panel. Select the cyan circle at the edge of the dome and press Enter. The command prompt reads

   ```
   Specify height of extrusion or [Direction/Path/Taper angle]
   <50.000>:
   ```

   Type **30** and press Enter. The 2D circle becomes a 3D solid cylinder.

3. The Millennium Dome features cylindrical towers in pairs. Type **MI** (for mirror) and press Enter. Type **L** (for last) and press Enter twice. The command prompt reads

   ```
   Specify first point of mirror line:
   ```

   Type **0,0** and press Enter.

4. The command prompt now says

   ```
   Specify second point of mirror line:
   ```

   Type **0,1** to specify a mirror line running vertically along the y-axis, and press Enter. Press Enter once more to accept the default (not to erase the source objects). Figure 17.16 shows the resulting pair of cylinders.

When you are specifying the mirror line, only its direction matters—the distance and units do not.

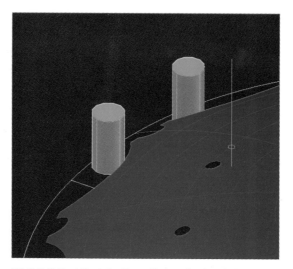

FIGURE 17.16 Extruding and mirroring one pair of solid cylindrical towers

5. You need to place six pairs of cylinders around the dome. Type **AR** (for array) and press Enter. Select both cylindrical towers and press Enter. Type **PO** (for polar) and press Enter. The command prompt reads

   ```
   Specify center point of array or
   [Base point/Axis of rotation]:
   ```

   Type **0,0** and press Enter. Type **6** (for the number of items) and press Enter. Press Enter twice more to accept the defaults and end the ARRAY command. Figure 17.17 shows the result.

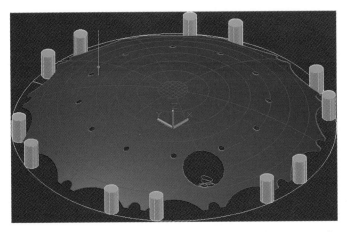

FIGURE 17.17 Arraying pairs of cylindrical towers around the dome

6. Switch to Wireframe using in-canvas Visual Style Controls menu so you can see through the dome. Zoom into the yellow vertical line with a hexagon around its midpoint; this represents a structural mast.

7. Hover the cursor over the Layer Properties Manager's title bar to open the palette. Double-click the Masts layer to set it as current.

8. Click the Extrude tool in the Solid panel. Select the hexagon at the midpoint of the vertical line and press Enter. The command prompt reads

   ```
   Specify height of extrusion or
   [Direction/Path/Taper angle] <30.000>:
   ```

   Type **T** (for taper) and press Enter.

9. The command prompt now says

   ```
   Specify angle of taper for extrusion <15.00>:
   ```

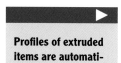

Profiles of extruded items are automatically deleted.

Type **1** and press Enter. Verify that Endpoint object snap is running and click the top endpoint of the vertical line to specify the height of the extrusion. Figure 17.18 shows the result.

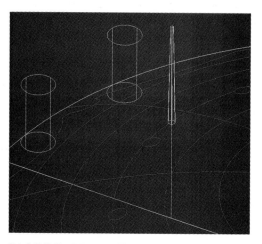

FIGURE 17.18 Extruding half of a tapering hexagonal solid mast

10. Select the Extract Edges tool on the Solid Editing panel, select the mast, and press Enter. Hover the cursor over the edges of the mast to see that individual edge lines are now coincident with the wireframe edges of the solid mast.

11. Zoom in on the hexagonal bottom of the mast. Type **J** (for join) and press Enter. Click points A and B shown in Figure 17.19 to create a crossing window that selects the lines, making a hexagon, and press Enter.

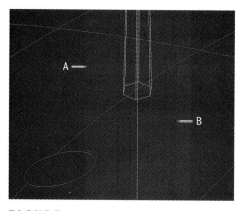

FIGURE 17.19 Joining six edges to form a hexagonal polyline

12. Select the Extrude tool in the Solid panel, type **L** (for last) and press Enter twice. Type **T** (for taper), press Enter and then Enter again to select the default one-degree taper angle. Zoom out and click the lower endpoint of the vertical yellow line to extrude the lower half of the mast down to the ground.

Lofting Solid Objects

Lofting is a modeling technique that lets you create a 3D model from a series of 2D cross sections. In the following steps, you will loft two ventilation towers from a series of circles and ellipses.

1. Hover the cursor over the Layer Properties Manager's title bar to open the palette. Double-click the Ventilation Towers layer to set it as current. Toggle off the Dome Membrane layer.

2. Switch to Shaded With Edges using the in-canvas Visual Style Controls menu.

3. Zoom in on the collection of blue circles and ellipses. Select the Loft tool from the drop-down menu under Sweep if Sweep is current on the Solid panel and press Enter. Select profiles A, B, C, and D shown in Figure 17.20 and press Enter. Open the grip menu that appears and choose Normal To Start And End Sections. Press Enter to end the LOFT command.

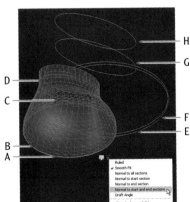

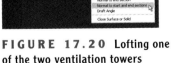

FIGURE 17.20 Lofting one of the two ventilation towers

You will union, rotate, and array the masts around the dome in the "Editing Solid Models" section.

The ventilation towers serve a pair of road tunnels passing under the Thames in London. These towers were in situ prior to the construction of the Millennium Dome.

Normal means perpendicular to the surface in question.

4. Press the spacebar to repeat the LOFT command. Select profiles E, F, G, and H shown in Figure 17.20 and press Enter. Open the grip menu that appears, choose Normal To Start And End Sections, and press Enter. Figure 17.21 shows the result.

FIGURE 17.21 Lofted ventilation towers

5. Save your work as Ch17-D.dwg.

Editing Solid Models

Solid editing tools provide an alternative set of modeling possibilities as compared with surface tools. Boolean tools (named after mathematician George Boole) allow you to union, subtract, and intersect solids (set theory terms) to create new forms. We will explore these tools in the following section and also discuss a variety of specialized solid editing tools.

Performing Boolean Operations

In the following steps, you will unify the top and bottom parts of the mast with the UNION command. You will then rotate and array 12 masts around the dome.

1. If the file is not already open, go to the book's web page, browse to Chapter 17, get the file Ch17-D.dwg, and open it. Switch to the 3D Modeling workspace if it's not selected already in the Quick Access toolbar.

2. Switch to Wireframe using the in-canvas Visual Style Controls menu.

3. Select the Union tool in the Boolean panel, click the left and right ventilation towers, and press Enter. A curve representing the precise intersection of these two forms' surfaces appears in the wireframe representation (see Figure 17.22).

FIGURE 17.22 Wireframe representations of two separate lofted ventilation towers (left) and single object (right) created with Boolean union

4. Pan over to the mast objects you extruded in the previous section. Hover the cursor over the Layer Properties Manager's title bar to open the palette. Double-click the Masts layer to set it as current.

5. Select the Union tool in the Boolean panel. Drag a crossing window through both masts solids to select them and press Enter. Although nothing has changed visually, the two solids have been unified as a single object. Zoom into the base of the mast.

6. Select the ribbon's Home tab and click the 3D Rotate tool in the Modify panel. Select the mast and press Enter. Click the lower endpoint of the vertical line, which is at the center of the mast, to act as the base point. A 3D rotate gizmo appears (see Figure 17.23).

7. Click the red ring to select the x-axis. The command prompt reads

   `Specify angle start point or type an angle:`

   Type **–14** and press Enter.

8. Press the spacebar to repeat 3DROTATE, then select the mast and press Enter. Click the same base point shown in Figure 17.23 and click the green axis ring to select the y-axis. Type **4** and press Enter.

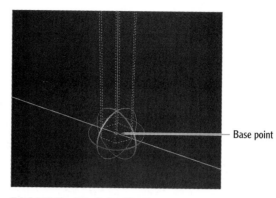

FIGURE 17.23 3D rotate gizmo displaying three colored rings representing the x-, y-, and z-axes

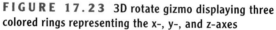

9. Zoom out and select the Erase tool in the Modify panel. Select the edges you extracted from the mast in the previous section and the vertical mast line (see Figure 17.24), and press Enter.

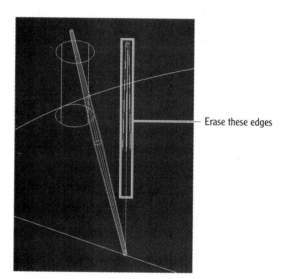

FIGURE 17.24 Erasing the edges extracted earlier

10. Type **AR** (for array) and press Enter. Select the solid mast and press Enter. Type **PO** (for polar) and press Enter. Type **0,0** (as the center point of the array) and press Enter. The command prompt reads

```
Enter number of items or [Angle between/Expression] <4>:
```

Type **12** and press Enter three more times to complete the command.

11. Hover the cursor over the Layer Properties Manager's title bar to reveal the palette. Toggle on the Dome Membrane layer. Switch to Shaded With Edges using the in-canvas Visual Style Controls menu. Zoom out to view the entire model. Figure 17.25 shows the result.

FIGURE 17.25 Arraying rotated masts around the dome

Editing Solids

Rather than having to edit a whole solid object, it is possible to select parts of the object (called *subobjects*) for editing. In the following steps you will offset a subobject, create an interior shell, and then use AutoCAD's Presspull tool on two faces to perform an automatic Boolean subtraction.

1. Select the Isolate tool in the Layers panel, select the ventilation towers, and press Enter. Zoom into the ventilation towers.

2. Select the ribbon's Solid tab, and then select the Offset Edge tool in the Solid Editing panel. Click the top face of the left tower. The command prompt reads

   ```
   Specify through point or [Distance/Corner]:
   ```

   Type **D** (for distance) and press Enter. Type **1** and press Enter.

3. The command prompt now says

   ```
   Specify point on side to offset:
   ```

Click the center of the top-left face to offset the edge internally. Click the top face of the right tower. Type **D** (for distance) and press Enter. Type **1** and press Enter. Click the center of the top-right face and press Enter to end the OFFSETEDGE command. Figure 17.26 shows the result.

FIGURE 17.26 Offsetting edges on the tops of the ventilation towers

4. Switch to Wireframe using the in-canvas Visual Style Controls menu.

5. Select the Shell tool on the right side of the Solid Editing panel. Select the side of the ventilation towers (not the offset top faces) and press Enter. Type **1** (the same distance you offset in the previous step) and press Enter twice to end the SOLIDEDIT command. A hollow interior shell is generated within each ventilation tower. However, the tops are still solid as the shell is inset 1 unit from all sides (including the top).

6. Select the Presspull tool on the Solid panel. Click point A in Figure 17.27, type **-1**, and press Enter. Click point B, type **-1**, and press Enter twice more.

7. Switch to Shaded With Edges using the in-canvas Visual Style Controls menu. Now you can see the voids you cut in the tops of the ventilation towers in the previous step.

8. Type **LAYUN** (for layer unisolate) and press Enter.

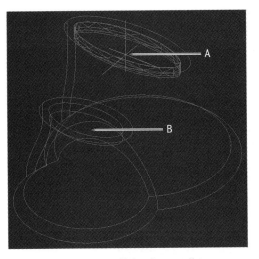

FIGURE 17.27 Using Presspull to remove the tops of the ventilation towers

9. Select the Thicken tool on the Solid Editing panel. Select the dome membrane and press Enter. The command prompt reads

   `Specify thickness <1.000>`

   Type **-0.5** and press Enter. The dome surface thickens into a solid shell (see Figure 17.28).

10. Save your work as Ch17-E.dwg.

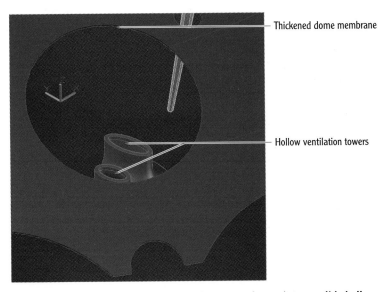

Thickened dome membrane

Hollow ventilation towers

FIGURE 17.28 Thickening the dome membrane into a solid shell

Smoothing Meshes

Mesh objects are represented by discrete polygonal surfaces that can be *smoothed*, meaning their geometrical forms can be rounded out. Mesh objects are ideal for representing organic or sculptural forms. In the following steps, you will convert the ventilation towers into a mesh by smoothing the geometry twice and thereby softening its edges.

> A common way of using mesh objects is to start with a *primitive* like a box, cone, cylinder, and so on and then smooth it. ▶

1. If the file is not already open, go to the book's web page, browse to Chapter 17, get the file Ch17-E.dwg, and open it. Switch to the 3D Modeling workspace if it's not selected already in the Quick Access toolbar.

2. Type **LAYISO** (for layer isolate), select the ventilation towers, and press Enter. Zoom into the area.

3. Select the ribbon's Mesh tab and select the Smooth Object tool on the Mesh panel. Select the ventilation tower solid and press Enter. Click Create Mesh in the warning dialog box that appears (see Figure 17.29). The towers gain a blocky appearance as the curvilinear solid is converted into a polygonal mesh.

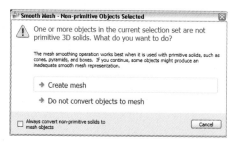

FIGURE 17.29 Mesh warning dialog box

4. Select the Smooth More tool on the Mesh panel, select the ventilation tower mesh, and press Enter. The mesh is subdivided and the result looks smoother (see Figure 17.30).

5. Type **LAYUN** (for layer unisolate) and press Enter.

6. Hover the cursor over the Layer Properties Manager's title bar to reveal the palette. Thaw the Cables layer, toggle on the Arena and Arena Roof layers, and toggle off the Layout layer. Figure 17.31 shows the completed project.

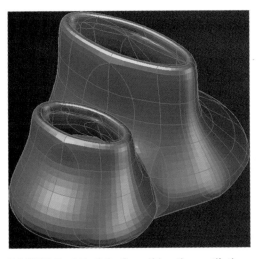

FIGURE 17.30 Smoothing the ventilation towers mesh again

7. Save your work as Ch17-F.dwg. Your work should now resemble the file of the same name that is provided on the book's web page.

FIGURE 17.31 Completed Millennium Dome 3D conceptual model

THE ESSENTIALS AND BEYOND

In this chapter you learned how to use a variety of 3D modeling toolsets, including surfaces, solid, and meshes. You learned how to create planar surfaces and how to revolve, sweep, and extrude surfaces from open profiles. You trimmed a surface with another surface and with edges you projected onto the surface in question. You also extruded and lofted solid objects, performed Boolean operations, created a shell, and thickened a surface. Finally you converted a solid into a mesh and smoothed the mesh to soften its edges and give it a sculptural appearance. In short, you now have the skills to model a tremendous variety of 3D objects in AutoCAD.

ADDITIONAL EXERCISE

Experiment shaping surfaces with the NURBS toolset. For example, convert the planar surface at the top of the dome model you made in this chapter into a NURBS object. Then rebuild the surface, giving it five CVs in both U and V directions. Show CVs and pull up the central CV to deform the surface, making it convex.

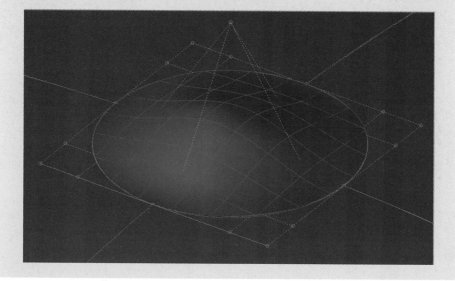

CHAPTER 18

Presenting Your Design

Wireframe, hidden line, and shaded views are helpful means of visualizing models during the design process. However, visual styles leave something to be desired when you are communicating designs to your clients. The general public has come to expect designers to be able to produce the kind of realistic computer-generated imagery regularly seen in movies. This chapter will help you learn to do that by teaching you how to create realistic presentation images using AutoCAD's advanced rendering system. Please keep in mind that AutoCAD LT does not have rendering capability and AutoCAD for Mac has a reduced set of rendering features compared to AutoCAD for Windows, which has advanced rendering capabilities that include global illumination, final gather, and exposure control features.

▶ **Assigning materials**

▶ **Placing and adjusting lights**

▶ **Creating renderings**

Assigning Materials

Materials describe the way objects interact with light. AutoCAD comes with an extensive library of real-world materials, including numerous types of concrete, metal, glass, brick, paint, leather, carpet, plastic, and so on. In the following steps, you will transfer materials from the Autodesk library to a sample model, and then assign them to objects layer by layer.

1. Go to the book's web page at **www.sybex.com/go/ autocad2012essentials**, browse to Chapter 18, get the file Ch18-A.dwg, and open it. This is a model of the author's house (see Figure 18.1).

2. Select the 3D Modeling workspace from the drop-down menu on the Quick Access toolbar.

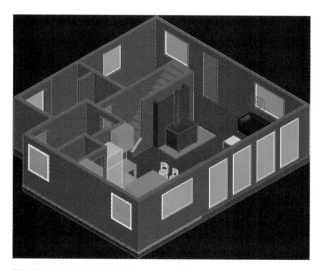

FIGURE 18.1 3D house model

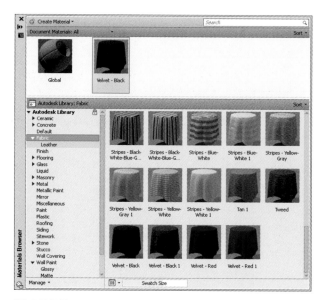

Materials Browser

3. Select the ribbon's Render tab and click the Materials Browser toggle in the Materials panel. In the Materials Browser palette that appears, select the Fabric category in the Autodesk library, scroll down the list of materials in the right pane, and click Velvet–Black to load it into the document (see Figure 18.2).

Single-clicking materials in the Materials Browser loads them into the current document. Double-clicking materials opens the Material Editor, where you can customize them.

FIGURE 18.2 Loading a material from the Autodesk library into the document

4. Continue loading materials by single-clicking the materials listed by category in Table 18.1.

TABLE 18.1 Loading materials from the Autodesk library

Category	Subcategory	Material
Flooring	Stone	Flagstone
Flooring	Stone	Flagstone Light Pink
Flooring	Wood	Natural Maple – Antique
Glass	Glazing	Clear
Masonry	Brick	Uniform Running – Burgundy
Metal	(none)	Chrome Satin 1
Metal	Steel	Stainless – Brushed
Paint	(none)	Black
Plastic	(none)	Laminate Light Brown
Wall Paint	Matte	Cool White
Wall Paint	Matte	Flat – Antique White
Wood	(none)	Beech
Wood	(none)	Birch – Solid Stained Dark No Gloss

5. Figure 18.3 shows all the materials loaded into the current drawing. Close the Materials Browser.

All drawings have a global material (flat gray) by default.

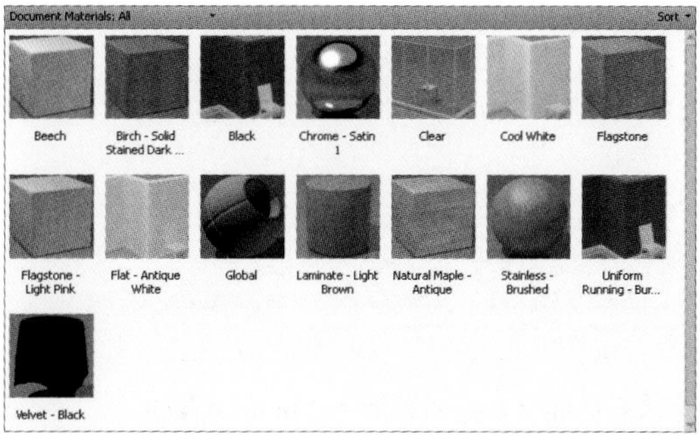

FIGURE 18.3 Materials loaded into the current drawing

You can also assign materials by dragging them from the Materials Browser onto specific objects in the drawing canvas.

6. Expand the Materials panel and select the Attach By Layer tool. Click the Layer header to sort the list of layers in reverse alphabetical order. Click the Layer header again to sort in alphabetical order. Drag materials from the left side and drop them on the right side according to Table 18.2 (see Figure 18.4). Click OK to close the Material Attachment Options dialog box.

TABLE 18.2   Assigning materials to layers

Layer	Material
0	Global
Brick	Uniform Running – Burgundy
Cabinets	Beech
Ceiling	Cool White
Ceiling2	Cool White
Counter	Laminate Light Brown
Defpoints	Global
Door	Birch – Solid Stained Dark No Gloss
Downlight	Cool White
Equip	Stainless – Brushed
Floor1	Natural Maple – Antique
Floor2	Flagstone
Floor3	Flagstone Light Pink
Seat-Cushion	Velvet – Black
Seat-Frame	Chrome Satin 1
Sink	Stainless – Brushed
Stairs	Birch – Solid Stained Dark No Gloss

(Continues)

TABLE 18.2: Assigning materials to layers *(Continued)*

Layer	Material
Stool	Beech
Stove	Black
Table–Glass	Clear
Table–Legs	Chrome Satin 1
Wall	Flat – Antique White
Wall2	Flat – Antique White
Window–Frame	Cool White
Window–Glazing	Clear
Woodstove	Black

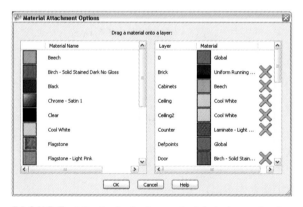

FIGURE 18.4 Assigning materials to layers by dragging from the left pane to the right pane in the Material Attachment Options dialog box

Texture maps are images used within materials to represent realistic surfaces.

7. Texture maps do not appear in the viewport in the Shaded With Edges visual style. Select Realistic using the in-canvas Visual Style Controls menu. Figure 18.5 shows the texture maps in the viewport.

8. Save your work as Ch18-B.dwg.

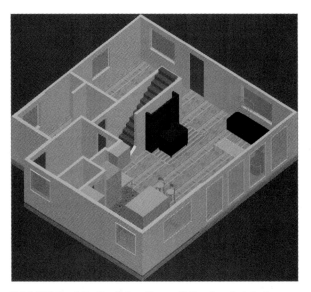

FIGURE 18.5 Using the realistic visual style to display materials' texture maps

Placing and Adjusting Lights

Without light nothing would be visible. AutoCAD uses what is called *default lighting* to illuminate objects in the viewport while you are building 3D models. The default lights are positioned behind the viewer and emit even illumination so that you can always see what is in the viewport. However, default lighting is not realistic and must be turned off as soon as you create artificial or natural light. You will add artificial lights (a series of spotlights mounted in the ceiling) and natural lights simulating the sun and sky light diffused throughout the atmosphere.

Adding Artificial Lights

In the real world, artificial lights are electrical lighting fixtures that are one of the hallmarks of the modern world. In AutoCAD, artificial lights include point, spot, and direct sources. Point sources illuminate in all directions, spot sources illuminate in a cone, and direct lights simulate light coming evenly from a particular direction, illuminating everything like the sun.

AutoCAD has two different lighting methods: standard and photometric. Standard lights were used before AutoCAD 2008 and are still available so that lights in older DWG files will still be compatible in the current version.

However, I strongly urge you to use photometric lights, which are much more realistic. Photometric lights use real-world lighting intensity values (in American or International lighting units), and light coming from photometric light decays with the inverse square of distance, just as light does in the real world.

In the following steps, you will first change lighting units to turn on the photometric lighting system, and then add a series of artificial lights to illuminate an architectural interior.

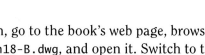

The absolute size of the model matters when you are using photometric lights. Natural light can easily overpower artificial light in terms of intensity.

1. If the file is not already open, go to the book's web page, browse to Chapter 18, get the file Ch18-B.dwg, and open it. Switch to the 3D Modeling workspace if it's not selected already in the Quick Access toolbar.

2. Select the ribbon's Render tab and expand the Lights panel. Open the menu that says Generic Lighting Units (used only for the standard lighting method) and select American Lighting Units (or International Lighting Units in metric). Figure 18.6 shows this menu.

AutoCAD for Mac users can change lighting units in the UNITS command.

FIGURE 18.6 Selecting photometric lighting units in AutoCAD for Windows

3. Click the word Top in the ViewCube to switch to a floor plan view. Choose Zoom Extents in the Navigation bar and switch to the Wireframe visual style using the in-canvas control.

4. Select the ribbon's Home tab and expand the Layers panel. Select the Turn All Layers On tool. Light fixtures (down lights) are visible in the viewport (see Figure 18.7).

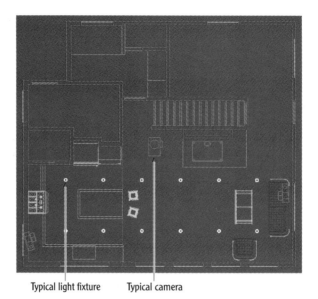

Typical light fixture   Typical camera

FIGURE 18.7 Viewing light fixture geometry on a floor plan

 5. Zoom in on the upper-left light by turning the mouse wheel forward. Click the roll icon in the ViewCube to rotate the drawing 90 degrees, as shown in Figure 18.8. Windows users select the ribbon's Render tab, and on the Lights panel, open the Create Light menu and select Spot. Mac users type **LIGHT**, press Enter, type **S** (for spot), and press Enter. All users select Turn Off The Default Lighting when the Lighting – Viewport Lighting Mode dialog box appears (see Figure 18.8).

Lighting - Viewport Lighting Mode

Sunlight and light from point lights, spotlights, and distant lights cannot be displayed in a viewport when the default lighting is turned on. What do you want to do?

➜ Turn off the default lighting (recommended)

➜ Keep the default lighting turned on
The default lighting will stay turned on when you add user lights. To see the effect of user lights, turn off the default lights manually.

☐ Always perform my current choice   Cancel

FIGURE 18.8 Turning off default lighting when adding the first artificial light source

6. The command prompt reads

```
Specify source location <0,0,0>:
```

Type **.xy** and press Enter. Click a point visually centered on the light fixture (but do not use center object snap).

7. The command prompt now says (need Z). Type **96** (the ceiling height) and press Enter. The command prompt now reads

   ```
   Specify target location <0,0,-10>:
   ```

   Type **.xy**, press Enter, and click the same center point you did in the previous step. The command prompt now says (need Z). Type **0** (the floor height) and press Enter. Press Enter again to end the SPOTLIGHT command.

8. Press the F8 key if Ortho is not already on. Type **CO** (for copy) and press Enter. Type **L** (for last) and press Enter twice. Click a point near the light fixture, zoom out by turning the mouse wheel backward, move the cursor down to the light fixture in the bottom row, and click in the drawing canvas to create the second spotlight. Press Enter to end the COPY command.

9. Press the spacebar to repeat the last command, type **P** (for previous), and press Enter. Type **L** (for last) and press Enter twice to end Select Objects mode. Click the start point under the last spotlight and zoom out. The command prompt reads

   ```
   Specify second point or [Array]
   <use first point as displacement>:
   ```

   Type **A** (for array) and press Enter. Type **6** (for the number of items) and press Enter. Type **F** (for fit) and press Enter. Move the cursor under the rightmost light fixture (see Figure 18.9) and click to specify the second point of the array. Press Enter to exit the ARRAY command.

10. Type **V** (for view) and press Enter. Double-click Camera 1 in the View Manager (see Figure 18.10). Click Apply and OK.

11. Click the Lights panel menu (a small icon in the lower-right corner of the Lights panel) to open the Lights In Model palette (see Figure 18.11). Select the first spotlight in the list, hold Shift, and select the last spotlight in the list to select them all.

12. Right-click the selected lights in the Light Lister and choose Properties. Select the Lamp Color property and click the icon to the right of the drop-down menu to open the Lamp Color dialog box. Select the Kelvin Colors radio button, type **5000**, and press Tab. The resulting color changes (see Figure 18.12). Click OK.

Point filters such as .xy, .xz, and .yz allow you to specify the listed coordinate values by clicking in the drawing. Typing the missing coordinate then specifies the 3D coordinates.

Placing lights within block definitions can help keep source and fixture together.

Real-world lamps are typically rated by a color standard and/or color temperature (measured in degrees Kelvin). The Tool palettes have a set of real-world lamps ready for use.

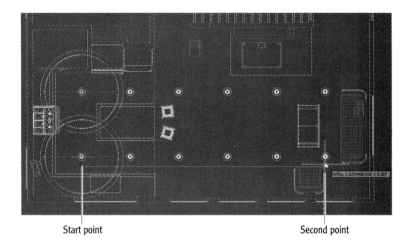

Start point   Second point

FIGURE 18.9 Copying spotlights in a rectangular array

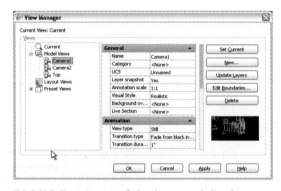

FIGURE 18.10 Selecting a predefined camera view

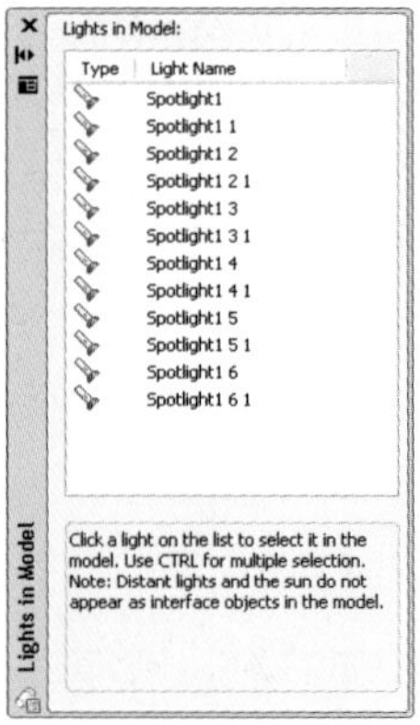

FIGURE 18.11 Selecting lights in the
Lights In Model palette

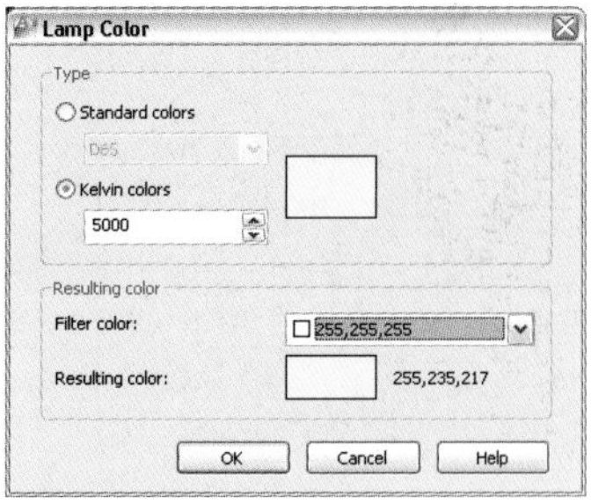

Lamp Color

Type

○ Standard colors

　　DGS

⊙ Kelvin colors

　　5000

Resulting color

Filter color: ☐ 255,255,255

Resulting color: 　　　　　255,235,217

OK   Cancel   Help

FIGURE 18.12 Specifying lamp color by temperature

13. In the Properties palette, change Lamp Intensity to **15000**, Hotspot Angle to **30**, and Falloff Angle to **60**. Figure 18.13 shows the resulting light glyphs in the drawing canvas. The outer orange cones represent the spotlight's falloff angle and the inner yellow cones represent the area of full light intensity. Close the Properties and Lights In Model palettes. Press Esc to deselect all.

◄

The viewport shows direct illumination only. Reflected and transmitted light must be rendered.

FIGURE 18.13 Selected spotlights reveal light coverage as seen in the camera view

14. Save your work as Ch18-C.dwg.

Simulating Natural Light

AutoCAD can simulate the light of the sun and/or the light scattered in the sky by the atmosphere for any location on earth and for any time of year and time of day. In the following steps, you will configure the model to use a simulated sun and sky with specific time and space coordinates.

1. If the file is not already open, go to the book's web page, browse to Chapter 18, get the file Ch18-C.dwg, and open it. Switch to the 3D Modeling workspace if it's not selected already in the Quick Access toolbar.

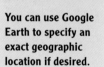

Mac users control Sun Properties in the Properties inspector.

2. Select the ribbon's Render tab if it is not already selected. Click the Sun Status toggle in the Sun & Location panel. The sun is on when the toggle is highlighted in blue.

3. Select the Set Location tool in the Sun & Location panel. In the Geographic Location – Define Geographic Location dialog box that appears, select Enter The Location Values (see Figure 18.14).

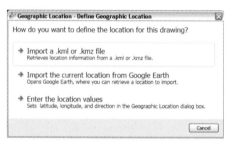

FIGURE 18.14 Using the Geographic Location dialog box to specify latitude and longitude

You can use Google Earth to specify an exact geographic location if desired.

4. In the Geographic Location dialog box that appears, click the Use Map button. In the Location Picker dialog box, click a point near Vancouver, Canada and the crosshairs will snap there (see Figure 18.15). Click OK.

5. Click Accept Updated Time Zone in the Geographic Location – Time Zone Updated dialog box that appears. Click OK to close the Geographic Location dialog box.

6. Open the Sky Off menu in the Sun & Location panel and select Sky Background And Illumination. AutoCAD automatically manages the color of the sky and degree of sky illumination based on your chosen time and space coordinates.

7. Save your work as Ch18-D.dwg.

Dragging the Date and Time sliders automatically repositions the sun as it would in the real world at the chosen time coordinates.

FIGURE 18.15 Selecting a city in the Location Picker dialog box

Creating Renderings

Rendering is the process of converting the geometry, materials, and lighting settings into pixels. Rendering can be a time-consuming process because it typically requires a lot of computation to perform. There are no rendering options on AutoCAD for Mac (just the RENDER command), and the resulting rendering quality isn't as realistic as that available in AutoCAD for Windows, where you have many advanced options. In the following steps, you will use AutoCAD 2012's advanced render settings for Windows to progressively create more realistic renderings.

1. If the file is not already open, go to the book's web page, browse to Chapter 18, get the file Ch18-D.dwg, and open it. Switch to the 3D Modeling workspace if it's not selected already in the Quick Access toolbar.

2. Select the ribbon's Render tab and expand its Render panel. Select the Adjust Exposure tool. After a few moments, AutoCAD creates a preview that gives you a rough sense of the level of illumination in a rendered thumbnail image. As it appears dark, change the Brightness from **65** to **100**. The preview brightens significantly (see Figure 18.16). Click OK to close the Adjust Rendered Exposure dialog box.

FIGURE 18.16 Adjusting exposure prior to rendering

The "Utah teapot" is the symbol of 3D computer graphics. See `http://en.wikipedia.org/wiki/Utah_teapot` for historical information on this symbol.

3. Open the Render Presets drop-down menu in the Render panel and select Low. Click the teapot icon to initiate the rendering process. Figure 18.17 shows the resulting low-quality rendering that appears after a few moments in the Render dialog box.

FIGURE 18.17 First test render using Low quality preset

4. Windows users should click the small icon at the right edge of the Render panel (or type **RPREF** and press Enter) to open the Advanced Render Settings palette. Mac users cannot adjust any advanced render settings. Scroll down in the palette and toggle on Global Illumination by clicking the lightbulb icon shown in Figure 18.18.

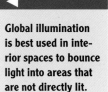

Global illumination is best used in interior spaces to bounce light into areas that are not directly lit.

Toggle on global illumination

FIGURE 18.18 Toggling on global illumination

5. Click the Render icon in the Render panel to create another test render. Figure 18.19 shows the result. The global illumination algorithm bounces photons off the floor, and this helps illuminate the ceiling. However, there aren't enough photons for a quality result.

6. In the Advanced Render Settings palette, change the number of Photons/light to **10000**. More photons will better illuminate the dark recess of the architectural interior. Click the Render icon in the Render panel to create another test render. It is much improved but photon circles are still visible on various surfaces.

7. Open the shadow menu in the Lights panel and select Full Shadows.

8. Open the drop-down menu at the top of the Advanced Render Settings palette and select High. Toggle on Global Illumination by clicking the lightbulb icon as you did in step 4. In the High preset, the scene will use *final gather,* which cleans up photon circles. Click the Render button in the top-right corner of the Advanced Render Settings palette to initiate a render. Mac users type RENDER and press Enter. Figure 18.20 shows the final rendering.

You will be prompted to install the Medium Images Library (700 MB) if it's not already installed when you initiate a render. For the purposes of this book, you do not need to install it.

Final gather can be used with or without global illumination. The final gather algorithm takes a lot of calculation (and thus time) but produces the highest quality results.

FIGURE 18.19 Global illumination bounces photons off the floor and onto the ceiling.

FIGURE 18.20 High-quality rendering using global illumination and final gather

9. Right-click the most recent output file name in the Render dialog box and select Save in the context menu. In the Render Output File dialog box that appears, open the Files Of Type drop-down menu and select TIF (*.tif). Type **Camera 1** in the File Name text box and click Save. Select the 24 Bits radio button in the TIF Image Options dialog box that appears and click OK.

10. Save your model as Ch18-E.dwg. Your work should now resemble the file of the same name, which is provided on the book's web page.

THE ESSENTIALS AND BEYOND

In this chapter you learned how to assign materials, create a photometric lighting simulation, place artificial lights, and assign space and time coordinates to sun and sky. In addition, you learned to create ever more realistic test renderings using global illumination and final gather algorithms to produce the highest-quality renderings.

ADDITIONAL EXERCISE

Render the Camera 2 view on your own. Change any of the materials or lights as you see fit to show off the space. Congratulations on completing all the exercises in this book!

AutoCAD Certification

Autodesk certifications are industry-recognized credentials that can help you succeed in your design career—providing benefits to both you and your employer. Getting certified is a reliable validation of skills and knowledge, and it can lead to accelerated professional development, improved productivity, and enhanced credibility.

This Autodesk Official Training Guide can be an effective component of your exam preparation. Autodesk highly recommends (and we agree!) that you schedule regular time to prepare, review the most current exam preparation roadmap available at **www.autodesk.com/certification**, use Autodesk Official Training Guides, take a class at an Authorized Training Center (find ATCs near you here: **www.autodesk.com/atc**), take an Assessment test, and use a variety of resources to prepare for your certification—including plenty of actual hands-on experience.

Certification Objective

To help you focus your studies on the skills you'll need for these exams, the following tables show the objective and in what chapter you can find information on that topic—and when you go to that chapter, you'll find certification icons like the one in the margin here.

Table A.1 is for the Autodesk Certified User Exam and lists the section, exam objectives, and chapter where the information is found. Table A.2 is for the Autodesk Certified Associate Exam, and Table A.3 is for the Autodesk Certified Professional Exam. The topics and exam objectives listed in the table are from the Autodesk Certification Exam Guide.

These Autodesk exam objectives were accurate at press time; please refer to **www.autodesk.com/certification** for the most current exam roadmap and objectives.

Good luck preparing for your certification!

TABLE A.1 Certified User Exam Topics and Objectives

Section	Exam Objectives	AutoCAD Essentials Chapter
User Interface	Access various tools to create, open, and publish a file.	1
	Identify and state the purpose of the main interface elements.	1
	Demonstrate the use of the tools on the Quick Access Toolbar.	1
	Define and set the workspace	1
	Describe the functions of InfoCenter	1
	Use the Application menu or Quick Access toolbar to open an existing file	1
	Describe the two primary spaces in AutoCAD.	1
	Use the Zoom and Pan commands to view different areas of the drawing.	2
Creating Drawings	Describe the two coordinate systems.	2
	Use dynamic input, direct distance, and shortcut menus.	2
	Use the Line, Circle, Arc, Erase, Rectangle, and Polygon commands to create and erase geometry in the drawing.	2
	Use object snaps to accurately place and create objects in the drawing.	3
	Activate and use the Polar Tracking and PolarSnap modes to more accurately create geometry at different angles in the drawing.	3
	Explain, enable, and use object snap tracking to position geometry in the drawing.	3

(Continues)

TABLE A.1 Certified User Exam Topics and Objectives *(Continued)*

Section	Exam Objectives	*AutoCAD Essentials* Chapter
	Describe the process of setting Length and Angle units	1
	Describe the Snap and Grid, Polar Tracking, and Object Snap settings.	3
Manipulating Objects	Use Grip modes to stretch, move, scale, rotate, or mirror an object.	4
	Use single clicks to add and remove objects from a selection set.	4
	Use a window to select only objects that are entirely enclosed by the rectangular area.	4
	Use a window to select objects that the rectangular window encloses or crosses.	4
	Use coordinates, grid snap, object snaps, and other tools to move objects with precision.	3
Drawing Organization and Inquiry Commands	Use layers to organize objects in your drawing.	6
	Use the Quick Properties palette to display and change the most commonly used properties.	7
	Use the Properties palette to display and change the properties of the selected object or set of objects.	14
	Use the Match Properties command to apply the properties from a source object to destination objects.	6
	Use linetypes to distinguish objects in the drawing.	6

(Continues)

TABLE A.1   Certified User Exam Topics and Objectives *(Continued)*

Section	Exam Objectives	AutoCAD *Essentials* Chapter
	Use the Inquiry commands (Distance, Radius, Angle, Area, List, and ID) to obtain geometric information from the drawing.	11
Altering Objects	Change the length of objects using the Trim and Extend commands.	4
	Create parallel and offset geometry in your drawing by using the Offset command.	4
	Use the Join command to combine multiple objects into a single object.	5
	Break objects into two or more independent objects.	5
	Apply a radius corner to two objects in the drawing.	7
	Apply an angled corner to two objects in the drawing.	2
	Use the Stretch command to alter the shape of objects in the drawing.	7
Working with Layouts	Identify the environments in which you can plot data and create a new layout.	13
	Create and manipulate viewports.	13
Annotating the Drawing	Use the Mtext command to create multiline text.	10
	Create single line text.	10
	Use different methods to edit text.	10
	Create text styles to manage text.	10
Dimensioning	Create dimensions using different options.	11

(Continues)

TABLE A.1 Certified User Exam Topics and Objectives *(Continued)*

Section	Exam Objectives	AutoCAD *Essentials* Chapter
	Use dimension styles to manage dimensions.	11
	Create and edit multileader styles and multileaders.	11
	Use different commands and methods to edit dimensions.	11
Hatching Objects	Add a hatch pattern to a defined boundary.	8
	Add a fill pattern or gradient to a defined boundary.	8
	Modify an existing hatch or fill.	8
Working with Reusable Content	Define and name a block.	7
	Specify the name and position of a block or drawing to insert in a drawing.	9
	Use DesignCenter to reuse the data in a drawing.	9
	Access tool palettes and use their tools.	9
Creating Additional Drawing Objects	Create and edit polylines with the Polyline command.	5
	Create smooth curves with the Spline command.	5
	Create ellipses and elliptical arcs with the Ellipse command.	5

(Continues)

TABLE A.1 Certified User Exam Topics and Objectives *(Continued)*

Section	Exam Objectives	*AutoCAD Essentials* Chapter
Plotting Your Drawing	Create and activate page setups.	13
	Plot design geometry from model space or from a layout.	14

TABLE A.2 Certified Associate Exam Topics and Objectives

Section	Exam Objectives	*AutoCAD Essentials* Chapter
Altering Objects	Create a radius between objects	7
	Trim and extend objects	4
	Break and join objects	5
Annotations	Work with Text: text styles, text justification, and multi-line text	10
	Set the Annotative property for objects	13
	Create and use Multileaders	11
Create Template Content	Hide and isolate objects	6
Creating Additional Drawing Objects	Create polylines	5
Creating Basic Drawings	Use Draw commands to create geometry	2
	Use object snap tracking	3

(Continues)

TABLE A.2 Certified Associate Exam Topics and Objectives *(Continued)*

Section	Exam Objectives	*AutoCAD Essentials* Chapter
	Use polar snap tracking	3
Dimensioning	Create dimensions	11
	Work with dimension styles	11
Drawing Organization and Inquiry Commands	Calculate the area of objects	11
	Change object properties	7
	Use layers	7
Isolate or Hide Displayed Objects	Use grips	4
Manipulating Objects	Copy, Move, Mirror, and Rotate objects	4
	Use selection set methods	4
	Describe and use arrays	4
	Use rotation reference angles	4
Layouts and Visibility	Create and Manage Layers	6
Printing and Plotting	Use page setup for plotting	13
Reusable Content	Create, insert and edit blocks	7

TABLE A.3   Certified Professional Exam Topics and Objectives

Section	Exam Objectives	AutoCAD *Essentials* Chapter
Altering Objects	Stretch objects	7
	Offset objects	4
	Trim and extend objects	4
	Break and join objects	5
Annotations	Work with Text: text styles, text justification, and multi-line text	10
	Set the Annotative property for objects	13
	Create and use Multileaders	11
Create Template Content	Hide and isolate objects	6
Creating Additional Drawing Objects	Edit polylines	5
Dimensioning	Edit Dimensions	11
	Work with dimension styles	11
Drawing Organization and Inquiry Commands	Calculate the area of objects	11
	Change object properties	7
	Use layers	6
Hatching Objects	Use hatching	8

(Continues)

TABLE A.3 Certified Professional Exam Topics and Objectives *(Continued)*

Section	Exam Objectives	AutoCAD *Essentials* Chapter
Insert and Manage External References	Apply External References	9
Isolate or Hide Displayed Objects	Isolate and hide objects	6
Manipulating Objects	Copy, Move, Mirror, and Rotate objects	2
	Describe and use arrays	4
Layouts and Visibility	Create and use Viewports	13
	Create and Manage Layers	6
Reusable Content	Create, insert and edit blocks	7

INDEX

Note to Reader: **Bolded** page numbers indicate main discussions of a topic. *Italicized* page numbers indicate illustrations.

S

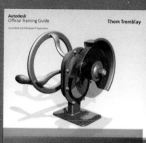
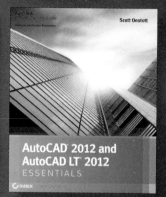